D1606850

Active Voices
I

Active Voices
I

James Moffett

with
Marie Carducci Bolchazy
and
Barbara Friedberg

BOYNTON/COOK PUBLISHERS, INC.
UPPER MONTCLAIR, NEW JERSEY 07043

MIDDLEBURY COLLEGE LIBRARY

ABA-1840

7/1988
Davison

Davison
PE
1121
A183
1987

Library of Congress Cataloging-in-Publication Data

Active voices I.

   Summary: Introduces the techniques of writing with a collection
of diaries, journals, autobiographies, research reports, fictional stories,
poems, and essays written by students in grades four to six.
      1. Readers (Elementary) 2. Readers (Primary) 3. English language—
Composition and exercises. 4. Children's writings, American. [1. English
language—Composition and exercises. 2. Children's writings] I. Moffett,
James. II. Bolchazy, Marie Carducci. III. Friedberg, Barbara.
IV. Title: Active voices 1. V. Title: Active voices one.
PE1121.A83   1987   428.6   87-11600
ISBN 0-86709-091-X

Copyright © 1987 by Boynton/Cook Publishers, Inc.
All rights reserved. No part of this book may be used or reproduced
in any manner without written permission except in the case of
brief quotations embodied in critical articles and reviews.

For information address Boynton/Cook Publishers, Inc.
52 Upper Montclair Plaza, P.O. Box 860, Upper Montclair, NJ 07043

Printed in the United States of America.

87 88 89 90 10 9 8 7 6 5 4 3 2 1

Acknowledgments

We are most indebted to those people who actually wrote the bulk of this book—the students. Their names appear in the Contents and in the text before what they wrote. We are also grateful to their teachers for creating the conditions in which writing of this vitality and variety can thrive.

All but a few selections came from the Chicago area—Naperville, Barrington and Evanston, Illinois. In Naperville we thank Rose Anne Hoekstra, Ruth Clemens, and Shirley Olejnik of Lincoln Jr. H.S.; Ruth Feightner, Edythe Johnson, Jean Bratek, and Laura Peterson of Naper School; Ruth Fawell and Ed Dlabal of Scott School; Marjorie Young, Jane Udell, and Elise Crowell of Maplebrook School; Rosemary Fitzpatrick and Lana Bassetto of Madison Jr. H.S.; Irene Rahder, Cynthia Macrane, and Lynne Caldwell of Elmwood School; JoAnn Smith, Sue Swanson, and James Wainwright of Mill St. School; Marcia Stone and Michael Zimmerman of Highlands School; Sandy Hill of Prairie School; Clare Jones of Washington Jr. H.S.; Joan Carter of Jefferson Jr. H.S.; and Melanie Raczkiewicz of Ranch View School. Teachers to whom we are indebted in Barrington are Diane Tyrpin and Leslie Williams at Grove Avenue School and Mary W. Atkins at Hough Street School. Marie Bolchazy arranged for the use of writing from the Naperville and Barrington Community School Districts.

Barbara Friedberg arranged for the use of writing in Evanston and supplied much from her own classroom. We thank colleagues of hers at Martin Luther King, Jr. Laboratory School who also contributed material: Gayle Rogers, David Sohn, Roberta Baldwin, Bette Mitchell, and Ellen Esrick.

Other teachers good enough to contribute were Irv Wasserman of Pacheco Elementary School in Novato, California; Sally Henry of Grace Church School in New York City; and William Winston of Joaquin Miller School in Oakland, California.

Thanks also to Adrienne Golinken of the Naperville District offices for typing that part of the manuscript—the majority—that was in children's handwriting.

Contents

LOOKING INTO 53

To the Student

Students in grades 4-6 wrote this book. It's meant to sample for you the many kinds of writing that you, too, may do at some time or other during these same grades. We also thought you'd enjoy reading what other people your age have written. We tried to choose pieces of writing that entertain while they illustrate.

We've clumped the writing into five main groups to help you get a picture of what the different kinds are and of how they relate to each other. Each kind has directions suggesting what to do and examples of it written by other students. Listed below are the five main kinds. They're the same kinds of writing *anybody* does, not just students, and you can find plenty of examples in books, magazines, and newspapers:

TAKING DOWN (diaries and journals)
LOOKING BACK (autobiography and memoir)
LOOKING INTO (reportage and research)
THINKING UP (fiction, plays, and poems)
THINKING OVER (essays)

(Don't worry if you're not familiar with all these names. You'll get to know them well from reading and discussing the examples in the book.)

Diaries are accounts you write down of events in your life soon after they happen. *Journals* are records you keep, too, but usually for a special purpose, such as collecting information to use later. Writing based on memories is usually either *autobiography,* when it features the author, or *memoir,* when it features other people or things. *Reportage* is information written up from visits and interviews. Add to it some digging in books and papers and you have *research. Fiction* covers all sorts of made-up stories. *Essays* are ways of writing what you think about things—your ideas.

Knowing about the kinds of writing you might do is, of course, only part of writing. What are you going to write about? For what purpose? To whom? At what length? The directions before each kind of writing should give you some help in dealing with these questions. But there are things you can be doing all the time that will also help—some alone, some with other people.

First, by yourself. Keep a writer's notebook and jot down in it at any time things you might want to save for your writing. These are notes for yourself, for later. If you put in it memories that come to you, dreams, story ideas, thoughts about recent events or things you read or hear, and so on, you'll always have plenty of things to write about. Writing is a form of thinking. All the things going on outside of you and inside at any moment are possible things to write about. Good writers of any age make use of everyday experiences and observations.

That's what you can do alone. Here's what you can do with classmates. Writing partners can help each other think about what they might write about. (A small group of three or four makes a good arrangement). You might take turns reading from your writer's notebook or explaining something you have in it. You can also discuss together which kind of writing illustrated in the book might be right for the material you have. Or you might talk over with your partners a writing project and see what ideas they have for going about it—like how to find certain information, or how you might get your finished paper to readers outside of school.

One useful way partners can help is by acting as an audience before you finish writing. Here are several suggestions about how to go about it:

1. Depending on the kind of writing and on other circumstances, you can all either read aloud your own drafts, read aloud each other's, pass around your papers to read silently and discuss later, or pass out copies to annotate as you read silently.

2. As you read or listen to a paper, think of a title for it and jot this down on a scrap of paper and compare later with others'. (The author should have a title but not place it on the paper.)

3. Let the author say what he or she wants help with or is wondering and worrying about.

4. Describe what you thought or felt at various points in the draft without necessarily advising.

5. Ask the author questions on what you don't understnd or are curious about.

6. Play with other possibilities. Tinker. Ask the group creative what-if questions about someone's draft. What if things were changed around or expressed in some other way?

You can also help each other with spelling and punctuation during these sessions. If you think something may be incorrect but aren't sure how to correct it, you can always say so and let the author check on it, either in a reference book or by consulting the teacher.

Finally, partners can help each other think of good things to do with finished pieces of writing. (It's a good idea to talk about this before or while you're writing.) Scripts, for example, are meant to be performed; how-to directions are meant to be carried out. Which writing might be read to someone out of school? Posted up somewhere? Printed up and passed around—in class and out-of-class? Done as part of a project? Put into a class or school newspaper or magazine? Where can your writing *go*? What can it *do*?

We hope that you'll enjoy this book. And we hope you'll try as many of these kinds of writing as you can. You'll discover that you too are a writer.

Active Voices
I

Taking Down

General Journal

Keep a lightweight notebook handy and write down in it any time all sorts of ideas and events that interest you enough to want to save. Put in the date when you write in it. Carry your notebook between home and school so you can write down things as they come to you—your reactions to events, your feelings and moods, observations of what is going on around you, stories you imagine, dreams, memories, lists and plans, and so on.

In this general writing journal you can store a treasury of ideas and experiences to rerun and make use of later. Some of this material you may want to read as is to certain persons, or let others read it on their own. You can choose what you let others, including the teacher, read.

Like professional writers, you can pick things out and rewrite them—fill them out, change them around, and polish them up for others to enjoy in various ways. Putting a lot in your journal notebook will keep you rich in ideas and material to use for all of the other kinds of writing to follow in this book.

Journal Samples
Kristen Cline

September 8

A long shadow fell across the sidewalk. I was scared. It was early evening and I was walking my dog. We were waiting for my dad to come home from work. I wanted to scream. A hand grabbed me and my dog started barking. Someone picked me up. Before I could stop myself I started to cry. The person asked what was wrong. When I looked up I saw it was only my dad.

September 27

The poor pigs' pie popped when poked or pinched with a pin.
A porcupine popped popcorn and played with a piñata.
A dumb dog dragged a dozen dragons into a dungeon.
A quick cow called for quite a few cups of chocolate milk.
Green geese that grow giant gourds go goofy for grape.
Don't drop the doll for my dog. Duffy doesn't like dropped dolls in the tub or he drains drowning dolls named Debbie.

October 10

Last year I went to the beach. I had never been there before. It was gorgeous. I could feel the sea air. It was so much lighter and more refreshing than the city smog which I'm used to. The sun was burning down harshly. It was then I decided to take a swim in the cool, glistening water. I swam much further than I knew I should have, when suddenly I was pulled down with great force. I spun around and around. I went deeper and deeper. I tried to scream, but I only choked on the water. I then remembered my father once told me about an undertow. I immediately got great strength within me and swam harder and faster than I ever swam before. I soon made it to the shore. My family was all gathered on the beach weeping. I saw a tear shimmer in my mother's eye. I ran to her for comfort and she let out a big cry of joy. I cried because I was glad to be back with them. Again, they carried me back to my soft bed with the big feather quilt. I was glad to be back.

October 10

Flag

Flag, stars, night, dark
scary, monster, hair, gorilla,
jungle, safari, explorer, hunt,
shoot, darn, upset, stomach.
food, peas, grass.

I sat in the basement by the sewing machine trying to figure out what I would be for Halloween. I decided to be a flag. I worked for a few hours on my costume, and then I put it on. I admired myself in the mirror and then marched upstairs like a soldier to show my family what I made. The minute my sister saw me she told me it was gross. Then she asked me what it was. When I told her she told me it was gross again, and then she laughed until tears came to her eyes. Then I marched up the stairs to my room, yelling, "Mom, Laura said my flag was gross." Then my mom looked at me and she couldn't stop laughing.

October 15

Lyn's wish had come true. She had gotten the time machine she wished for. She traveled everywhere she had ever wanted to go, bringing back fancy clothes and old dolls from the places she went. She soon had the biggest doll collection in her school.

October 18

She thought all the kids would envy her, but when she told them they just laughed and said it was only because she was spoiled. Then she realized the problems of a time machine. For instance, what if she went some place and couldn't get home? Or what would happen if she were some place and lost her time machine? But the worst question she thought of was what if her friends stopped liking her?

October 19

Later that night Lyn decided she wanted her friends back, so first she put all the fancy clothes and dolls away in her closet. Next she wrote notes to all her friends that said she wanted to play with them again. Then she did the one thing that was hardest for her, and that was to throw her time machine away.

October 20

Dear Journal,
I've decided today that I hate school. I'm sick and tired of all the homework I've been getting lately. I bet we're going to play scatterball in gym again. Why can't we play something fun like basketball? I can't wait until 2:45, when school is over.

Kristen

P.S. I think I'm gonna barf.

Only Eleven

Wesley Hsu

I have a love,
And she's all that I need.
I will conquer any obstacle to win her heart;
She knows of my presence but never speaks to me.
I'm scared when I'm near her,
But she doesn't seem to notice.
She accepts me as a mere existing pupil.
The way I'm acting now,
She'll never notice me;
And if I don't improve, she'll find somebody else,
Leaving me with a broken heart,
Without realizing my admiration for her.
Her beauty shines throughout the day,
And my eyes long to see her.
If she's gone
I begin to feel weary,
Her presence keeps me going.
I long to have her for a wife,
So I may see her every day.
I could speak to her whenever I please,
But there still is one more far worse problem.
I'm only eleven.

Journal Excerpts

Wendy Ramsbottom

Strange Incident

February 26

The strangest thing happened to me today. I have never really been good friends with Susan Quick. She sits in front of me in English. She and I know each other, but we've never been good friends. What she did was give me a sticker at the left of the page. It isn't much, but I thought that was pretty nice of her to give something away to someone she wasn't really good friends with.

Her Description

About 4'10", brown hair, short hair, brown eyes, dresses well, and has pale skin.

The Girl Who Was Kidnapped and Killed

March 2

Over the past weekend a 10-year-old girl named Jeanine Nicarico was kidnapped from her home. She was home sick recovering from the flu. A man came in and kidnapped her. She was home alone because her parents were at work. But her mother called every hour to make sure she was ok. At lunchtime her mother came home and ate with her. She was last heard when she called her mother at 1:20 p.m. and told her mother about a TV show that she was watching. When her older sister Kathy (14) came home at 2:40 p.m. the door was broken down. Kathy went in, and when Jeanine didn't answer her calls, she set her books down and ran to her next-door neighbor, and they called the police and her mother. After two days of searching for Jeanine, they found her dead along a highway.

A Ghost or Something That Scared Me

March 14

Between the shadows of my room and between the starlight that shined in the peeks of my windows, I saw something weird, like a ghost.

March 15

It was not white, it was black. But it had a white outline. When I closed my eyes and then opened them, it wouldn't go away. The worst thing was that I *really, REALLY*, had to go to the bathroom. What do you do when you've really got to go? I eventually made it to the bathroom, but I really had to go. What an experience!

The Day My Brother Made Me Pass Out

March 16

This past Friday, Scott, my brother, told me that he could make me pass out. And of course, I said that I did not believe him. So he said come here and stand against the wall. So I did. He said, "Now lean over and breathe deeply twenty times and then stand back up again." When I stood up, he pushed on the upper part of my stomach and I just fell over onto the floor. I was out only for about five seconds, but for the next half-hour I was real dizzy.

What happened was that when I leaned over and was breathing hard, all the blood quickly was going to my brain, and when Scott pushed on my upper stomach, it stopped the blood (with oxygen) to my brain, causing me to collapse. But I know for one thing that I'll never do that again and I'll listen to my brother from now on.

Changes

Aimee Roupp

Slowly the sun rises,
beam by beam,
light by light,
waking the day
ever so quietly.
The fog becomes
grey mist,
another form
of
soft rain
changing
yet again
into
a
rainbow.

Special Journal

In addition to a general journal, you might keep a special journal on a subject that you expect to hold your attention for some time—a hobby, strong interest, ongoing project, or subject you think about. Title a separate notebook, and write in it only about that subject, picking up each time where you left off. This kind of journal allows you to develop some subject a long way gradually without trying to write about it all at once and without knowing where you're going to take it.

You can invite others to read it as you go and give responses and suggestions. Select parts that stand well alone and present them in some way to others, rewriting if necessary. Or summarize some of it for others.

Scenes from World War II
Wesley Hsu

September 8

The sun shone brightly as the three groups of Dauntless dive bombers flew across the Pacific Ocean. The bombers had just been launched from the three American carriers *Hornet, Enterprise,* and *Yorktown. Yorktown* was already suffering damage from earlier attacks by the Japanese. It was 1941 and the Japanese had secured many islands in the Pacific. They were working to capture Midway. The Japanese had a huge force under the command of Yamamoto, the commander-in-chief of the Japanese Imperial Navy. The first carrier striking force was under the command of Nagumo. He had four carriers. Right now the Dauntless dive bombers were on their way to destroy the carriers. They carried tons of bombs. The Japanese were already busy with the torpedo bombers. The fighters were already busy finishing up the job when the dive bombers came screaming from the sky. The Japanese were unprepared for the attack. Their fighters were low from slaughtering the torpedo bombers. The dive bombers quickly released the bombs and turned the carriers into blazing infernos.

September 9

artillery
shell
damage
London
Churchill

As the bombs ripped through the building, people ran for the nearest bomb shelter. Screams and cries for help could be heard over the sound of the anti-aircraft artillery, and the noise only added to the drone of Luftwaffe airplanes flying overhead. Shells crashed into streets, spreading fire and flame. A small boy ran from his burning home holding his ears because of the terrible roar of the artillery. London was under siege by the Nazis attacking from France. It was June 4, 1940.

The next day a limousine pulled up in front of St. Paul's Cathedral.

September 10

Winston Churchill stepped out. He slowly shook his head as he sadly walked through the streets. Whole blocks had been wiped out. The streets were deserted. Rubble lay in piles in empty lots. What was left of St. Paul's Cathedral lay in a big heap of ashes. Winston Churchill slowly got back into the car. He knew that they could never win the war without supplies from England's powerful ally, the United States. But soon they too would be at war. Unknown to him or the United States, Japan had plans already for a raid on Pearl Harbor. The United States would soon be Britain's best ally. But as of now, he only could hope the United States would help Britain in the dreadful war. England really needed help to defend herself against the powerful Nazi navy and army.

September 13

All was quiet as the sun rose, people began to get up, stretch, and attend to their daily chores. A few hours later, the small Polish village was awake. Children went to school. Men worked in the fields. Everything was normal.

A young Polish man who was busy cutting his crops stopped and listened. Far away he could hear a humming sound. It sounded like an airplane. As it came closer, he could tell it was more than one plane.

Suddenly the attack began. Junker 880's and Hienkel 111's appeared from nowhere and began bombing runs. Bombs fell everywhere, setting the fields on fire and turning houses into blazing infernos. There was no place to hide. No bomb shelters. Nothing could stop the Germans. People ran wildly. Finally, the air attack ended as quickly as it had come. The people calmed down but not for long. Marching could be heard. German foot soldiers! Tanks charged into the village firing shells. The soldiers were like locusts, spreading everywhere and destroying what the bombers missed. The village was taken in three minutes. The Germans faced no resistance. The Second World War started with this swift one-sided battle. The rest of Poland fell within a week, but Germany didn't stop there. Hitler's armies kept driving until they captured France, Belgium, Finland, Norway, and were never stopped until they tried to invade Britain.

Britain stopped them with only a miracle. The Germans were

strangling it. They fought them by sea, they bombed from the air, and they cut off every supply line with the use of the German U-boat. Britain was still hanging on stubbornly, never thinking of surrender. Britain never collapsed in the time between 1939-1945, but during that time a *lot* happened.

September 14

As rocks fell and dust flew, the tired and hungry soldiers fled from the cave. Only one got to the next cave, however. Before the dust settled a Japanese machine gun cut the rest down. The lone surviving soldier looked out of the cave at the bodies of his friends. He thought of his family back in the United States. He sighed at the thought of his wife. Ever since Pearl Harbor had been attacked he had served in the Marines. Now he was stranded in a cave on the island of Iwo Jima. He couldn't get out of the cave without any smoke cover. He listened to the drone of airplanes in the distance. Suddenly a shell struck the cave entrance. It started an avalanche. Rocks cascaded on his head and knocked him out.

Soon the cave gave way and he was buried alive. He died instantly. He was one of the many Marines who served faithfully but never lived to see the day Japan surrendered.

Story Journal

Make up a story as you go along, in installments. Each time you write, pick up where you left off and continue the story. You don't have to know exactly where it's going when you start. This way you can write a longer story than you could at any one time, and you have time in between to recharge your imagination.

Read your story aloud to others in to-be-continued fashion. Then, perhaps with their help, pull it all together and touch it up after you've finished, so that you can make a book out of it.

A Door in the Woods

Mark Schwartz

September 11

One day my friends and I were playing baseball. It was my turn to bat. I hit the ball. The bat went flying into the weeds. I went to the weeds to find it. When I looked in I heard a small voice. I looked down and saw a small man. He said, "Follow me." So I did. He led me to a door in the woods. He opened the door slowly. It creaked and vines snapped. Suddenly a bright light shined straight in my eyes.

September 12

I closed my eyes. When I opened them I was in a room. The room was very big. There was a huge red rug on the floor. Also, there was a couch. In front of me there was a fireplace flaming. Above it was a moose head. It seemed as if I was inside a castle. I turned around to ask the little man a question. He was gone. I found him in a dining room. I asked him, "Where am I?"

He answered, "In the land of Cicera."

"Where's that?" I asked.

September 13

He answered, "When the moon is full and the North Star is beneath the moon it is directly between." The little man took me to a room. The room was huge. (It seemed huge.) Each wall was made of one big mirror. He told me to stand in the middle of the room, so I did. Expecting to see my reflection, I looked over at a mirror. All I saw was green smoke hovering over the middle of the room. Suddenly a bright ray shot down directly at me. It went right through me as if I wasn't there.

September 14

I felt nothing. I walked back towards the little man. I felt something swinging by my neck. It was a cloak. It was long and black. The man told me, "Say 'Silar.'"

"Silar," I yelled. Unbelievably I started ro rise.

September 15

I started to float back to the main room. I flew in front of the fireplace, still flaming. I questioned, "How do I get down?"

"Just say 'Silar' again," he responded. So I did. I floated down with ease.

"Why did you bring me here?" I asked.

He answered. "To help save us from the Lord of Spectres."

September 16

He continued, "You are now Thorg the Warrior!" He touched me delicately with a golden sword gleaming in the sun. When it touched my shoulder it gleamed so brightly that it blinded me for a moment. When I had regained my sight I had everything. I had a sword, a helmet, a shield, bow and arrow, and a dagger. I asked, "Why do we have to fight the Lord of Spectres?"

"Because he's trying to take over Cicera and be king." He continued, "That's not true, because you're going to be king." After this he bowed in respect.

September 20

"What am I to do?" I asked.

"Go to Spectre Valley, you'll meet him there. I warn you, be ready for anything."

"When shall I leave?" I inquired.

"Tonight."

"One more question: How am I to get there?"

"Follow Raging River until you get to the woods, then take Spectre Trail until you come to a clearing. There in the center should be a throne. Wait there."

September 21

Black Evil

So that night I left on my journey. I got to Raging River and followed it. I arrived there at the woods at about midnight. What was ahead of me was a black forest. I found the trail and started down it. On both sides of me were millions of huge red oaks. As I peered into the woods I felt a chill, as if someone was following and watching me. The trees cast weird shadows on the path from the crescent moon. The silence was an eerie feeling. Every step I was ready for something to jump at me. I closed my eyes, trying to forget how scared I was. A hawk cried high above. I opened my eyes slowly. I was in a clearing. As I looked around I saw a huge, golden throne in the center. Cushions of silk were tacked on it with silver tacks. It gleamed brightly in the moonlight. I gave a sigh of relief when I found I was out of the woods.

September 22

I stood waiting for at least half an hour. Clouds started to form overhead. Suddenly there was a clap of thunder. The throne glowed as if it were on fire. On it sat a tall, mysterious figure.

All you could see of the figure was his—or should I say its?—face. He wore a long white robe that had a hood which was up. His eyes were nothing more than thin slits glowing along with his robe. He held an old, rugged staff which had a brass snakehead on top. He squinted at me with his eyes gleaming down at me. A chill crept down my spine.

September 24

He said, "Set down your weapons." So I did, hoping there would be no fighting.

"You fool, why are you trying to stop me? No one can."

"Because I stand for what I believe. You're just a stupid spirit who thinks he owns the world," I replied.

"Shut your mouth or you'll pay," he insisted.

"No," I argued, "I have as much right talking as you have."

September 27

Suddenly two bright, red rays were shot directly at me from his mysterious eyes. As quickly as possible I grabbed for my heavy shield. (It weighed at least 15 lbs.)

September 28

I drew it up in front of me, kneeling. The rays bounced off but left two heavy black marks from the heat.

"Ah, I'm surprised that a being of your size can use such a shield. You still can not stop me. For if you touch me with the blade of your sword the forest will come against you. Everything and anything in there is evil. You can not escape me, the Lord of Spectres!"

After this he drew up his snake staff and yelled something in a different language which I could not understand.

September 29

All at once twigs started to move, as if they were crawling. A beam of light in the shape of a sphere came out of the mouth of the snake's head. Out of the sphere came lightning bolts piercing every twig. They lit up the whole clearing. Then suddenly the sphere disappeared. All that was left was a mass of smoke. It drifted away in the wind.

September 30

I looked back. All of the twigs, big and small, had turned into snakes. There were hundreds of them slithering towards me. Not knowing what to do I darted as fast as my legs could carry me toward the spectre. Then realizing what to do, I drew my sword, which was very sharp, and sliced the staff in two, unaware that I had hit the spectre. Then I realized that I had hit his left hand. It started to crinkle and get smaller, like a sheet of paper getting wadded up. A purple glow surrounded the hand. All at once it started to melt, drip by drip, as it formed a puddle in the weeds. It seeped slowly into the ground. The grass blades turned into spikes.

October 1

As I turned to see where I had dropped my shield all of the snakes turned back into twigs.

"The blade of your sword has touched me. As I warned you, all forest creatures and living things will come upon you!"

Again he said something that was in another tongue. This time I knew what he was saying. Everything started to encircle me. I yelled with all my might, "SILAR!"

I started to climb up into the sky. Arrows were flying, voices chanting. Something pierced me suddenly in the back. I screamed as I fell in pain. My head hit with a hard thump. . . .

"Son, Son. Are you all right? Wake up please. I will not harm you."

I opened my eyes slowly. A tall man with grey hair and a full beard was stooping over me.

"Ohhh!" I moaned, "My head and Ohh! my back."

"Lie still. No use in hurtin' yerself anymore."

"What happened, uh . . . uh . . .?

"Orgre, yep, Orgre Bozla."

"Orgre, what happened?"

October 4

"Apparently you were shot with an arrow and hit your head. You were unconscious."

"Where did all of those things go?"

"I guess I scared them away. Why don't you come to my place for the night?"

"I would be pleased to. Thank you very much," I answered.

After about a 10-minute walk we arrived at this house, which was made of stone.

"By the way," he started, "what is a youth (to be exact, 13) like you doin' out in these dangerous parts, son?"

"I was sent here to conquer the Lord of Spectres. I'm from Cicera, or originally I'm from Naperville, which is in Illinois, which is in the United States, which is on Earth, which is in the Milky Way."

Journey Journal

If you travel somewhere, keep a day-to-day record of what you do, see, feel, and think. Your "trip" doesn't have to be an actual journey, however. It can be any activity or experience that you are involved in over a period of many days or weeks, like taking part in a sport or a play or a club or beginning a new job or hobby. Trace it as it goes along. You'll enjoy later looking back at what it was like blow-by-blow. It may be entertaining or even helpful to others. So write it in such a way that others can read and understand it. Also, summarizing it might make a good story or thought piece.

Florida Trip
Jeff Skahill

December 16
Travel Day
Naperville to Chattanooga, Tenn.

We left about 1:00 P.M. and stopped about 1:00 A.M. As soon as we started down the road we had to go back to get some cookies my mom made for our grandparents. We went to Indiana first then played "Do You Know Your Father?" into Kentucky. (I'm writing in the car and there are a lot of bumps.) Something happened to our shock and we had to stay in Indiana about an hour longer. We ate at the Waffle House. I had to talk my parents into letting me have shrimp. They were pretty good. I also got salad, which I took one bite of and went back to my shrimp and french fries. We moved past Kentucky into Tennessee late in the night, or you could say very early in the morning, and then stopped at a gasoline station which had a hotel in back of it. My dad was the first in bed while my mom, sister and I took turns using the bathroom.

December 17
Chattanooga, Tenn. to Venice, Fla.

We left at 7:00 A.M. and ate breakfast at Burger King. I had some eggs that were cold, so I only ate a little bit. I've been pigging out on Jolly Ranchers.

We ate lunch at Cordell, Georgia, and I had a hamburger in Wendy's.

We stopped at a gift shop and got a few postcards, which will probably go to Nick or a friend in N.C.

We got to our grandparents' house at about 10:00 P.M., and it is so neat. Everywhere you look there's a door leading to a room. The house is colored a weird pink paint but it isn't bad or anything.

They have a huge swimming pool in a gigantic screened-in porch. They have a jacuzzi in their bathroom which I'm bound to go into one of these days.

December 18

I never thought taking a shower could be so much fun. They have a sliding glass door on the stall. The stall is so big three people could fit in at one time.

I let my feet dangle in the pool, but it's not heated yet, and my feet got very cold very quickly.

My grandmother told me there's a boy around my age next door, but I'm having enough fun as it is right now. I took a few pictures of the pool and the house, then I jogged about a mile and drank a huge glass of milk then went to sleep for a few minutes.

My sister, mom, and grandfather went shopping and I jogged a little while longer.

Later in the day after letting my legs dangle in the pool a while I walked about a mile with my mom around the neighborhood. I almost caught a little lizard but he was too small and too fast. Sometime in the near future I'll take a jar and put a lizard in it for a while then let him go before we leave.

I finally got to go in the wondrous jacuzzi, and I was the first one. Nobody had ever gone in it before, so I had to tell everyone how it was. It was *heaven* and I mean *heaven*!!

December 19

All morning my sister and I helped my grandfather unpack some stuff. They just moved in about a week ago, so we had to carry everything in the house.

My grandfather collects mugs and some of them are really weird and x-rated.

Grandma broke her ankle and has to use a walker, so Jennifer (my sister) and I pretend we have a broken leg and walk around with it.

We went to the Venice Beach and got a bag full of shells and coral. Jennifer would stand with her back to the Gulf of Mexico. I was supposed to tell her when a big wave was coming, and her pants got *soaked* because I didn't tell her.

The plumbers came to fix the pool because the filter didn't work, and we can probably swim in it tomorrow.

My grandparents got a new RCA television which is remote controlled.

December 20

The pool was finally ready to be swum in, and I had to put *two* layers of plastic bags on my fractured arm so my splint wouldn't get wet. As hard as we tried my splint still got *drenched*!

While this was happening some workers were putting palm trees fifty feet tall in a park across the street. When they hit an electric wire all the electricity in the block went out for a little while. When the wire finally snapped, the hole started to smoke and there was a loud snap.

Before I tell you about this I have to say that I love crab legs. We decided to go to a seafood restaurant. I ordered crab legs, and the waitress told me they were small because they were running out, so my sister had shrimp instead of crab legs, but I stuck with mine and they were excellent.

December 21

Today Jennifer and I swam our brains out. Between the rafts we got last night and just swimming laps we got a lot of water. All day we tried to dunk each other on the rafts until my mother made me get out because I kept coughing and sneezing while my lips turned *blue*.

I also finished the book *Westing Game,* which on a scale from one to ten I would give a 10½! It was a mystery, and I just love mysteries, but I don't like the Hardy Boys. I'm going to do a partner book report with Nick as soon as we do five reports.

Our grandparents have a tradition of having breakfast then a dinner about 3:00 P.M. and then just having snacks for dinner. I like it but I snack too much between dinner and night. There wasn't that much to write about.

December 22

Today was a very boring day. We swam all day, so I don't know if I can write a page, I barely finished yesterday's.

I liked the book *Westing Game* so much I asked my mom if we could go to a book store that she and my sister had gone to the night before because my sister has a book report due when we get back, and I looked for some other Ellen Baskir books (she wrote *The Westing Game*), but they didn't have any of her books, so I looked at Twilight Books, which are horrors and found a new kind of horror book that is called *Dark Forces,* and the book I got is called *Devil Wind.*

I guess you could call it good but it's nothing next to *The Westing Game*, which I could read three times in a single week.

December 23

I couldn't believe that in two more days it's Christmas, but it's true! Usually you think of Christmas as a cold and snowy time of year, but in Florida you put a tree on your back porch and decorate it. Then if you want you can take a dip in the pool, ha, ha!

My mother, sister, and I went to downtown Venice, and it is really nicely built. They have little islands in the middle of the streets with palm trees and posterboard candy canes on it.

Venice is where the Barnum and Bailey Circus stops, so they had all these signs saying the circus is coming or something like that on Jan. 13.

When we got back the boy next door came over and asked if I could play. I couldn't say no, so we went to his house, and he wanted to play trucks. I felt babyish playing on our hands and knees. Finally I just said, "Do you want to go outside?"

He said okay, and we shot some baskets until I practically was bored to death, then I finally went in.

December 24
CHRISTMAS EVE

All I can think about right now is the ghetto-blaster sitting in front of me that I unwrapped only about ten minutes ago.

We decided to open our presents tonight because we are going to our other grandparents early tomorrow. Everyone got nice gifts, like my sister wanted an electric razor for her legs and she got it.

I was so surprised when I saw a ghetto-blaster. (If you don't know what it is: a rectangle-shaped box with a speaker at each end. There is a tape recorder with a radio above it so you can tape songs off the radio very quickly.) At the sight of the box I had to ask my mom to pinch me. I paid so much interest in it I didn't see what everyone else got, so I went and asked.

Early in the day we went to a seafood place, and I had snow crab again. This is the best trip I have ever had.

December 25
CHRISTMAS!

We left at about 10:00 A.M. and arrived at about 1:00 P.M. As soon as we got there we opened more presents and I got a bunch of pennants (which I collect) and a few football shirts that I really like.

It's really cold down here, and when I saw how cold it was in Ill. I whispered to myself, "I'm really glad I'm down here."

We had turkey when we were in Venice and there was a lot left over, so we had it for lunch and we were getting tired of it. Then we got here and we have turkey *again.*

I can't wait until we get home so I can buy a cartridge or some tapes with all·the money I got. My parents told me that if we go to Disney World (or Land, I don't know) we will go on Thursday because my grandma is going to the hospital and my grandfather will be the only one home.

December 26

We left early in the morning with my grandmother to St. Petersburg, and after two hours of driving we found a restaurant with food (there were only hotels). We ordered our food, and I think he forgot about us, so we told him after forty minutes of waiting. After we ate we wandered around a dock with little gift shops and found a pier called "Pelican Pies" which had pelican's left-overs all over.

When we left, my grandmother told us about a bridge that was knocked down by a barge on a foggy night. A bus was coming and didn't see the bridge was down, so they flew off the edge of the bridge and couldn't get out. There were forty-four people killed. We drove over a bridge that was right next to the broken one, and it was scary enough just seeing the bridge suddenly end like that, but those poor people in the bus.

When we got home at about ten it was half-time for the Aloha Bowl, and Penn State was trailing 10-3. Then they came on the field and late in the 3rd quarter they kicked a field goal for 10-6. Then with three minutes to go, touchdown. Penn State wins and my dad owes me five dollars. (We made a bet on who was better—Penn State or Notre Dame!)

December 27

We went to a shopping center called Roses and I got a tape by a group named "Loverboy," which has a few of my favorite songs. We then headed for a mall called Lake Park Square. We got a few little things and headed back home.

Late in the day we borrowed three-wheelers from our neighbors and went riding, which a lot of people do in Florida. We went to the edge of the woods where people feed the ducks. When we got there people were feeding three little raccoons. All of the ten or fifteen ducks hobbled up to me and wanted food. I didn't want to feed the ducks as much as the raccoons, so I threw a few pieces of corn flakes away from the raccoons. Only about five ducks went for it, so I walked up to the raccoons and put some flakes in front of them, but as soon as I did the ducks came running up to the food and pecked at the raccoons; so they ran away and the raccoons only got a little bit of food.

We saw a duck that must have been in real pain because he was hopping around on only one foot and he wouldn't eat. Then on the way back I stopped to watch a squirrel run around me with food on his mind. My mother yelled, "Don't touch him, he might bite and have rabies." As I watched, the squirrel jumped on my tire and climbed up it then jumped off.

December 28

Today we went to Walt Disney World. We left at 8:30 and got there about 10:30 A.M. because of all the traffic going to the Magic Kingdom and Epcot Center. We had to wait for an hour to get in, then the first ride we went on was "Space Mountain," which my mother hated. I kept telling my dad we were not going to go in the front cart, but sure enough we got it. After the ride I decided it wasn't as bad as I thought.

"Space Mountain" was neat because of the way you're always inside and can't really see where you're going. There's a big dome which you walk into and see all these things that RCA has made (the producer of "Space Mountain") then go into a huge room that looks like the planetarium but bigger with the laser-pictured roof.

When we got in the eight-person cart the first thing we did was go through a tunnel with blue blocks of light shooting out at you (you'd have to see it to believe it) then faster and even faster until you go flying down a hill then do a few spins and dips and climbs. Then it's over.

We went to a ride called the "Pirates of the Caribbean" where you sat in a boat and pirates were shooting cannons at a village and there would be a big boom. Then from beneath the water a machine would shoot water up to make it appear a cannonball landed in the water. Later on the ride, more pirates were in town and burning as they sang, "Yo, ho, ho, we're pirates of the Caribbean, yo, ho, ho, it's a pirate's kind of life." (I think that's what they said.)

When it started to get dark we took pictures of Cinderella's castle and a beautiful Christmas tree, then went to see a show called the "Country Bear Jamboree," where the bear would sing some funny songs which had a long line (like the rest of the rides).

We then went to the "Haunted Mansion." A bunch of people would walk into a big room and a voice would say "Welcome to the most terrifying mansion you've ever seen. The object: to get out." Then a door opened and we all went through it to where all these chairs sat. Everyone climbed in, and we were off. As you traveled through the mansion ghosts and gobblins popped out at you and also hitch-hiked on your chairs.

I could write a story about Disney World but my hand is getting tired.

December 29

We made plans to go out for dinner at a seafood place, and I told myself I've had enough crab legs so don't get 'em.

When we got there we had to wait a while, so we went into the bar and saw these people who just got their drinks and were called for their table. So they asked if they could hold it for a minute.

Ten minutes later the same thing happened to us.

I ordered shrimp and they were huge. It was like two shrimp coming from the same tail.

Notre Dame beat Boston College in the Liberty Bowl, so I don't know who's getting the bet money but I hope I will.

On the way to dinner I made a bet for five dollars with my dad that Boston College would beat Notre Dame, and God cursed me for betting, and I haven't ever won a bet from my dad.

December 30

All we did was sit or sleep all day because my grandmother, mother and dad went to Orlando to return a gift that was too small for my mother. My grandfather was telling jokes all day and finally he went to sleep and so did the two of us.

When I woke up I was in a real grouchy mood, and when everyone got home the littlest thing bothered me (the same thing happened at Disney World because I was so tired).

My parents told me that they ate at some kind of future restaurant and really liked it, but they said that all they did was drive (it takes about an hour from my grandparents' home to Orlando) and then returned the gift to get a larger size.

That night we watched some English comedy which was so stupid it was funny.

December 31
Travel Day
Leesburg to Nashville

We left at 7:00 A.M. and stopped about 6:00 P.M.

We stopped at a hotel that had an exercise room and an indoor pool for only $29.00, but it was filled, so we went to the Howard Johnson's down the street.

The first thing we did was check for postcards, which I forgot to take. We watched a show called *Zapped!* with Scott Baio and Christopher Atkins which was rated R for good reason (the hotel had HBO).

We went over to the McDonald's and my sister and I split 20 McNuggets. It filled us both up for about an hour, but then we started to get hungry, so we split a donut.

After a while *Cannery Row* got boring and I fell asleep (I didn't stay up until midnight) but at 1:00 A.M. some party people came home and woke us all up.

January 1
Travel Day
Nashville to Home!

We left about 8:30 A.M. and ate at McDonald's again. I had a Dunkin' Donut chocolate-filled donut from the day before and a glass of orange juice.

We took off for Kentucky and an hour later we got there and I was asleep at the time. Kentucky went by fast, and we were in Lafayette, where Purdue University is, and we ate at a place called Godfather's Pizza. The pizza was good but Baby Pac-Man was better (they had arcade games there).

I think we were in the car too long because before we got out for dinner we were laughing at my dad's jokes.

We got home and Santa had come because gifts were all over the floor under our tree.

Journal Summary

Look over some journal you have kept for a period of weeks or months and decide what the gist of it was, the main things that stand out for you now. Write this summary by blending your separate entries into a single, shorter story of what happened that brings out your main points and leaves out unimportant details. You might present to others both the journal and the summary or the summary only.

Making Stories and Friends
Shelly Heldreth

I am a person who loves to write made-up stories. I wrote about my orange and purple skunk. She can't spray but everybody is scared of her. She loves the snow. I also wrote about the Different Zoo. All its animals were owned by a mad scientist. He was always trying things on the poor animals. The cow had such long hair it couldn't see. I wrote about the horse who went to school. It wore blue cords and purple jeans. It liked math but hated homework. I wrote about my baby cat. I fed it some milk and it grew and grew and grew. It didn't stop growing. We put an ad in the paper. The owner came by, and it turned out to be the mad scientist from the zoo.

I also wrote about myself and how I felt when we moved here from Ohio. At first I was so lonely I ached. It slowly got better. The more I was here the lonelier I got. I missed my friends. Then one day we got a phone call. It was Marcey. She was coming! I was so excited! I hoped she would bring Susie (her dog). Finally the day came when she was coming. Her mom and dad came too, of course. We had such fun.

Now I have new friends. I still miss the old friends. It doesn't hurt much when you have friends. One of the sayings I like best is "Make a new friend but keep the old one. It is silver, the other is gold."

What I Do
Angie Zeedyk

You might say I'm one of those people who loves horses and to ride. I ride English and am pretty proud of how much I am accomplishing so far. I've been in two shows already and pulled away a first place ribbon. You can also say I'm a person who cares a lot about poems and detailed writing. I write, and it makes me feel better and even more confident of myself. I also like ice skating. My ankles are a little weak (I can only go backwards, do a slow turn, and go forward). I also like to watch snow and rain storms. They are relaxing, and when I go to write I can give the feeling of it along with mine too.

Working It Off
Jenny Connor

After reading my journal, I have found that most of my life revolves around gymnastics. It is really hard work, but it makes me feel free from any other troubles that I might have. I also learned that I am not usually in a bad mood, and if I am I can usually make it into a joke. For example when my locker jammed I wrote a poem about it. Here it is:

Lockers

Lockers, Lockers, Lockers, Lockers.
Sometimes they will drive you bonkers.
I used to think they'd be great
But then I came and met my fate.
Lockers, Lockers, Lockers, Lockers.

Or when we were about to start something new, and I didn't know anything about it, in my journal, instead of saying "I feel like crying," I said that it was just because we hadn't started it yet.

Looking Back

Memories

Look around at your surroundings until something you see reminds you of an event or person or place from your past. Jot that down briefly. What does that memory in turn remind you of? Keep the chain of memories going. These are just notes for later, so you don't have to write full or correct sentences or think about spelling till later. Just get down a lot of memories.

Afterwards, talk over your notes with a partner or two to decide which of the memories might be best to develop for others. Try out certain memories by telling them to each other in as much detail as you can recall. Sort out the memories that seem most promising to write about further. You might pick out one memory and jot down everything else you can recall by way of new details about it. How did things and people look? What did you hear and feel? Or you might connect several memories that at first appear separate and jumbled. What connects them? Should the order be changed?

Now write up the memory or memories into a complete story or poem for some audience you picture in your mind. Use your notes but feel free to go as far beyond them as you need to make your recollection come alive and become clear to others. Try out this draft on partners and revise for a final version to print up with other memories as a booklet. Or rehearse and read aloud to some people in or out of school.

This activity may result in one of the following kinds of writing called autobiography and memoir. You can do it many times because we all have lots of memories, and this is a good way to get them out so you can use them for your writing.

Memory Notes
Katherine Robison

Fee Fee	Chip & Dale
Goo Goo	No Cupcake & Boxer
Laundry	"I'm older than you."
No diapers	"Only by a minute!"
Becka	Do dishes
Bobby	skinny
twin	clothes
Kim D.	No brush hair
	Play games
	wanting to be skinny
Mrs. Nocho	snarls
Mrs. Ponemba	freckles
Red	pretty
operation	running
"No Homework"	jogging
Mrs. Crowell	friends
I love you	Acceber
Club	"Freckle Face"

Rebecca

Katherine Robison

When Rebecca and Kalyn were little we used to hide when my mom wanted to change our diapers. Kalyn, my older sister, is about one year older than I.

Well, Kalyn, Rebecca, and I would go downstairs into the laundry room and would hide in the laundry. Kalyn would hide in the bottom of a basket, then Rebecca would put some clothes on Kalyn then she would lie on Kalyn. Then I would take a washed blanket or towel and put it on Rebecca. Then I'd take another blanket or towel and put it on me. My mom would go crazy.

Memory Notes
Mike Bremmer

I won it
it was electric
I was elected for winning it

best athlete in class
3rd grade
close run
50 yd. dash ⎫
600 yd. run ⎬ had to win to run
beat fastest runner in school
Mrs. Haffner
3rd & 4th grade mixed
40 children in class
lived in Woodbridge
St. Scholastica

Pencil Sharpener
Mike Bremmer

On the day of May 21, 1981, I won a prize for my class. I had to run the 600-yard and 50-yard dash because I was representing my class. I was elected because I was in track. I was a sprinter and long distance runner. We ran the 50-yard dash first. I was in last place for the first 20 yards. I started looking at the back of the kid in front of me and soon I was in second place. My coach had told me that would work. In the last ten yards I pulled ahead of the fastest girl in the school to win.

The 600-yard run was next. I thought it should be called a dash because it was short. When I started to fall behind I just thought to myself, "Mike, you're representing your class," and I pulled ahead again.

The prize I won for my class was an electric pencil sharpener.

Memory Notes
Kaati Brehm

Buttons   calling her Sara
Sara   all wanted her
licking my face   barking around us
mom liking her   took her home
in a basket   cute as can be
called them over   had fun with her
on the floor   agreeing
all said yes   I tried to ride her

disagreeing
hated bikes
name for it
dug under fences
falling asleep
liked to gnaw on wood
long drive
had puppies
lively
brother and I fishing
sleeping in kitchen
needed a dog

one year on Feb. 12
wanted a dog
loved her
white and black
wire-haired terrier
female
jumping
wagging her tail
what to name her
loved the car
was good pet
never bit anyone

The Dog Poster
Kaati Brehm

The dog poster in our room reminds me of when we got our dog, Buttons.

We drove up to the pet store. It was a long way away from where we lived. When we finally got there, my brother and I were half asleep. We went inside and started looking around. I went over to a basket on the floor. I looked inside and there was a cute little wire-haired terrier. I called my mom over and told her I liked this one and asked if we could get it. We all agreed to get her. When we left, the dogs who had been sleeping woke up and started barking like crazy. I was very excited and I almost asked if we could get them all, but I didn't because we were leaving.

On the way home we decided to call her Buttons. My mom wanted to call her Sara, but she was overruled by my brother and Dad. We finally decided on Buttons, and her middle name would be Sara.

Memory Notes
Beth Adams

diaper
baby sit
Coleen Kelly
Sit and play with hair

spider
Pink box (taped)
chocolate chip cookies (bet)
Green ghost

Red can	fun
Fudge Brownie & Tea	Tom
Barb	allergic
Got to go	yell
High heel clogs	Bell-yell
yell	Christmas card?
pushing her down	spider web (Halloween)
Chocolate	Homework!!
Red curly hair	

Fudge Brownies and Tea
Beth Adams

In the first grade and second grade I had a teacher who I thought was the perfect person. I used to try to do everything like her. Her name was Mrs. Rafferty. One time my mom had invited Mrs. Rafferty over after school for tea. I almost went crazy when my mom told me that. I insisted on making fudge brownies, they were my favorite dessert. So I made the brownies the night before, and the next day I wore my best dress, did everything she wanted, and didn't do anything that she didn't tell me to do. Then it was time to go home because Mrs. Rafferty couldn't get out of school until three. I was going out the door, and she told me to stay, so I stayed, and she said if I would wait a minute she would give me a ride. I just about flipped. When she drove us home my Aunt Barb was there, and I found out that my Aunt Barb and Mrs. Rafferty were friends in college. That was just about the best day in my life.

Susie's Cat Takes a Bath!?!?
Mary Dalrymple

One day Susie Osing and I decided to give her cat Justice a bath. We ran the water until it was warm and then filled the wash tub. Justice was locked in his cage so he couldn't run away. We brought him (Justice) near the water. He made a weird noise and clung on to Susie for dear life. Gently we eased him into the tub. He was *scared*!!! Susie poured some Clairol herbal shampoo on him and scrubbed it in. He looked like a foam monster! We rinsed him off with cups full of water. He had a fit, but I didn't get too wet because I had a raincoat on! Susie did too, but the zipper did not work, so she took a bath. Her clothes were sopping. We dried him off and he ran upstairs like a speeding bullet. Boy, was that an experience, but afterward he smelled really nice.

Incident in Your Life

Tell an incident that happened to you some time in the past, an incident being a specific event that took place only once, on a certain day or mostly on one day. Let events reel by in your mind like a movie. Take notes on some, then pick out an important one and write down all you can remember about it. Tell it aloud to a partner or two and let them ask questions about what they want to know more about or don't understand. Write up the incident now in a way that will bring out for others what makes it important or interesting to you.

Think of who might want to hear or read this. Include it in a book of other memories.

Frog Fights
Kim Dietz

I remember putting slightly old frogs in different kids' window wells. Then we'd get a slightly young snake. We would have fights in the summer with one kid's frog and another kid's snake.

One time a snake started to swallow the frog's front left leg. The frog tried to pull his front leg away. Then the snake swallowed the frog whole. We saw a big lump go down its throat. Near the middle of the fight I went down in our basement and looked out the window for a close-up. Then my brother came down. It was excellent! Afterwards I was guessing why the frog let himself go. I guess it either gave up or lost its strength. We had the fights at different kids' houses. It was fun! (But grossing!)

When My Cats Had to Go
Barbara Yacobellis

Once I had ten kittens and one cat. They lived in the basement. But one day they ripped the curtains and the couch, they even spread their kitty litter all over the room. My mom said that the cats had to go. So my dad sold all the cats to a pet store, all except one. Her name was Bessy-May-Moocho. I was so happy when we got to keep one cat. After we fixed up the basement, Bessy-May-Moocho lived there. And she died down there in the exact same place she first stood on.

When I Went Water Skiing
Mike Mueller

It was noon when I got up on water skis. I got up three times without any trouble. The lake water was calm, but in back of the boat it was very rugged. But I had no trouble at all. However, I was terrified of the walleye, muskie, and northern pike.

My cousin came along with me. He had water skied before. This was my first time ever, and Paul never got up, and I was out there in the middle of the lake. I forgot all about the walleye, muskie, and northern.

Thanksgiving
Chris Sims

About two years ago we went down to Springfield, Illinois for Thanksgiving. The forecast said, "Possible ice-covered roads and blizzardy conditions." We weren't sure if we would make it.

About an hour later we left. We went down the road, and the wind was blowing hard. It was real boring, so my brother and sister went to sleep. I didn't. First of all, I love traveling. Second of all, I always stay awake when any kind of storm comes. After a while it got boring to me, so I just dozed a little.

After about three and a half hours I woke up. My brother, sister and mom were still asleep. My dad said, "These roads are slick." Just when we came up to a bridge a car stalled in front of us. All the other cars were driving on the side because there was no ice. Finally, after about an hour, we got there.

Our aunt and uncle had a feeling we would be late. We talked a bit and then, since it was late, we went to bed.

The next morning we woke up to a big surprise. We woke up to five feet of snow. We were real excited till we heard our relatives couldn't come. It was a little upsetting but we had Thanksgiving together.

A Jewish Evening—"Hmmm!"
Caroline Dehnert

We started off by reading from a small purple book. First Papa read, then Brother read, and around the table. "Baruh Elo Hay Nu! Baruh Elo Hay Nu!" When it was about time for me to read, I didn't know what to do and got cold feet. I didn't know how to read Hebrew, but I could read the English translation on the left. "Caroline, read your part in English."

"Okay," I replied nervously. It was the first time I had ever been to a Seder. Everything was different. Luckily I knew a little Hebrew and spoke it whenever I could. They seemed impressed and said, "You can read the Hebrew translation parts sounded out in syllables." Now I was impressed. I finished with a roll on my "R" and then we started around the table again. Every couple of pages or so, we blessed some bitter tasting grapefruit wine and took a sip. I took a gulp. My mistake! It was so ... bitter tasting. Probably vintage '84! I thought I was getting drunk! Finally we finished reading half of the book. Thank God! I thought I was about to fall asleep.

Shelly and I were the cleaning duet. I held a bucket under a person's hands while Shelly poured lukewarm water over them. I handed them a towel and they dried their hands. Interesting! Then the mother brought out the food. It didn't look so bad. There was a raisin and nut casserole. Pretty good pink lemonade, American. Halleluiah! Fish and carrots, which were really mushy and soaked in wine. Hard-boiled eggs, and of course matzoh, and matzoh-ball soup. What's Passover without matzoh? "Dessert time!" called Mother. It was pretty good. Dates in some kind of juice. "Thank God, it's over," I thought.

"Eldad, get out the books!"

"What!" I thought, dumbfounded. Oh no, not that purple book again! "Please, God, no!" I thought and looked up at the ceiling.

"Baruh Elo Hay Nu!" shouted Grandpa, reading as fast as he could.

"Sounds like a broken record!" I murmured. I sat listening and reading, staring at the clock. Tick faster! I thought earnestly. Finally it was over and time to hide the half piece of matzoh. "Here comes the fun part!" I cried to Shelly and Eldad. "Don't kill each other trying to look for it!" I knew where the matzoh was, I saw the mother hide it. I was tempted to tell Shelly but didn't. She wouldn't have found it anyway. Eldad jumped into the kitchen and found it before I could have said, "Shalom!"

It was time for me to go. I thanked them for inviting me and left. When I got home and saw my bed, I cried, "Halleluiah!" and jumped in faster than you could've said "Good Night."

The Chilling, Unforgettable Day
Cheryl Pasbach

It was September 26, two days before my birthday. But somehow I didn't really feel like living, guilt building inside of me like a wall made out of blocks. My sister had died the day before. I felt I was the cause of it, which made it worse.

I was going to church and couldn't let Amy, my sister, go with me, even though she wanted to go so bad. She was only a child of three years. When I got home, she wasn't there. I asked my father where she was. He said she was out playing. So I went out and looked for her, but I couldn't find her anywhere. I went to every apartment complex and asked people if they'd seen her. There was no sign of her, so I went home to see if she'd gone home. When I came home, Dad said that he was going to pick my mother up from work.

A few minutes later Dad came running in with Amy in his arms. She was coughing and very pale. I was scared and didn't know what was going on. Dad quickly ran to the neighbors, who were paramedics, but they weren't home. Dad ran back to the apartment and looked up the hospital. I ran outside and screamed for help. My friend, who wanted to be a nurse, came and did something to her stomach. It seemed to work, but a minute later she turned pale again. A few minutes later an ambulance came with one fire truck and a police truck. Boy, was I confused. What was wrong and what was happening? My mother had just gotten a ride home. The ambulance went off with Dad, Mom and Amy.

Two hours later my parents came home and announced that she was dead. I ran out of the building with my dad trying to catch me. I thought it was my fault because I didn't let her go to church with me. When my parents caught me, they told me she was found in our car with the windows closed. It was 90° and even hotter in the car. She choked. They didn't know the cause and had an autopsy done on her.

A week later we found out she had choked to death on her own fluids. It was because of its being so hot in the car. The weird thing is that we didn't even know she could open the car door. So how did she get in the car?

Horrible Happening
Helene Harrison

It was one of the worst things that had ever happened to me. It was a warm summer's day, and I hardly expected what I saw when I walked around the corner of the house. It had been a pleasant Sunday. We brought my grandfather over from the retirement home he was in. I had just come from the kitchen. My mother had been making chicken cacciatore, which smelled delicious. And now, what did I see when I come around the corner of the house? My grandfather on his hands and knees and my brother's dirt bike lying on the ground nearby. When I saw this, my heart was clutched with claws of fear.

I went over to him, and he asked me to help him get up. For such a frail-looking old man he weighed a lot. I simply couldn't get him up. He had been saying, "Don't get your mother or father," because he knew they would be angry when they found out that he, a man in his late seventies, had been trying to ride a child's dirt bike. I motioned to my brother, who was coming around the corner, to get my parents. I should have gotten them in the first place despite his commands.

My parents came, and they were angry. My father got my grand-father into the car and we went to the emergency room. We then waited a long time, and the doctor's verdict was that he would need a new ball joint in his hip socket. It was a serious injury.

After that it was never the same. He went from one hospital to another, then from one nursing home to another. Now he spends his life in a bed, in a dimly lit room, in a nursing home.

The Story of the Missing Part

Jennifer Hoebeke

One Saturday afternoon I became sick, and everyone thought I had the flu. After four days I still had a low fever and pain on my right side. So my parents decided I'd better see the doctor.

The doctor sent me to the hospital and said a surgeon would check me over. The doctor said it was my appendix. So I had x-rays and blood taken out. And then at 6:30 I had my operation. I was in the operating room for an hour and in this other room for an hour. The next day I had something to eat. It was jello, soup, crackers, ice cream and milk.

The second day I started to walk. It was hard to walk because I had I-V. The third day I had my nose tube out. It felt a lot better. The fourth day I read the letters the children wrote. The fifth day I had my staples, tubes and stitches taken out.

The doctor said, "You may go home tomorrow." And I was glad. Saturday I called my dad and told him that I was coming home. My mom, dad, and Audrey came to pick me up. The nurse wheeled me out to the car. When we got home I got a present from my family. Then Audrey played with me.

Play Accident

Ajay Naidu

When I was two years old and living in our Skokie house my uncle and aunt were staying with us. I was playing near our outside backyard wooden gate. It was open, so I decided to close it. I went over to the heavy gate. I tried to close it, but it wouldn't budge. I tried to brace against something, and my hand found the hinge area. I pulled with all my might. The heavy door came unstuck and hurled closed, slamming my thumb in it. I bellowed so loud my uncle ran outside to look what had happened. He quickly undid the gate, yelling for my aunt and grandma to call my mother. My mother rushed home and then rushed me to the hospital. I had a contusion and had to wear a splint for four weeks.

My First Fossil
Seth Finnegan

When I found my first fossil it was on the beach, and I thought it was a firecracker. It was about a centimeter high and a quarter of a centimeter wide with a glossy grey center, and it was round and white. I showed it to my father, and he said, "That's not a firecracker, it's a fossil crinoid!"

I said, "What's a fossil crinoid?" So he explained that a fossil crinoid is an animal that has a stalk that attaches to a rock or something and at the other end of the stalk is a crown of tentacles used for catching food and that they still exist but they are called sea lilies. At that time I was about 5½ years old. Now I am 10 and I have probably well over 1000 fossil crinoids, trilobites (and for those of you who don't know what a trilobite was, a trilobite was a three-segmented animal somewhat like a woodlouse and an ancestor of the horseshoe crab). I have fossil shells and coral, and many other assorted fossils. I think this incident changed my life because before this I had never ever heard the word *fossil,* and now I have over 1000 fossils.

Tummy Pains
Karl Siegfried

One of the most important events in my life happened when I was eight years old, and the important event was my getting appendicitis. It was in the spring of 1982, when I was in Mr. Watterholt's homeroom, at King Lab School.

It started when I began having tummy pains, except they were on the right side of my body, instead of the left. Just my luck, stomach flu was going around, so all the doctors dismissed it as that.

Soon the tummy pains got so bad that I had to miss school and stay home, which I was *so* depressed about (hee, hee, hee!). Well, one night they got really awful, so my mom and dad had to drive me to the hospital in my pajamas.

All the doctors *still* said it was stomach flu, when finally a brilliant surgeon named Dr. Swan said that my appendix had already ruptured and that they would have to operate immediately. By then it was about 7:00 in the morning, so when one of the doctors put the anesthesia mask on my face and told me to count to ten, I was out before I even got to one.

After a few days Mr. Wetterhold came to visit me and bring me get-well cards from the other kids. When he came, I was so excited I forgot all about my pain, but I fell asleep in the middle of his visit.

Since my appendix ruptured before they could get it out, that portion of my body was filled with pus. To get it out, they made a second incision and stuck a small straw into it, to let the pus drain out. One day a doctor came in with four nurses, pulled down the sheets, and quickly yanked out the straw.

Instead of stitching all my incision up, they just let it heal by itself. I had to wear a gauze pad over it and change it every day.

I shall never forget the experience of going through an operation and living in the hospital for two weeks.

An "Almost" in Third Grade
Kim Meyers

I can remember a boy in third grade named Mark Furman who was funny but at times a troublemaker.

Well, one time during outside recess, Mark, I guess, wanted to be noticed. The way he wanted to be noticed was to pull a stray dog's tail that was on the playground. When he finally grabbed the dog's tail the dog bit him on his bottom.

It was so funny, I started to go to the bathroom in my pants. As fast as I could I ran into the school and to the bathroom.

Boy that was sure a close one!

Phase of Your Life

Tell about some important experience or situation in your life that went on for several months or years—some phase that seemed to have its own beginning and end. Use the memory-notes technique to get started. Or summarize a journal you kept during that phase. Tell the story aloud to a partner or two and let them ask questions. Use their responses to help you write the finished story. Do they understand what made this a phase? Think of a title that indicates what the phase was about, and use that to guide you as you write.

Include it in a memory book, or make it a part of your
full autobiography.

My First Semester in
Junior High School
Carol Kantayya

The first thing that bothered me was the large appearance of the school. It certainly scared me, but later on I realized that the layout of the school was pretty easy to get around in. Once I got to know where my different classes were, the size of the school decreased fifty times.

The large amounts of homework surprised me. Every day my back pack would be copiously flowing with books, folders, and notebooks. Eventually, I got used to the large but mostly easy amounts of home-work.

During this semester I had different feelings about each class. Certain classes were much harder than others. I thought all the classes would be tough, but that was not necessarily true. For example, to me social studies is much harder than math.

I also learned a lot about being responsible. At the beginning of the year (Aug.-Sept.) I decided to get involved with school activities, so I joined the *Lance* staff. Turning in stories for the newspaper before the deadline helped me to be responsible in turning in my assignments on time.

After five months of junior high, I have finally realized how to handle my problems. All in all, my first semester turned out to be a good learning experience for myself.

My Early Life
Shelly Yogev

My name is Shelly Yogev, a Jewish name which means "mine." I was born in the Hadassa Hospital located somewhere in the city of Jerusalem. When I was born on June 30, 1972 I weighed 7.2 pounds and had blue eyes. I was three and a half years old when I moved from Israel to the U.S.A. I didn't know any English and thought there was only one language, so on the first day I went to nursery school I walked up to someone who looked nice and began to talk. I still remember the expression on her face and how she ran to the teacher crying because she was so scared. That's how I met my best friend. She taught me many words in English and I'm very thankful to her because of that.

When I moved here to the U.S.A. I moved into a townhouse on Brown Street in Evanston. When I was about six I moved to a big house on Payne Street, and just a few weeks ago I moved to a big flat on Park Place. When we moved here we only planned on staying for a year or so, but my father got a good job and so did my mother, so we decided to stay longer, and every year we stay the harder it gets to say we will move back. I doubt we will, and I hope not. I've been living here in the U.S. for 8½ years now and never want to move back. When I entered kindergarten I was scared out of my wits. I didn't know what it would be like. When I entered the classroom and looked around, I was about to run out. I turned around and was ready to run when a short skinny Japanese-looking woman walked in and said, "O.K., class, come and sit on the rugs."

As the year went by I became very attached to her (my teacher—I forgot her name) and at the end of the year I didn't want to leave. I was on the verge of tears when my mother reassured me and told me I could see my teacher next year. I left slowly and unhappily, and the last glimpse I saw of my teacher she was wiping her eyes.

The first thing I did when I took a step into the Timber Ridge school was to run down to my old room. I hid behind the wall, jumped out and shouted "SURPRISE!" Then I just stood still. My jaw dropped. My eyes popped out. There in my old room, my favorite room, was nothing. Nothing but a few rays of sunshine and a chair that sat in the middle of the room with nothing but a cobweb strung across it. I will never forget that sight as long as I live. I thought my favorite teacher had gotten fired, but a few days later I saw her at the JEWEL (grocery store), ran up to her and hugged her. When she saw me she picked me up and smiled. I told her the whole story, and she told me she wasn't fired, she had just changed schools. I was relieved to find that out, and every time I was at that store I would race around the whole place looking for her. But I never found her.

I remember the day my family and I took a plane and moved here to the U.S. I remember when I tried spaghetti for the first time and asked for seconds and thirds. After I finished eating I got up and wobbled down to the end of the plane to go to the bathroom. I remember I heard a man's voice saying something, and then I felt the plane tilt downward. I went flying with it. The next thing I knew I had gone to the bathroom on the floor of the plane. I left it there, got out of the bathroom and went to my seat. I looked outside and saw cement, gravel, ground. I was excited but went up to my mom and said, "Mom, did we forget something and come back?"

"No," she said. We got off the plane and began our life here in the U.S.

I have two brothers, one older than me and one only five. I have always been jealous of my older brother, and he is jealous of me many times too. That's the cause of most of our fights. When I was young my brother and I barely ever fought. As we grew up we began to fight more and more. As we grew older we grew out of fighting. My younger brother is really sweet. He is funny and nice to be with. He has just entered kindergarten and is always talking about it. He brags to me that he doesn't get any homework, and I'm just about to kill him when he smiles, and then I just can't hit him. Both of my brothers are very nice, and we try hard to live happily together.

When I lived in Israel my brother and I would get into a lot of mischief together. For example, one time we played Popeye. My brother was Popeye. I was Olive Oyl, and our dog was Bluto. My brother decided to act out a scene from Popeye when Popeye is fighting with Bluto over Olive. So my brother began to fight with our dog, and it wouldn't have been too bad if our dog wasn't a German shepherd. My brother had gotten all chewed up, and I had sat there the whole time trying to look like Olive. My brother and I got into other things like when we drew train tracks all over the living room walls because my brother's train didn't have tracks. We were nicknamed "Shovavim," which means *mischievous people* in Hebrew.

My Early Life

Shane Mecklenburger

My name is Shane. I was born August 31, 1973 at 1:05 p.m. I weighed 6 pounds, 8 ounces. I had brown eyes and curly blond hair. When I was first born, these were the people in my family (some are dead now). My two grandmothers and grandfathers, my great grandmother and grandfather, my four aunts and uncles, my father, my mother, and my sister.

Here are some stories about my early life that my family and I recall.

When I was very little I was sitting on a changing table and cooing while my mother was working in the kitchen. Suddenly she heard terrible choking sounds from the other room. She ran in to find me choking on the table. My sister walked in, and my mother told her to call a friend who had four accident-prone boys. By that time I was turning blue, so she hung me upside down and patted me on the back. That didn't work, so she waited a while then got impatient and put her little finger down my throat and flicked out the button I had swallowed.

Another time my sister and I were playing tag, and she chased me down the stairs. I was going so fast I couldn't stop, and bang! I was bleeding, so they took me to the hospital, where I got six or seven stitches.

I remember also the time I first learned how to ride a bike. We were having a cookout and we invited some friends over, and I really wanted to learn how to ride a bike. So one person (his name was Jack) took one training wheel off and told me to ride that way, so I did. Then after a while he took the other one off and said, "Now try it." I did and it worked.

One time I was going fishing and I had to go to the bathroom. So I ran really fast, and to get there you have to jump over a three-foot wall, but my foot got caught on a rock and I slipped and did a flip and landed on my elbow. I was crying, so they took me back and called the paramedics. They said to go to the hospital.

When I got to the hospital I had broken a bone and taken a piece of nerve with it.

One time my family and I were on a trip to southern Missouri. We were in the middle of nowhere and it started to rain hard. Then lightning flashed and thunder rolled. Then I looked across the field we were next to and saw a house that looked as if it were on fire and that's what I said. My stepfather said, "That's not smoke, it's a twister." Sure enough, it was and it was heading straight towards us! So my stepfather got us into a ditch on the side of the road and opened all the doors and windows of the car. Then he put a blanket over us. By that time I was crying and praying for us not to get hit. Fortunately the rain stopped, and the tornado turned and we got back safely.

Well, I'm 10 years old now and I weigh 72 pounds and I'm 57 inches tall and I have brown straight hair and brown eyes.

Autobiography

Tell a series of important or typical events that capture the story of your life. Don't summarize a lot of facts and dates. You may want to include some incidents, phases, or other memories featuring you that you have already written. Place these in the order that they happened unless you have a reason to put them in another order that you make clear. Let a couple of other people read a draft and talk it over with you before doing the final version.

Pass it around in class and show it to friends and relatives. Make it into a booklet or include it in a book with others' autobiographies.

The Many Lives of Kimberly S. Cullen
Kimberly S. Cullen

My Life in Kindergarten

I called a friend of mine butt-brain in front of my teacher. I was sent to the doggy corner. This was a big doghouse in the room, and if you were bad, you had to sit in the doghouse for the rest of the day. My kindergarten was in Salisbury, Maryland, and it was Beaver Run School. I learned a lesson because my friend ignored me completely before I moved to Tennessee.

First Day

I screamed and kicked. I would not set foot in that classroom. My teacher helped Mom drag me in. The kids were staring at me as if I was crazy. Everybody was sitting on little carpets, so Mrs. Morgan got out a little rug for me to sit on. My mom stayed with me that day and helped me calm down. By three weeks I calmed down and soon I enjoyed the school. This happened in Holston View Elementary School in Bristol, Tennessee, in first grade.

Big Feet, Big Foot

Ever seen Big Foot? I've seen Big Feet. This was in Holston View Elementary School in Bristol, Tennessee. I was in Pod B, second grade, and my teacher was Miss Mimi Tilly. Our principal had an operation. When we found out she was coming back to the school the next week, the school planned a welcome back ceremony for the principal. By the tennis court there was a big spot filled with trees. One day at recess, some bulldozers came and started to clear the area. The next day they were finished. The men had left a little island in the middle of the circle. On the island were little fir trees. But we were not done yet. The school had to make a small trench around the circle and put a fence in it. When we were finished, we went inside the school. The next day we all looked at the circle. Suddenly a boy screamed. We ran to see what was the matter. He shrieked, "I saw Big Foot!"

Maura Ruane asked him, "Are you nuts?" The boy shook his head and pointed to the fence, which was trampled on and lying on the ground broken. "I also saw Big Foot!"

Mrs. Daniels gasped when she saw them. "This man must wear a size twenty in shoes!"

"Really," laughed Miss Grace, "I thought it was Big Feet!" Everybody laughed, but then there was a rustle in the bushes and the thud of feet. Some of us screamed and ran out of the circle. After that the circle was closed down and we had the ceremony on the stage.

The Leprechaun Attack

On St. Patrick's Day something very mysterious happened in Mrs. Cullen's third grade class. This happened in Maplebrook Elementary School in Naperville, Illinois. When my class went into the classroom, it was a mess! Broken pieces of chalk were everywhere! Totes were dumped on the tables and chairs. Most of our chairs were gone, and we found them in Mrs. Hansen's class. Some of the totes had green feet in them cut out from green construction paper. Some things were stolen, too. On the chalkboard, weird drawings were drawn. By the look in Mrs. Cullen's face, I could tell she didn't do it. We cleaned up the classroom. But the next day it happened again. Papers were ripped into shreds lying on the ground. Even some tables were turned over. So my class decided to write the "creatures" a letter in order to teach them a lesson. We wrote about how they hurt our feelings and destroyed things and would they please stop it. We left it on the chalkboard overnight. The next morning the "creatures" had written a letter back. It was written in a very messy handwriting, and every word was written backwards. It talked about what they eat and how they sleep. The letter also apologized for doing mean things to us. They said they would leave tonight at six p.m.

I was riding my bike at six p.m. and I saw a green light flashing by. I followed it until it went up in the air.

Brace Yourself

I had to get braces in fourth grade. But I didn't tell anybody except Mrs. Udell. I went to my orthodontist every day for four days after school. I usually kept my mouth closed. Still, nobody knew about my braces. Finally, all my braces were on, and my class was at the front of the room talking with Mrs. Udell. Then Mrs. Udell said, "Quiet, everybody; Kim has something to show us." Everybody quieted down and looked at me.

I opened my mouth a little and said, "Brace yourself!" Then the eraser fell off the edge of the chalkboard right on Jenny Murphy's head! I burst out laughing; I couldn't help it. Everybody saw my braces and called me brace-face, tinsel teeth or railroad tracks for days. Now, I can't wait to get the braces off! This happened at Maplebrook Elementary School, Naperville, Illinois.

Slip 'n Slide

Christy, Kristina and I went sliding on our butts and stomachs. This happened at Lorado Taft, De Kalb, Illinois. It was our fifth-grade trip, and my instructor, Gene, wanted my group, the Bears Group, to learn how to use showshoes. But first we had to go down this really steep hill. It went almost straight down! But it slightly curved and slightly slanted. Gene went first, followed by Mike, Keith, Sean and Cheryl. They went sideways. Christy pushed me down the hill. "Christy," I hollered. I caught a branch and slowly walked sideways.

"Is it easy?" Christy called. I nodded my head. So Christy followed me going sideways. Kristina went after Christy. But then Kristina slipped and fell on her butt and slid down towards Christy. Christy started to run, then she slipped, but then held onto a branch. Then Kristina bumped into Christy, who lost hold of the branch. Both of them were sliding on their butts towards me. I just stood there, and Christy caught hold of my legs, and I flopped right on my stomach in the snow. We went sliding down the hill so fast I felt we could beat Superman in a race any old day! He could fly and Christy, Kristina and I could slide down the hill. Christy and Kristina were sliding on their butts; I was sliding on my stomach. Then I started screaming; we were heading right for a huge pile of snow. Suddenly—swoosh—we ran into it. Gene wouldn't let us go back to our bunks and change, so we spent the whole morning in wet clothes.

August 23, 1982

August 23, 1982 was my sixth-grade orientation at Lincoln Junior High. Jenny Waters and I left early so we could make it on time. When we got there, there were already lots of kids. Most of them were sitting on the risers or chasing each other around the gym. Jenny and I sat in the middle of the risers, where most of the kids from Maplebrook were. Then Mr. Raynett came into the gym and talked to us about Lincoln. Then, he said, anyone's last name that began with A-D go to the first table by the stage. I ran to line up. When it was my turn to go up to the table by the stage, Mrs. Mackay asked me my full name. When I told her, she gave me my schedule. I went back to the risers and compared schedules with Jenny. I felt like crying; Jenny and I didn't have any classes together. We didn't even have the same teachers. Then I got lost while looking for Mr. Kelso. Probably the happiest thing that happened was when I met Debbie Holic.

Eyewitness Incident

Tell anything you saw happen once, some brief incident you merely witnessed as a bystander. The incident does not have to be unusual or dramatic, just interesting or memorable to you for some reason that you bring out. It might involve animals or something else in nature as well as people.

Could this fit in with any of your other writing? Or you and others might make a collection of your eyewitness accounts, perhaps clustered around certain themes suggested by the incidents themselves.

The Hawk

Shane Mecklenburger

The great wings of the beautiful brown and white hawk spread. His talons loosened their strong grip on the top branch of the towering, skeleton-like oak. The wings gave a great swoop down and then up to lift the bird into the cloudless sky. It flapped three more times with feathers rustling in the wind as it rose through the air. It flew over mountains and valleys with small streams branching off in all directions.

Suddenly it spotted the unfortunate prey. Peacefully sat the small white hare, twitching its long whiskers. It smelled something. It spun around only to find two huge yellow claws shooting at him. He sprang to the side but the wary hawk caught him in the air. The hare squirmed and kicked with his powerful hind legs. The claws loosened from pain to let the hare go free. The hare shot to his hole, too late.

The hawk grabbed him by the shoulders and flung him over on his back. The helpless hare was then torn to shreds and killed by piercing of the neck. The hawk took him in his claws and flew off again to his giant nest in the oak.

Memoir of a Place

Get your memories going and focus particularly on places. Pick a place that has a special meaning for you or that you have a lot of interest in. Jot down all the details that you can remember about it. Tell what the place is like and show how you feel about it. Help your reader to visualize it and grasp what goes on there.

Include it in a book with other memoirs by you or others. Submit it to a magazine or newspaper as a feature.

Lorado Taft

Kevin Rose

On the bus
I did a scavenger hunt.
As I drove up

I had butterflies
Twirling in me.
I walked toward the dorm.
Wind whistled in the trees.
Every step I took
Had a little crunch
From dried-up leaves.
I smelled wet moss
On the trees.
Here and there were puddles
From melted snow.
Our dorm was big
With a million bunks.
Going home was sad
But there was no choice.

Fire

Chris Derylo

We all sat down near the bonfire after dinner in the woods. We were telling stories while the fire crackled and snapped as if someone were breaking twigs. I looked across the fire and could just make out people's faces through the orange glow. The warmth felt good on my cold feet, legs, and arms. I smelled the burning wood. It had a sweet, piney, and crisp outdoor odor.

We were getting tired so we put out the fire and went to bed.

My Lovely Time at Lake Moraine

Christa Pohlmann

Last summer my whole family went to Canada. My favorite place was Lake Moraine. One day we went there I climbed up the hill of rocks in the lake and found a perfect place to sit. There were lots of flat rocks to sit on, but I found the best one. The scenery was beautiful. There were some trees in among the rocks. The lake was clear turquoise because of the glaciers that melted in it. The pine trees which were on the nearby mountains were a luscious green. In my place you could hear hardly anybody talking. A peaceful feeling came over me when I sat there. Now and then I could hear the high-pitched twittering of birds. Unfortunately this beautiful and serene time was interrupted by my father's call from the bottom of the hill for me to come down.

The Beach
Cindy Pierce

I run past the door
while I think how it once
        smashed my finger.
I yell good-bye
        as I
                whizz
down the hall to the elevator.
In the elevator
I think about the sign
        that says
"Children should be
accompanied by parents."
        Ignoring it
        I press the button,
Towel in hand.
I run down the ramp to
        the beach.
The soft sand feels good
        on my feet.
But soon I get to
        the water
where there are many crushed shells.
I run past the shells
        where it is smooth
                again.
A large wave comes,
        knocks me over by
                its force.
Water gushes
        into my mouth.
I come up coughing.
I notice now that
        I'm freezing.

I go back to the
            beach
        to dry off.
My mom is waiting
    with some snacks.
I eat and throw
    the crumbs to
        the seagulls.
When the crumbs are gone
    they follow me for a minute
        thinking I have more.
At 3:00 a.m. the next
        morning
    with a flashlight
we search the beach for
            shells.
    We find
    a starfish,
with sizeable shells,
                and a crab.
Many strange things
        wash up on the beach
that we don't want to touch.
    Another
        day
            has
                begun.

Candid Camera

*Pretend you are a camera and show what some person
looked like at a certain moment. Describe the person so
that your reader can visualize him or her exactly. Do the
same thing for an object or apparatus that interested you.
Draw mainly from memory, but fill in some detail from
imagination if you want to.*

*Ask someone else to draw a picture from your descrip-
tion, and post up the two together. Or include in a
booklet you put together of other sketches and reportage.*

Four Candid Shots
Ajay Naidu

Mod

The Mod wore a slim army coat with a large British flag on the back. He had his hands in his pockets with his fingers shuffling around in them. Underneath was a Levi jeans jacket. And under that was a spotless clean ivory white shirt with an olive leaf on the left chest. He also wore some pinstriped gray and black pants that were held up by a checkered belt. His shoes were black and were shaped like the front of a Western man's boots. His hair was black, which made a contrast against his pale white face that had scars on the forehead and jaw. Slowly he drew a cigarette from his pocket. He tried to ignite a match. But when it broke he cursed and put back the cigarette. When he spoke, he spoke in a cockney accent that sounded like he came from West London. As I marked all these points about him he saw me and looked disgusted. He gave a snicker and tramped off.

Scooter

The scooter leaned against the post. I could see why it was chained at least five times by the back wheel. It was magnificent! It had a Union Jack on the front plate, which was a gleaming black color. The plate reached to the back of the scooter under the glittering mudguard that had a black and white checkered mudflap attached to the back of it guarding the rear tire. The front of the plate had right next to the Union Jack two large stenciled letters. The letters were GS. Jutting out of the plate on both sides were an infinite count of mirrors of all different shapes and sizes. At the bottom of the plate was the front wheel. It was small but had a large mudguard over it. At the top of the plate were the handlebars. There was a visor right above the top light. At the end of the handlebars were brake levers, two lights, and two tassel grips. Directly even with the handlebars was the seat. It arched up about two and a half feet. And last of all, attached to the rear mudguard was a flexible flag pole that reached about five feet up with a coontail on top of it.

Vegetarian Sausage

The sausage was brown and about three inches long. It smelled fantastic. The sausage had lines that looked like little rivers that had dug little canyons everywhere. That little sausage could entice a man who had sworn to fast! It had been cooked to perfection on a griddle. I bit into it. It tasted scrumptious. To be precise, it tasted like soy. It was a vegetarian one, but it was just as good as the real thing!

Tornado

The sky turned pale green. The wind was blowing extermely hard. Our car sped along the highway. We were in Lonoke, 11 miles from Little Rock, Arkansas. We pulled off the road with a screech. We said a prayer. Outside the wind was picking up. Soon the green began leaving the stormy sky. The air became cold and light, rather than the dangerous warm, humid, heavy air. We got back on the now-wet, slippery highway and drove to the nearest rest stop, which was called Stuckeys. We called our nearest friends in Little Rock and left after we had a snack and heard the weather report.

The Old Man
Shelly Yogev

He was a tall, strong grey-haired man with a short grey beard hanging from the end of his thin hairy chin. There were several wrinkles on his face and there was a big gloomy smile that covered it. His nose was big and red, and the only friendly look he had was in his big blue eyes. As he smiled you could see his old, ugly yellow teeth. His shoulders were as broad as an ape's, and muscles bulged out all over his legs and arms. His chest was big and strong. It seemed as if he held a knight's shield in front of it. His stomach was big, and his feet were a size twelve. His muscular arms could lift 395 pounds with ease. He looked fiercer than a mob of dogs.

Sketch of a Person

Drawing on your memories, tell what some person you know well is or was generally like. Tell typical things they did or do. Use their actions and habits and words to sketch the main lines of their character or of their relationship to you.

Include this in a collection of your other sketches and memoirs.

Busie
Emily Steel

Busie is the Polish name for grandma. Busie is very important to me because she is my grandma. Busie is about 65 years old, weighs approximately 100 pounds, has silver-blue eyes, white hair, tan skin, wears glasses, and is about 5 feet 2 inches tall.

She took my cousin Paul and me to Poland. When we were there we visited relatives. We stayed in Poland for a month. We went to Katowice, Dolzyce, Wabbrzych, Krakow, and Warsawa.

Often Busie would sing when she was walking, cooking, or sitting in church. When we visit her in Florida she treats us like spoiled children. When Paul and I were in Poland she treated us like grownups.

When my family was in Florida Busie wanted to have something special for my brother and me, so she signed us up for a candy-making class. In the end Jamie didn't want to go to the candy-making class, so only Busie and I went.

In Poland Busie asked Paul and me if we wanted tea, which was what the adults were drinking. Paul and I were very pleased that we were not being treated as spoiled children.

My Parents and Pets
Tori Landau

My parents are the Master and Mistress, or King and Queen, or Grand Majesties or WHATEVER you want to call it.

My father is a handsome tall man. (He looks like a cross between Christopher Reeve and Mikhail Baryshnikov, and the best of both.) He's kind, humorous (with such corny jokes that a crow could feast for days!) and has an air about him that makes him perfect. He also has brown hair, blue eyes, and steel-rimmed glasses that make him look mild-mannered.

Mom, on the other hand, is imperfect. She has frizzy black hair, green-brown eyes, and either glasses or contact lenses on for vision. She is only about 5′5″, and she locks the bathroom door when she weighs herself, so I don't know her weight. She is a computer freak and is getting her Ph.D. this moment (10:31 a.m., 10-28).

I have had about seven pets, not counting numerous goldfish. In order they are: Quicky & Fanny, guppies; Quickly, the tadpole; Milkey, Twigger, Sinbad and Merlin, who were anoles. Twigger was my favorite pet of all. He was also the most intelligent. I was able to teach him a few tricks, such as displaying his aggressive mating act on command, lying quietly on his back in my hand, and shaking claws. I really miss him.

Quickly, the tadpole, was a very fun pet to have. I happen to take medicine. I had put an empty pill bottle in his tank so that it would float. Quickly used to use it as his house.

Nicky
Emily Halderman

My brother is often referred to as a dragon. At least it seems like he's a dragon sometimes, but really he's a fairly nice little boy. He's got bright strawberry blond hair that shines like a gem in the sunlight. His eyes are a bright blue. Not greyish like mine, but a vivid blue! His skin is very fair and burns pretty easily. One cute thing about him is that he says a lot of funny little things without really knowing that he's being a comedian. Here are some things he said: My mom had told my brother to get out a bag of carrots for the hamster because the hamster was running very low on food. He went to the refrigerator and pulled out a bag of parsnips. He frowned and said, "Aw shoot! These carrots aren't ripe yet!" Also, my mom asked my brother what Valentine's Day was. He replied solemnly, "Valentine's Day is the day when you send signals of love." (It made me think of a traffic light flashing, "Love! Love! Love!") He said many many more things but these two were my favorites.

Looking Into

Baby Days

Ask older relatives or family friends to tell you about yourself during the babyhood time that you don't remember. Write this down first as notes, then write up these notes in your own words.

Exchange with others who have done this also. Add it to your autobiography.

Basic Facts About My Babyhood
Eddie Siew

My name is Eddie Siew. I was born in Denver, Colorado July 31, 1973. I was born prematurely and weighed only about 5.6 pounds. So they put me inside an incubator. They fed me by sticking tubes down my nose and sent food through the tubes. They put me inside the incubator for about three days. When they took me out I had enough body fat to protect myself and weighed about 5.8 pounds. I was about 1 foot 6 inches tall.

When I was taken out of the incubator, I right away developed jaundice and had to be put under an ultraviolet light. Jaundice is when your skin turns yellow, because there is bilirubin in your blood. They put sun glasses on me to protect my eyes from the light. When they put them on, I looked like a mean bandit taking a tan. There was an American girl that was under the ultraviolet light next to me. The nurse was joking and said, "No hanky panky!" They put me under the ultraviolet light for three days. After that, they kept me for two more days. Then we went to my new home. I went home to a nice house in Denver.

Two weeks before I was born, my maternal grandmother came to take care of me. When I was born, she fed me formula milk for about three months and helped change my diapers. During those three months, I did not do much except crawl around, cry, and say, "Aaa, Aaa" wherever I went. When I was six months old, she started to feed me baby food. She always gave me any flavor except spinach. I would spit it up at my mom or my grandmother. I grew my first tooth when I was nine months old. When I was one year old, I had four teeth. My mom started giving me a little table food, like rice, vegetables, and some ground meat at the age of one.

In 1974 Dad got his Ph.D in Pharmacology. He got a job as a research fellow at Stanford University. When I was one and a half, we moved to Palo Alto, California. We moved into a small apartment with nice neighbors. I liked to suck my thumb a lot, so my mom bought me a pacifier. I liked it so much I started to collect them.

Oral Story

Ask older relatives or friends to tell some of their memories of their youth. Write this down in their own words by recording, transcribing, and editing, or by taking notes and going over these with the person right after he or she finishes. Use the words of the speaker, who should be the "I" of the memories. But you may add a short introduction, if you want, telling who the person is.

Read your story to others. Make a collection of these with other students.

My Aunt's Memories
Kim Hermanson

When I was at home with my brother we had a little store made out of cardboard. There we sold colored sand. We used to go down to a special place and shovel up the pure white sand. When we got home with the sand we would color it with beet juice that made it a lovely pink, onion water, and other dyes. When we colored all of the sand we went back to our store and sold it to the people who came with the jars so we could put the sand in it. Most of the time we were not paid with money, we were paid with safety pins. I forget why we were paid with safety pins though. Once in a while we were paid with a few pennies, but not very often.

When our grandmother was a very little girl it would be so funny when she dressed her cats up in doll clothes. When she was finshed she would get one of the boys to nail a few boards together and make a carriage. Then she would take the cat and she would put it in the carriage and pull her around the yard, sidewalk, any place she could find. Our mother used to do that too, and you should have seen her face while she was pulling the cat around in the carriage.

Seven Lives to Go

Jeff Watts

My grandpa, Maurice Watts, lives in Elmhurst, Illinois and has a summer house at Apple Canyon Lake. He is always either inventing new things or making jokes. He is also very good at ping-pong, so whenever he comes over I play against him. He is also very handy with tools and at fixing things. In fact, I remember when he made a see-saw and my brother and I would play on it. Also, he made a tire-swing and a little horse like the ones at some playgrounds. When we go to his summer house I get to drive his boat and water-ski while he drives the boat. Whenever he comes to our house, he always either fixes something or makes something neat. He has also had quite an unusual childhood. So Heerrree'sss Grandpa:

I once had a horse and I was riding down a riverbed when my horse got stuck in quicksand. I didn't think we would get out very easily, but my horse kept pushing and pushing, and the quicksand loosened, and we finally got out.

But now this is the horse that almost caused my downfall. I had it hitched to a little cart and it ran away with me. It led the cart toward a train track. Well, the cart tipped over, and I was left with the cart on the railroad track unconscious and there was a train coming.

Luckily, the engineer could see the cart, so he braked the train and got out. Then he found me unconscious on the track and brought me home.

Now it turned out I had my back broken, but out on the farm, since I could wiggle my toes, they didn't take me to a doctor. So it was not until I came up in the draft in World War II that I found out my back was broken. There were four crushed vertebrae in the lower lumbar section and I could have well been a cripple for life but I wasn't.

The army doctor said that the fortunate thing that happened to me was that I hadn't seen a doctor, because if they had seen the condition of my back, they would have felt it necessary to operate, and in those days in the country where I live, I could have well been left an invalid.

Now a cousin of mine had received a little cartridge gun, and we were playing with it, and my finger got shot. I can remember yet seeing just that pearly-white bone for a minute until the blood started coming out. We were only two blocks from a doctor, so we ran over to the office, and he wrapped it up. Well, it turns out, the gun wadding had hit the bone, and seven days later I came down with lockjaw. I was the ninth lockjaw case they'd had in this hospital, but I was the second one that ever survived. They said I was worse off than any other patients they had. As a result of that I was in the hospital delirious for seventeen days that I don't remember anything about. My mother was told that I didn't have a chance to live. But I did. So when you add up my horse problems, and my gunshot problems, my mother used to think I had nine lives, but she told me not to use the other seven.

Tell me, Grandpa, how many trips have you had?

Well, you might say this—when your dad was growing up, we traveled in the United States and we had our children in every state but Hawaii. My excuse for not going to Hawaii is my camp trailer just wouldn't make it—too much water! Then since the children left we started traveling abroad.

We've been to Russia, England, Ireland, Scotland, Denmark, Sweden, Norway, Finland, Germany, Austria, Yugoslavia, Italy, the Netherlands, Spain, Portugal, Egypt, Greece, Israel, Japan, Hong Kong, Fiji Islands, and some others that I can't think of now.

Lillian Greenwood

Rosemary Latshaw

My great-grandmother's name is Lillian Greenwood. She has grey hair and loves to crochet. She also likes to bake pies, cakes, cookies, and tarts. She collects music boxes and hummingbirds. My great-grandmother loves to play cards. She writes letters a lot and has very neat handwriting. Doing kind deeds for other people is one of the many things that makes her a likable person.

When I was a young girl, I had one brother and three sisters. We lived on a farm, and in the summer, I had to rake fields and drive the horses. I also had to do things around the house. I'd do the dishes and help my mother out with the laundry. I had to churn butter, which I didn't like to do but I did anyways. I'd sit there for a half-hour churnin' and churnin'.

We went to Greenbrier School. It was a big school, just one room. It went up to eighth grade. There was a big stove right in the middle. I remember my teacher's name was Mr. Humphrey. There was just one teacher for all of us. You had slates to do your homework on. We wrote with slate pencils and an eraser. We had a spelling bee once at school, and I won that. We had fifty-two words and I didn't miss any. We had the most fun when we went to school.

I liked to be outside. In the summertime we picked blackberries. We'd can 'em and make jelly. Sometimes my sister and I would go fishin' in the creek. We had an old-fashioned rope swing and we'd always play on it. We always had a playhouse outside and we played house in it. I used to like to play in the snow. We'd slide down the hills and build snowmen. We had a sleigh pulled by a horse that we'd ride in. That was fun.

I learned to crochet when I was about nine years old. After I got a little older, I helped make quilts and things like that. All the kids would get a big ball of yarn and we'd go to a place with a loom. We'd make a rug and sell it in the spring when everybody got new rugs.

We lived about eight miles from any town. When we went shopping on Saturday, we had to go by horse and buggy because it was too far to walk to town and we didn't have cars. On Sunday, we went to church and Sunday school.

I used to help my mother bake in the kitchen. In them days, people used to make lots of bread. I guess not much happened in them days, but that was how it was.

Family Anecdote

Retell in your own words some incident that is told in your family about one of its members. Ask relatives to recall some story that is passed around because it's comic or dramatic or otherwise memorable. If the story is not already familiar to you, write it down right after you

hear it. If it is familiar, write it down from your memory,
perhaps reinforced by another's retelling for you.
   Exchange one or more of these with others and make a
book of them.

A Runaway Dog

Mary Whitehead

It was Christmas, and my dad and his brother wanted a dog. One
day while they were in the kitchen they saw an ad cut from the
newspaper that said, "Dog, free to a good home." The night before
Christmas my dad slipped downstairs when he heard a dog barking. In
the morning it was no surprise. They got a little grey schnauzer, a year
old.

About a week after Christmas, my dad's brother was playing with
their dog in the backyard. The dog started getting mad and bit my dad's
brother. My dad's brother was only four years old, so he didn't know
what to do. So he bit the dog back, and the dog ran away and that was
the last they saw of him.

A Stay at Ellis Island

Jenny Connor

When my grandma was about five years old, her family came over
from England, which is where she was born, to the United States. All
boats coming into the United States had to stop at Ellis Island, where the
people on the boats could be examined for any diseases that they might
be bringing into the United States. Her father told her to say that she
felt fine even if she didn't. She felt fine, but told the man that examined
her that she had a sore throat, just to see what would happen. After she
told him that she had a sore throat, he asked her to say "Ah." She said it
in a real scratchy voice. He asked her if that hurt, and she said yes. Then
she and her family had to stay at Ellis Island for two days. Her father was
mad at her for making them stay there, on Ellis Island, when they didn't
have to.

Vegetable Soup

John Meiser

When my mother was little her least favorite meal was vegetable soup. Her mother made vegetable soup one night and my mother refused to eat it. Her mother told her she couldn't get up from the table until she ate her soup. Since it was summertime it was a real bummer for my mother because she couldn't go out and play after dinner. After everybody had left the table, my mother was still there with a cold bowl of soup in front of her. She decided she was not being treated fairly so she ran away from home.

My mother had walked about six blocks and decided to take a rest. While she was sitting, a neighbor walked by. She thought for sure the neighbor would run home and tell my mother's parents.

When my mother finally decided to go home she discovered not only that the neighbor didn't tell my mother's parents, but that they didn't know she was gone. The vegetable soup was still there and she had to eat it.

Poor kid!

A Burning Experience

Anant Setlur

This is a story about an early childhood event for my father. Once when he was a young boy in India his family used to celebrate a festival called Holi. On this day the country celebrated the spring time with song, dance, and good food. Another tradition observed on Holi was to have a big bonfire, which symbolized the burning of the old and unwanted things and the harvesting of the new. The kids used to eagerly wait for this day because it was a lot of fun gathering old boxes, paper, and other combustibles, and having a big fire. There even used to be a competition among groups as to who would have the largest bonfire.

One "Holi" day the kids were all having a lot of fun around the bonfire. It was late in the evening and the fire had almost died when one of the kids who got overexcited pushed my dad into the fire. It was a terrifying experience which he will never forget as long as he lives. He must have been in the fire for a minute, but it felt like a lifetime. He was dancing over the smoldering embers because he was barefoot. He shouted for help, and it felt that no one out there knew what to do.

Finally, he felt a big tug on his arm and the next thing he knew, he was out of the fire. Fortunately, he was not badly burned.

The Waterfall
Arjun Natesan

My mother and aunt were living in a hill station in India. Here is a story of one of her adventurous days there.

My mother Revati and my aunt Chiccu were starting off for a walk. They had no idea where they were going, so they just headed to their usual waterfall where they played a lot. Today they decided to climb to the top of the waterfall. The had never tried that before. They climbed over about a hundred rocks to get to the top. They sat down and rested for a while at the top and then they walked on. They heard some noises ahead so they peeked through a couple of bushes. They were really surprised at what they saw. What they were looking at was a Tibetan temple with seven or eight flags outside it.

They slowly and cautiously tiptoed to the entrance and went inside. They were in a large hallway. In the center of the hallway was a big box covered with silk cloths and a sacred Tibetan book on top. They were lucky that there were only three or four men inside there. They kept walking through the hallway until they came to another. This room was empty but was vastly decorated. They were scared to stay in this unknown temple any longer, so they sneaked out the same door they came in. When they got home their mother gave them the spanking of their lifetime.

A few days later my mother was alone, so she went to that same waterfall. She wanted to know where the water from the waterfall went, so she followed the river. As she was walking at the river's edge she saw a pipe. On the other side of her was a man filling up a little pool with the river water. My mother is not a good swimmer. When she was playing around in the water, the pipe suddenly gushed water out and my mother swallowed a few tadpoles (yuk).

Family Stories
Paul Etzbach

Great, Great, Great, Great-Grandma

My great-aunt Glady remembers her grandma telling the story about her grandma starving two times in her life. The first time was when she was four years old and they were coming to America from Poland on a sailing ship and they ran out of food halfway here. The second time was during the Chicago Fire. They were watching the fire coming and for some reason the only thing they saved was a new headboard they had bought for a bed. Their house burned to the ground and they had to live under the sidewalk until the houses were rebuilt. All her family had to eat was stale bread, which was divided equally.

Great-Aunt Zada Mae About Her Grandma and Grandpa

They left Selma, Alabama with a group of people in a wagon train. Their destiny was Tyler, Texas. It took months. The wagons had to stop often to rest the horses. When it rained, the wagons couldn't go very fast, and often the rocky trail caused the wagon wheels to break. They had to stop and fix them. There were other misfortunes such as the wagons being cold at night, and it seemed someone was always sick with a cold or cough. Each wagon was responsible for cooking its own meals and building its own bonfire. Zada Mae said to me that as a child she thought the journey sounded like a lot of fun, but to her grandparents it was a real hardship.

Aunt Carole

My Aunt Carole was an exchange student in Paris, France. She went to school there for six weeks. She was 16 years old and lived with a French family. She really enjoyed herself. The daughter of the French family then decided she would like to be an exchange student and lived with my aunt's family.

My Grandpa's Journey
Marla Kramen

My grandpa, Al Bloom, was born in Warsaw, Poland about 1907. He was very poor. Grandpa's mother came from a rich family, and her father was unhappy when she married a poor baker. They had five children, but because of immigration laws they had to leave two children behind. They left the oldest and the baby.

Grandpa remembered the long trip over on a boat. He landed on Ellis Island near the Statue of Liberty. After going through the checkups on the island, he had to live in a place called Hell's Kitchen in New York. It was called Hell's Kitchen because everyone was very poor and lived in crowded tenement buildings. Grandpa had to sleep in a bed with his two brothers. In Hell's Kitchen each group, like Italians and Jews, lived in a separate area, and Grandpa was once beaten up because he went into a wrong area.

After Grandpa's dad died, his mom got sick and he had to live in an orphanage for a while. Because the orphans were given cast-off shoes to wear that didn't fit too well, Grandpa developed bad feet. When he was twelve he had to quit school to work. He pulled heavy carts for 25 cents a day.

The family wasn't able to get the other children out of Poland because World War One began not long after they got to America. Finally, the older boy got to France during the 1920's, and he died in World War Two. The youngest child came to America in the 1930's, but he couldn't get used to his new life and he has spent his entire life in mental hospitals.

Grandpa read a lot of books even though he had to quit school. He sent my mom and uncle to college and always told us how important it is to learn. I will never forget him.

Biography

Interview some older person to get the story of his or her life. Have some questions ready to get the person going and to prompt them if they run out of thoughts too soon. Ask them for the main events of their life or of one important part of it. Ask them things about their life that you are curious about. Take notes or tape-record.

Retell in your own words when you write up the interview. This means that you tell the person's story "in the third person"—that is, refer to your person by "he" or "she."

Include your biography in a collection of others done by classmates or in a collection of other community information that may come out of some of the following kinds of writing.

Grandmother's Life
Billy Zukauskas

My interview was with my grandmother, Virginia Bosgraaf. Her maiden name was Trowlridge.

She was born on March 13, 1923 in Chicago. She was the fourth of five children. She had two sisters and two brothers.

Her father was killed when she was three. He was shot in the leg by someone trying to steal his paycheck. He died of lead poisoning caused by the bullet.

When she got older, about ten, she would go to the bakery in the morning for her mother and buy twelve hot rolls for 25 cents for her family. The boys would get three each, the girls and mother would get two each. Her older sister lived with her grandmother.

Her mother would play the piano. She could play any song she heard by ear. They liked to sing.

In the winter she would go ice skating at the lagoon near her house. She loved to be outside. In the summer they would take a streetcar anywhere they wanted to go. It would cost three cents to go to the beach. She would go to the 79th Street Beach in Chicago.

She had a dog named Queenie. Queenie would follow her everywhere and would sleep under her bed. At the park Queenie would follow her up the steps of the slide and slide down after her. Queenie would walk across a large field on her hind legs for a piece of candy. When Queenie had puppies my grandma's older brother, John, would sell them for a quarter each.

My grandma belonged to the Chicago Park District and won a blue ribbon in broad jumping when she was eleven years old. She loved to read and would read five books a week.

In winter they heated their house with a coal stove in the dining room and kitchen. When it was cold they would cook on the wood stove in the kitchen. When it was warm they used a gas stove.

They would go to the show every Saturday for ten cents. T.V. wasn't invented yet. Sometimes they would visit their grandmother on Sunday and go to Lincoln Park Zoo and have a picnic there. They would go to a carnival when it was in the area. They could rent bicycles for a quarter an hour. They would rollerskate and play games, like jump rope, hopscotch, piggy-move-up and baseball.

During World War II she worked in a defense plant office. They made lift trucks, and their company received a Navy E Award for excellent work.

She was engaged for four years during the war while her future husband fought in Europe at Anzio Beachhead. He was 375 days in front line duty. He was in the Fifth Army Infantry.

Granny
Stacy Huckabay

My great-grandmother Maudie Jan Dodd was born in 1890. Her mother died when she was eight years old, and her father was a country doctor in the backwoods mountains of Arkansas.

As a young girl she went with her father on his rounds and sick calls. Maudie became a good midwife and delivered many babies in her lifetime.

When she was twenty-two years old she married Arthur William Watkins. Bill was very poor and joined the Army. He fought in France during World War I.

After the war they bought a farm way up in the mountains. They grew peanuts and tobacco. They also grew a garden and raised chickens and cows.

Maudie and Bill had nine children. The fifth one died of whooping cough when she was two years old, and the ninth child, born when Maudie was fifty-one years old, died shortly after birth.

My mother remembers my granny brushing her long white hair that she could sit on. Granny never cut her hair except once when the children brought home head lice from school.

She insisted that all her children go to school. Some of the children went to college even though the family was very poor.

Granny loved her gardening, raising chickens, making quilts and crocheting.

At Christmas time presents were not put under the tree. The children stayed in bed and Granny brought each one their Christmas presents. Each child received one toy, usually a doll for the girls and a toy car for the boys. They also received a big red apple, an orange, and some hard candy. These were very special because they only had apples in the summer when they grew them and they never had oranges. The Christmas apple and orange were store-bought.

Granny died in 1979 at the age of eighty-nine.

My Lawyer of a Grandpop
Susannah Beary

My first memories of my tall, handsome, whitehaired grandfather, Frederick Wayne Ford, are posing with him for a picture, when I was six. He always "takes a big bite" out of my neck and says, "I wouldn't trade you for a forty-shilling dog and a brick watch." Sometimes I turn it around and ask him that as a question! He also tells a lot of jokes. My favorites are

> My name is Johnny Johnson. I come from Wisconsin. I work in the lumber yard there. Whenever I walk down the street, all the people I meet say, "What's your name?" And I say, "My name is Johnny Johnson. I live in Wisconsin. I work in the lumberyard there. Whenever I walk down the street all the people I meet say. . . ."

> They were all gathered 'round the campfire, and little Johnny said, "Grandpa tell us a story," so Grandpa said, "They were all gathered 'round the campfire, and little Johnny said, 'Grandpa tell me a story . . . '"

One of 74-year-old Frederick Wayne Ford's childhood memories is of his father running for State Superintendent of Schools. "I came home from school every day, folded campaign letters and hauled them to the post office on my little wagon. I was very happy when he was elected."

My grandfather considers his marriage to my grandmother Ginnie and his appointment as an attorney for the federal government in the Department of Justice and then as chairman of the Federal Communications Commission (F.C.C.) as special memories.

At the age of twelve Grandpop was a page (messenger) in the West Virginia State House. Many years later he was put in charge of getting the 1954 Anti-Communist Bill through the U.S. Senate. His past experience in a legislature was invaluable in this successful effort.

Grandpop spent several summers in a tent with his father in army camps. He learned many lessons that were useful years later in World War II, when he was in the Air Force teaching cadets how to be officers. He also traveled quite a bit, including a trip to Tokyo, Japan as an observer at the International Conference on Extension of the Cable from Honolulu to Southeast Asia.

Grandpa restored three different historic homes in Alexandria, Virginia. My mother once said, "We never have to worry. Daddy can be a carpenter, plumber and electrician."

I feel very fortunate to be Frederick Wayne Ford's granddaughter because he's an interesting person and made an important contribution to society. However, more important is that he's lots of fun, and I love him very much.

My Aunt's Childhood
Sarah Olden

It was fun interviewing Mary, my aunt. She is 22 years old, and she is a senior at Texas Christian University.

Mary told me that she was annoying when she was little. She used to sit in the doorway between the dining room and the kitchen.

Also, when she was in kindergarten she learned some songs. After dinner she would practice the songs in her room, which was right next to her sister's room. Her sister was studying one day, and while her sister was studying Mary started singing. Her sister got mad and yelled at Mary and Mary yelled at her. So Mary would get her sister back by writing Batman and Robin all over her sister's homemade pillow. She also jumped all over her bed with her dirty shoes on.

Some of Mary's funniest times were mostly at church and school. In church, Mary and her friend Gail were acolytes. Between Sunday School and church, there is a thirty-minute break. During the break, Mary and Gail would stop at McDonald's across the street and get coke and McDonaldland cookies. Since there wasn't enough time to eat all of the cookies, they gave the rest to the other girls who weren't acolyteing. After a hymn, one of the girls sat on their last and only Grimace. The girl picked up the crumbled Grimace, patted it, and gave it a funeral *right in the middle of a church lesson.* Mary and Gail saw the funeral.

Again in church, Mary and Gail were sitting in the back row. Gail decided to sing alto to make the hymn sound prettier. She was concentrating on the alto so much that she didn't sing the right words and instead of singing "eternal consummation," she sang "eternal constipation." Everyone in the back now laughed. Nobody knew what they were laughing about either.

Now for school. Once in high school, one of Mary's classmates was going to try a test on the teacher. He sat in a row next to a window. Nobody else was sitting in that row, so when the teacher looked away, the boy moved to the next seat. When the teacher turned around he didn't notice that the boy had a new seat. When the teacher looked away again the boy moved to the next seat. The teacher still didn't notice. So on and so on until there were no more seats left to move to. He put his books on the table and jumped out of the window. Later that day the boy went into the classroom, picked up his books and the teacher never noticed.

Once a group of students glued the teacher's coffee cup to the desk. When the teacher couldn't get his cup off the desk, he pretended he didn't want it.

Some neat and scary experiences were fun to listen to. Like when Mary told me about her first trip on a plane alone. And she was only eleven years old! One experience I didn't enjoy listening to was when she almost drowned when she was little. She was playing on some rocks next to a river, and suddenly she slipped off into the water. She couldn't get back up until finally she pulled herself up on a rock. Very scary!

It was real fun interviewing Mary, anyway. What an exciting childhood!

Blue Waves and Thoughtful Memories: My Grandpa's Story
Christina Dermody

Dedicated fondly to Grandpa and Grandma Dermody.

My grandpa is a stranger to some.
But to me he is the one I trust, the one I know.
No others like him, not even close.
So quiet but able to understand.

My Grandpa took me to the beach once. Now as I look back on it, I really don't think I gave him enough credit.

As we were driving he pointed out farmers' lands, dry rolling hills, and funny, tall, scrawny trees. Soon the countryside was covered with hardy brush, out of which jumped a jackrabbit right in front of the pickup! Grandpa stopped just in time, and the jackrabbit crossed the road to safety.

The mist was just rising from the ocean, two and a half hours after we had left the house. We located a fishing site, checked our gear and climbed down the cliff on a worn, rocky trail. We found ourselves on a corner of land with a perfect view of the ocean. In sea water pools among the rocks we saw colorful starfish, abalone shells of bright hues, and all sorts of interesting rocks.

Grandpa climbed up several shelves of rocks and stood high above the water. He cast his line. Then he turned, picked up a stick, and poked it into a shallow pool. A squid came out, surprising Grandpa! He called me, and we poked around in the pool some more but didn't find the squid again. Then Grandpa climbed down to some lower rocks, and I sat next to him.

Later we climbed a rope to a small beach below; he cast and put his fishing rod in its holder. He glanced off, saw a group of sea lions, and called me to see them. Then he went back to his fishing. I sat there transfixed by his determination and the perfect grace of the fisherman's art. Gradually my thoughts wandered to what Grandpa had told me earlier today. . . .

"I never have given up on anything. I don't think by nature that I am that way. I've hung in there."

I see my grandpa as a strong person, just as his immigrant parents were. His father was a born Irishman and his mother was from Scotland.

Grandpa was born in Cleveland, Ohio in 1921. His father, a railroad man, moved the family to Omaha, Nebraska, then to Caliente, Nevada, and finally to Long Beach, California.

Growing up during the Depression years meant homespun fun, "funny" clothing, and hard work. Grandpa's fun was swimming with friends, and climbing and swinging in a fig tree. In the summer his clothing was a pair of bib pants. Grandpa explained, "Shoes? What are shoes? No, no, we used to take the shoes and shirts away and run around in bibs, and toughen up our feet all summer. Nature puts on her own soles! Walking on hot pavement, railroad tracks, and running through rocks. I remember going to grammar school in a rich neighborhood, and they all made fun of my clothes. That left an impression."

As a child Grandpa worked hard picking berries and oranges, trying to make money to help out his family. . . .

I noticed Grandpa studying a rock. I went up to him, and he said, "This is a whale vertebra." As he went back to his fishing, the vertebra reminded me of the skeleton of Grandpa's education. . . .

Grandpa remembers a favorite high school teacher who thought that he had a special talent for zoology and offered to help him through college. Grandpa felt that he needed to provide for his parents instead of going on to school.

Since there were few jobs and little money during the Depression, Grandpa graduated from school in 1939 and joined the Civilian Conservation Corps (or C.C.C.). He helped on building and rebuilding bridges, roads and missions and worked in National Forests for wages to send back to his family. . . .

I realized that times were not always so good for Grandpa as they are today. . . .

After Grandpa left the C.C.C., he married and survived a very serious accident. He backed a truck over a cliff, broke his neck and was temporarily paralyzed. After an eleven-month recuperation, Grandpa started studying surveying because he could no longer do his original job. He had to leave his wife and two children in Lompoc when he was offered a surveying job with Pacific Gas and Electric in San Francisco. . . .

I looked back and saw a shark in Grandpa's hand. He told me that a shark is a primitive animal that has adapted to its environment and survived. . . .

The day ended too soon for both of us. As we drove home Grandpa pointed out some deer and a coyote. I was reminded that Grandpa had always loved animals and farming. . . .

Until he graduated from school he had seen little green except for the top of a pool table. When his father-in-law died in 1947, he had a chance to farm. He learned by watching and asking people who had made a good profit from farming. The most important part of cultivating the land to Grandpa was paying the bills! He said that the reward of farming was, "You are your own boss, you can see things grow, and you can see the kind of work you do." Grandpa will always be one with the animals and the land.

After selling the ranch Grandpa worked with the Cornellius Cattle Company, rode horses, worked cattle, and met some very famous and interesting people. He told me, "I worked with a very nice man, Mr. Harvey McDonald; I should have wrote a book on him. He was an old timer; he was up in his 80's and a very interesting man."

To keep up with the farm life Grandpa had left, he had a cat, dog, horse, bird, and two Shetland ponies for the grandkids. For fun, Grandpa would hitch the Shetlands to a wagon and call it a "Shetillac"!

When we got home we went to his garden and Grandpa admired his roses. I was wondering what advice he might give me, when he said, "Try to be honest in all that you do . . . be a gracious person, be a nice person; there are an awful lot of mean people in this world. Try to learn as much as you can. O.K?"

Even now I can still hear those words. I will carry them, and the memories of that day at the beach, with me always.

The Way It Used to Be

Interview an older person about what life was like and how things were done when they were young. Prepare some questions about things you are curious about, but let them ramble some too. Record in some way what they say and write this up afterwards in your own words. You can move some things around for better organization if desirable.

Do this several times alone or with others and make a collection. You might try to cover a certain ethnic community. For such a collection you might write some commentary about what you see in the responses. This could be an introduction to the whole or headnotes between interviews.

My Mom's Childhood Christmas Eve
Eric McDonough

When my mom was a little girl, the whole family went to her grandparents' home on Christmas Eve for a huge feast. Her grandmother and aunts worked for days preparing the food for the dinner, which didn't consist of meat, since the Catholic Church didn't allow people to eat meat on Christmas Eve. Some little bread-like balls had to be soaked in water for days to make them soft enough to eat. They were all Lithuanian recipes that went back many years.

My mom had to stay in the kitchen with the women while they got dinner ready, and the kitchen door had to stay closed. While the women got dinner ready, the men were in the living room decorating a huge tree. Every year they'd put my mom's electric train around the tree and all the gifts from Santa Claus. My mom thought Santa Claus brought the same train Christmas and took it back to the North Pole afterwards.

Before dinner, it was the Lithuanian custom to break bread with each other. The "bread" was rectangular and more like a wafer, though, that could be easily broken off. It pretty much melted in your mouth like a Communion wafer and didn't have any taste.

After dinner my mom was allowed into the living room to see what Santa brought her. When she was a toddler, Santa had brought a buggy with a huge doll in it. She was so jealous of the doll, she threw it out of the buggy and crawled into it herself. When she was older she was really disappointed, because she thought she barely missed catching Santa. She saw her stocking hung on an inside doorknob and somebody closing the door. She rushed down the stairs, but when she opened the door all she saw was one of her uncles.

Christmas Day was spent with her mother and father. The family started out the day by going to Christmas Mass. After Christmas dinner, the more practical clothing type gifts that were wrapped and under the tree were opened.

Life on the Farm
Todd Delahanty

My grandma always lived on a farm. She attended a one-room schoolhouse. It had grades one through eight and one teacher. There was not a school bus, so she had to walk three-fourths of a mile to go to school. She went to school for seven months. If she was late for school she would get a paddling when she got home. There was not a lot of homework because the kids had a lot of chores to do.

The chores she had to do were to milk the cows, wash the dishes, gather the eggs, etc. The house didn't have an indoor bathroom, and they had to use corn cobs or old catalogs for toilet paper. There wasn't any electricity. There wasn't any heat in the bedrooms, and they had thick feather beds.

For a treat she got to go to her uncle's house. They could travel there in a horse and wagon. Her uncle lived twenty-five miles away. She also remembered a railroad called Rock Island, and she thought it was a treat to hear the whistle as it went by, but she never rode it. The games she would play indoors were dominoes and checkers. The checkers were homemade. They would use red and white corn for men. They could never play cards and they could never sew on Sunday. The outdoor game they would play was usually ball. There weren't any restaurants or hotels. For money they would sell cream, eggs, and chicken, but they wouldn't get much money.

For Christmas she didn't have a tree or stocking. The thing that they would do was on Christmas Eve she would put her plate where she sat and on Christmas there would usually be an orange and some candy on the plate. There was a tree at her school, and they would decorate it by making paper chains.

When my grandma was eight or ten they got a Model T car. The gas tank was under the front seat. When they were low on gas they would back up a hill. There was no roof on the car so they got wet when it rained and cold in the winter because there was no heat in the car.

Folk Cures and Recipes

What cures for ailments and recipes for cooking have been passed down and handed around in your family or community? If you know some already, write them down. If you need help, ask relatives or friends, take notes, and retell what they said. Make a book out of cures and recipes that you and others have collected this way. Put this book together with others done on the community.

Bringing Inside Chicken Pox Out
Shelly Heldreth

My grandma told that her mother used bacon grease to bring inside chicken pox out. She took a bacon rind and fried it for five minutes, then she took the grease and rubbed it all over the person with the inside chicken pox. She let them sleep all night with the grease on and when they wake up in the morning the chicken pox should be out.

Sore Throat
Paul Etzbach

My great-aunt Glady said to help a sore throat you take one teaspoon apple cider vinegar to one-half cup lukewarm water. Then you gargle with it. Don't forget that medicine that tastes bad works.

Backaches
Arjun Natesan

Pranyamam is the Indian name of the breathing exercise we are going to talk about. You should always do it early morning. To do it you should kneel down and be relaxed. Then take a deep breath, hold your breath, and breathe out loudly. The professionals breath in for about five seconds, hold their breath for about three seconds and breathe out for about seven seconds. There are also different finger positions that you should keep your fingers in:

1. Your thumb and your second finger should form a circle while the other three fingers stay straight.
2. Same as the last one but the other three fingers bend inwards.
3. Make a usual fist but put your thumb in the fist.
4. Make a fist lying vertically and the thumb pointing up.
5. Just like the third one except you should hold vertically up near your abdomen with your knuckles touching each other.

During the exercise you should keep your mouth closed, and you should do it non-stop. This was given to me from my grandma.

Biting Fingernails
Julie Rzepka

My mother, Kathy Rzepka, says a cure for biting fingernails is to take an unripe apple and peel the skin off of it. Next you rub the apple on your fingernails and let it dry. Every time you go to bite your fingernails you will stop because of the awful bitter taste of the apple. Use this system until you are cured from biting your fingernails.

Bites and Stings of Insects
Todd Kilbaugh

We were on a camping trip in Michigan when I was stung by a bee. My Uncle Bob was an outdoorsman. He immediately took a handful of fresh gooey mud and slapped it on the bite. It took the sting out, and as it dried it took out the stinger.

Temper Tantrums
Todd Kilbaugh

Mr. Joe Loperfido believed that cold water on the buttocks of children would cure their temper tantrums.

What you do is fill one sink with ice cold water. Then take one hyper child and pull his pants down and drop his backside in. In no time at all you have one calm child!

Boils
Anant Setlur

This is a cure for boils. According to my father, you take a particular type of rosewood and make a paste out of it. You make a paste by rubbing the rosewood on a flat and hard stone with a little water on it. After a while it will become a paste. Then you apply the paste on the boil. Warning. If you touch anyone with the paste on you, you will stick to that person for five days.

High Fever
Jenny Peters

My great-grandma, Aurand, would put peeled onions on the bottom of her child's feet, tying them with strips of an old sheet. The child would be put to bed and covered warmly. Usually, the next morning the fever would be broken and the onions were partially cooked.

Poll and Survey

Select a subject that you want to know other people's opinions on. Write this out as a question or as a set of questions. Then ask of whatever people you want responses from—maybe a particular group, or maybe a mixture of people for comparison. Record answers.

Pull the answers together and write up the results. Part of your summary might be in the form of numbers and percentages, maybe charts or graphs. Some quotations might be good for illustration. Summarize also in your own words the gist of what people said. Weave this together with any figures or quotations.

Post this up, or put it in a newspaper. Or make it part of a bigger project like consumer research on a product.

Favorite Sport

Ron Eisenstein

I interviewed fifty people about the question "If you had to play a sport after school which sport would you play?" My prediction was that baseball, soccer, and basketball would score high. Surprisingly basketball did not score high at all.

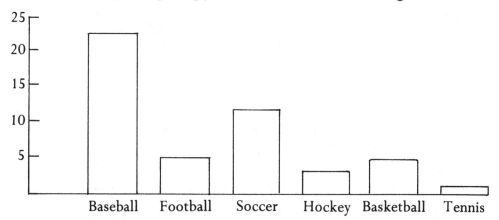

What a surprise! Basketball only got five votes. As I suspected, baseball and soccer scored high.

Favorite After-School Pastimes

Josh Ehrenfried

The Question—
After school, when you get home, what do you like to do most when it is your own choice?

Prediction—
My prediction was that most of the fourth graders would want to play with a friend because then you can play a game, watch TV or do anything else together.

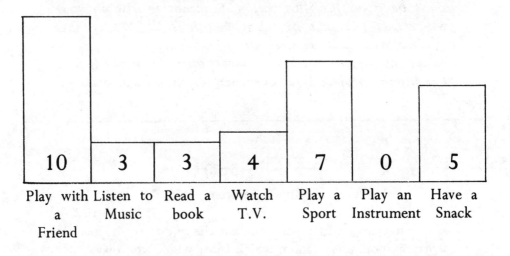

| 10 | 3 | 3 | 4 | 7 | 0 | 5 |

| Play with a Friend | Listen to Music | Read a book | Watch T.V. | Play a Sport | Play an Instrument | Have a Snack |

I had predicted that out of 25 third- and fourth-graders, five would like science, eight would like math, six would like reading, and six would like gym. It turned out that twelve liked reading, eleven liked math, and two liked something else. I was surprised!

Favorite Kind of Movie

Mike Gwinn and Ryan Foran

We asked 98 students in grades 2 to 4, "What is your favorite kind of movie?" Thirty-nine of them said Comedy, 7 said Horror, 18 said Action, and 22 said Adventure. Sports and Musical both got six.

We predicted in the beginning that Comedy would win, and we were right.

Question: What is your favorite kind of movie?

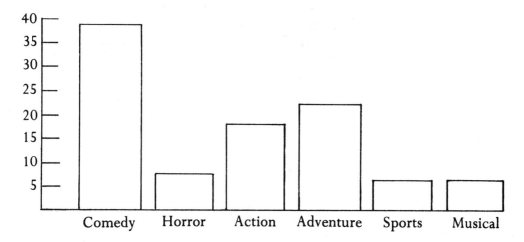

Favorite Subject
Karen Lizars

I had 25 third- and fourth-graders choose their favorite subject of the day. Forty-four percent liked math, 48% liked reading, and 8% liked other.

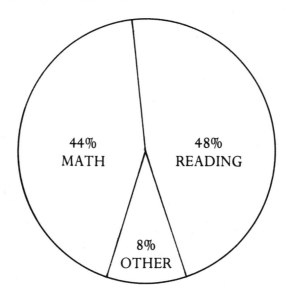

Winter Feelings

Josh Copland and Mark Nelson

As we all know, winter has started. We are coming to the heart of it, and how much snow we get is anybody's guess. We wanted to get some idea of how people feel about winter.

How do you feel about the first real snow in '82? Mrs. Baldwin answered that she can hardly wait until it's here. Why? "Because I like to wear heavy clothes."

We got Saul Kalos' reaction to winter: "I like winter a little bit because I used to live in Hawaii." Haakon answered: "I think it's excellent because it's more active. You can throw snowballs."

Mrs. Holloway says she likes lots of snow ... at least 12 inches. She doesn't think there is enough right now.

Survey of Readers

Emily Steel

I did a survey of different kinds of books to find out what books ten- and eleven-year-old kids liked most.

Twenty-five people were interviewed (including me) and thirteen of those twenty-five people chose fantasy. Four of the twelve people left chose science fiction. Two of the eight people left chose biographies. One of the remaining six chose autobiographies. No one chose history, and the five people left chose other.

What Books Do You Like?

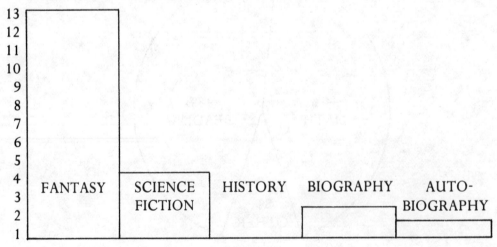

Interview Sketch

Interview someone in your community outside of your family and write up your notes or recording as a sketch of the person. Choose someone who interests you because of what he or she does or knows or represents. If the person's setting is important—where he/she lives or works—arrange to have the inverview there and make some notes on it too. Prepare some questions to get at your interest, but be prepared also to come up with new questions once you've heard some of what the person has to say.

Write up. Mix some direct quotations with some of your own restatement of what the person said. Blend summary and quotation without referring to your questions unless you have a special reason. If you want, you can shift things around to go under certain topics that threaded through the interview. At some point describe the person and the place as much as seems worthwhile. A sketch shows what a person or his or her occupation is like. Give a fitting title.

Your interview sketch might go in a newspaper or into a book about your community. If you choose a person for his or her profession or job, your write-up could go into a book showing what different careers are like.

Mr. Bernie Arbogast

David Vogel

Mr. Bernie lives in Naperville, Illinois. He is a custodian at Naper School.

I think he does a lot of hard work to try to keep our school the cleanest in town. He mops up the floors after everyone comes in from recess and cleans up all the crumbs and bags after lunch in the lunchroom.

He has to go down to the boiker room and check on big fans and water tanks to make sure that the rooms in the school get enough heat in the winter and stay cool in the summer. Today Mr. Bernie took us down to the boiler room and showed Jason K. and me two big fifty-year-old water tanks filled with boiling water. The boiling water heats the rooms. It was very stuffy in the boiler room, but we enjoyed seeing the heating system of the schoo. He took us to a room behind the boiler room He told us in the boxes that were down there were light bulbs of all different sizes, so when a light bulb burns out he can replace it with the right size.

"I like to keep thinbgs clean. A long tome ago I would wash my car in the river by Eagle Street. I would drive into a shallow spot and use a sponge. In fact everybody in town used to wash their cars down in the river by Eagle Street."

There is a swimming area here in Naperville which used to be a big quarry a long time ago. Now it is a concrete pool which has two diving boards and a big slide in the middle and a sandy beach.

"When the beach was built there were railroad tracks and hand cars and big chips and rocks that were taken out of it. I always tried to bring rocks up. So I worked hard.

"There was a swinging bridge. Kids used to swing across the water. They took it donw in the early 40's. But we had fun sometimes long ago. We picked corn by hand. We had shotguns to shoot rabbits and pheasants.

"Jason K., who is in your class, his grandmother and my wife played baseball on a team. They traveled from city to city."

There was a lot of information that I didn't know before I interviewed Mr. Bernie. I was surprised at all the equipment that he had to keep up with. Jason and I were so surprised at all the things that were down there. We kept looking at each other and saying to ourselves, "Wos, we could never keep up with all that." But Mr. Bernie can because he works hard and still has fun.

Roving Reporter

Choose a place outside of school that interests you, visit it at a good time, and take notes there of what you see, hear, smell, and touch. This might be a nature spot, a store or office, a street corner, any place you like. Write down in your own kind of shorthand as much as you can record this way of what you observe and what you feel there. Don't concern yourself at this point about organiz-

ing this; just get a lot of material down.

Use these notes later as the basis for telling what went on there, what it was like, and what you thought or felt about what you observed. Let others experience what you experienced there. Let them get to know your place. You can organize this either by the time order in which things happened or by features of the place, taken one at a time.

Include your piece in a newspaper, or post it in your classroom with a photo or drawing of the place. Combine it in a booklet with other pieces about the community such as elders' stories and folklore.

The Wedding

Ted Reavey

I went to the wedding of Pete and Daty Reavey, now a very happy couple.

At the beginning of the wedding, instead of the Wedding March they had a lady sing. Unfortunately, the lady forgot part of the song.

Then Katy finally came down the aisle, looking half nervous and half happy.

Then the priest started talking. He was wearing a white robe. As he talked he sounded as if he never took a breath. He also looked and sounded serious.

As a matter of fact, everyone looked serious. Then everyone stood and started a prayer for Pete and Katy. It was for good luck and happiness. Then we all sat.

Peacefully, a relative got up and read a little from the Bible.

As he was reading, Pete and Katy were whispering to each other.

Then the priest started reading from the Bible. He read about Adam & Eve. And then he started congratulating Pete and Katy. He was saying things about how they finally made it.

As he was saying this, Pete and Katy were making goo-goo eyes at each other.

The priest kept on thinking of things to say, so it dragged on a lot!

Finally Pete and Katy exchanged rings. Then they went to a table. First Pete blew out a candle. Then Katy blew out hers, but she dropped it. And Pete reached all the way across the table and caught it. Some people said, "That's what he's there for." Then they both walked back.

Suddenly the priest took out a golden cup. He poured two drinks in it. And then he put a lot of crackers in it. He ate a couple and gave one to a lot of people.

After that he made another blessing.

Then the whole crowd stood up for a blessing.

Then we made a final prayer.

The priest gave another blessing. And then he gave an Irish blessing. And finally he let them kiss.

Doctors' Building

Tracey Schroeder

This is Tracey Schroeder reporting at my father, Dr. Keith E. Schroeder's office in the Doctors' Building connected to Humana Hospital in Hoffman Estates.

The atmosphere I'm observing is extremely busy and tense. People are running all over the place, carrying papers, files, reports and messages and trying to get things done.

There are many voices talking at once, many secretaries typing, and many phones ringing. My dad is rushing from room to room, and I hardly see him.

People are limping in on crutches, wearing casts, or going into examining rooms, the x-ray room or the cast room. I hear someone having a cast taken off right now. The machine looks like a giant saw. It's terribly loud and sounds scary.

My dad is an orthopaedic surgeon and must take care of my bones, so I am sitting in front of the x-ray room. A man just walked in wearing a hospital gown and holding the back of it together because there's no tie there.

The huge, heavy metal door just closed, and I can hear the lady who does the x-rays telling him what to do. On the door is a sign that reads something like: "Do not enter while door is closed and x-rays are being taken. Thanks."

The man who puts most of the casts on keeps walking past me. Sometimes he stops, looks at my paper, and asks me a few questions. He's wearing surgical clothes, probably so he won't get his regular clothes dirty from putting casts on. It's a pretty dirty job.

The atmosphere suddenly got quiet. Everyone has something to do, quietly. The only sounds are a few voices, typing, a phone ringing, and once in a while a cough or sneeze.

There are many people in the waiting room, reading silently or watching TV. There are some babies crawling around and one crying.

As I sit here, I notice many plaques and awards hanging on the wall. I think they were very well earned. The jobs of the people in this office are very stressful and hard on them. They work all day and give their full attention and all their effort.

I appreciate these people and have learned a lot from them. This has been a great experience for me, and I have enjoyed it.

Feature Article

Choose an activity or enterprise that interests you, like a factory, business, laboratory, farm, government agency, etc. and arrange to interview a key person there and to tour around as you talk. If you don't know someone who can help you visit an unfamiliar place, go to a place where a relative or friend works. Record or take notes on the interview, and jot down notes also on the activity and place. Prepare some questions to satisfy whatever curiosity you have about the activity.

Pull your information together later into an account of what goes on at that place. Quote from the interview occasionally and mention details to give flavor and back up things you want to show. Your write-up can follow the order of your visit or be organized around features of the enterprise or around stages in the activity run there.

Sometimes the activity may be complicated enough to require more than one visit or interviews with more than one person. Alone or with a partner, visit at different times that afford different information, and interview several people knowing different things about the operation. The enterprise may, for example, have different phases occurring at different times and areas and involving different people. To help you, the organization may have a booklet to hand out which you can draw some information from (mentioning the source). You can also discuss with others how best to put together all that you have found out into a smooth description of the activity that shows your reader what it consists of.

Your feature article can go into a newspaper or magazine or be included in a booklet about community enterprises. Or just print it up and distribute it.

An Independent Company

Christa Pierce

The business I interviewed is Dee Pierce and Associates, which happens to be owned and operated by my father, Dee Pierce. This business is a manufacturer's representative agency, and its main function is selling products of twelve different companies. These products are not sold to small, independent retail stores, but are sold to wholesalers, distributors, and major chain stores such as Osco and Walgreen's.

The kinds of companies represented by my father are in the categories of school and office supplies, ribbon and crafts, and closet accessories. For all of these companies, his selling territory includes Illinois, Wisconsin, and Minnesota. However, he also covers Michigan, Indiana, North Dakota, and South Dakota for a few of his companies. My dad's business gets paid a commission on its total sales from each of the twelve companies he represents.

Before starting his own business, my dad worked for eight years with a different firm. In the summer of 1979, he started his own agency in the living room of our former house. The main reason for using our house as an office was to keep the expenses down. However, he liked having an office in our home so much that, even after the business was secure, he decided to stay in our home. After a few months he converted our basement into an office. A home office works very well for this type of business because my dad travels to his customers; they don't come to him.

In the beginning my dad started with only two companies, and my mom was his secretary. As the business grew, my father hired a secretary and another salesman. Recently, he hired a saleswoman for this office and an independent salesman for Michigan. My mom now takes care of the bookkeeping and accounting.

The office space in our home is very professional and is much like any other office. There are three individual, carpeted offices, a sample storage area, a sitting area, and a bathroom. The equipment includes a copy machine, postage meter, electronic typewriter, refrigerator, four desks, many file cabinets and brochure cabinets, and very importantly, phones.

An average day at the office for my dad often starts at 6:00 a.m., when he gets a head start on paperwork before phones start ringing. Other employees arrive about 8:00 or 8:30 a.m. Many phone calls are received. Customers call to place orders and call with questions or problems concerning orders for products, or shipments from the factories. The salesmen may call to set up appointments to show and sell products; fill out listing forms for customers listing specifications of different products; write letters to follow up after appointments; and sort and put away samples of products needed to be given to buyers so they can recognize the quality of the merchandise. They also attend trade shows in other cities at different times of the year.

After interviewing the people involved in this business, I realize that it is difficult to learn. The salesmen don't work for one company only; they work for several. One company alone has over one hundred products, and each product has many different specifications, such as, color, size and pattern. That's an awful lot to learn and keep track of. I really respect my dad's hard work in starting and building such a successful business!

Metromedia Telecommunications Inc.

Melissa McTernan

Metromedia is a very busy company. It is one of the two suppliers of cellular service in the Chicago area. Cellular service gives you the ability to have a telephone in your car that operates just like a telephone in your home or office. It is very convenient for people who travel or are in their cars often.

Follow me into the switch. The switch is a large computer that runs the cell sites. Cell sites are radio transmitters that send messages to and from your car phone to the Mobile Telephone Switching Office, or the MTSO. You see many computer control terminals. They are being monitored by switch technicians. The switch tells how each cell site is working.

While I was at Metromedia I interviewed some important people. Diane Astrella has worked with Metromedia for two years. She is Customer Service Manager. Some of her responsibilities are that she interacts with customers, receives billing problems, and activates and deactivates into the switch. Her most difficult situation is dealing with an unhappy customer. She enjoys her job because she says it's challenging.

Jim Walters has worked at Metromedia for three years. His position at Metromedia is Business Manager. His responsibilities are financial reports. He handles budgeting and the budget analysis. The most difficult situations are those where people act as if he doesn't know what he's talking about. Mr. Walters is satisfied with his job and thinks it seeks reality.

John Fugi has worked at Metromedia for four years. His position at Metromedia is Vice President and General Manager of Paging, which is a separate part of the company. Paging is a system that allows you to send one-way messages to people who are carrying "beepers." His major responsibility is the day-to-day operation of paging. His most difficult responsibility is dealing with upset customers. He is satisfied with his job and thinks it covers all aspects of business from sales to delivery.

Larry Harris, Director of Network Operations, has worked at Metromedia for three years. His major responsibilities are to maintain system quality and provide adequate growth of the system. Dealing with legal aspects is one of his most difficult situations. He enjoys his job because he says it provides ample rewards.

Brian McTernan has worked at Metromedia for over two years. His position at Metromedia is Executive Vice President. His responsibility is General Manager for Cellular 1 in Chicago. His most difficult situations are negotiating with Illinois Bell Telephone Company and attending partnership meetings in other cities. He enjoys his job because it is challenging.

In today's society cellular service enables us to always be in touch with our family, friends, and relatives. It is mostly popular for business people to keep in touch with their clients and offices.

Research Article

Choose a subject you want to know more about. Make a list of questions you want to find answers to. Write each question on a 5 x 7 card, and write notes on it about what you find out toward answering that question. Include also the sources of the information. Get help from your teacher or librarian about how to find books and magazines or

*other sources of information on your subject. Interviewing
an expert is one way of getting informed. If the subject is
something that is rapidly developing, like some things in
science and technology, try to get the most up-to-date
information, which is usually found in periodicals—magazines, newspapers, newsletters, and specialized journals.*

*After you've gathered your information, organize your
notes and decide which points about your subject should
come before others and which should go under others. An
outline might help to fix in your mind this sequence of
topics and the ranking within a topic. Try your article as
a talk to some group. Speak from your notes and outline.
Ask for response from your audience to help do your next
draft. If you tape your talk, you can revise that into your
article, taking the audience commentary into account. Try
this draft out on some readers to see if it needs further
improvement. Look at a book or article that cites sources
in footnotes and lists them in a bibliography. Follow that
form for your own.*

*Print up copies to distribute and submit for publica-
tion. If there is a particular group, like a club, that deals
with your subject, you might read your talk to them as a
lecture.*

Witches
Ranee Chaturantabut

A witch is a person that studies witchcraft. A witch is called the
devil's servant and is said to be possessed by the devil. A man witch is
called a wizard or a warlock.

Witchcraft is the power to harm others by supernatural or magical
means, and the power to change or affect the course of happenings.

The first witch was found during the fourth century A.D. Witches
were found in England, France, Germany, America, Greece, New
England, Japan, China, Scotland, Sweden, Switzerland, and Britain.

There were many tests for witches. People believed that all witches
had a witchmark, which was caused by a blood-sucking imp. A needle
was pricked into bumps, moles, or pimples that were said to be

witchmarks. If it did not bleed it was a witchmark and the person was a witch.

Matthew Hopkins, an Englishman, used a trick needle that disappeared into a handle and never touched the skin. He accused many innocent people and in 1645, 68 so-called witches were hanged.

Another test was to see if the person could say the Lord's Prayer because witches were known to only be able to say it backwards.

Witchcraft in America was mostly found in Salem, Mass. The witchcraft of Salem started with an informal club of 11 young girls who were taught witchcraft by a freed slave. The children started barking like dogs and throwing fits. They were said to be bewitched and were called "The Afflicted Children." The Afflicted Children were forced to tell who was bewitching them. So the girls started a roll call that grew and grew. Twenty-two people were burned and over 142 were arrested.

Cotton Mather was a prominent minister who wrote many books about the Salem witchcraft trials. He was born in 1663 and died in 1728. He wrote a book called *The Wonders of the Invisible World*. It was about trials and executions of the Salem witches.

A witch trial is a trial for witches to prove if they are guilty or not guilty of witchcraft. Confessions and tortures took place at every trial. There was the dunking stool and tearing flesh with red-hot pincers. Also, the accused witch was forced to reveal the names of other witches.

An accused witch, proven guilty at a trial, would be tortured, strangled, and burned. They would be stripped and beaten with rods and sometimes get wooden wedges driven under their fingernails and set on fire. They then would get burned. Green wood was often used to make the fire burn slower because people believed that witches deserved to die in prolonged agony.

Judges that seemed too easy on their prisoners were thought to be on the witches' side and also got killed. That is why most accused witches had a slim chance of escaping.

Most people think that witchcraft ended a long time ago, but there are still people today that believe in witchcraft.

Alex Sanders is the leader of an ancient religion called "Wicca." Many people believe that they can gain wisdom and witch power by signing up as members of Wicca. Alex Sanders is known as the "King of Witches."

Sybil Leek is a member of Wicca and is known as Wicca's Wonder Woman. She works on potions in an old antique shop she once owned in England. Members of Wicca say that they are good witches and worship a moon goddess and a horned goat, not the devil.

The French Horn
Sally Francis

The French horn gives a medium warm mellow tone that blends well with woodwind instruments. It is the connecting link between the brassy drama of the band and the rich elegance of the orchestra. Its tone can be sweet and loving. The French horn can play from as high as a trumpet to as low as a tuba.

Development of the French Horn

Thousands of years ago cavemen discovered that by blowing through a hole in the side of an animal horn and forcing air through the opening they could produce sounds that were useful in sending messages short distances. Since buzzing the lips into the opening produced the louder sounds, this was the method most used by early people, and it is how sounds are produced on the French horn today.

To make a sound loud enough to travel many miles a very large, long horn was needed. People living in the Alps of Switzerland play wooden Alpine horns twelve feet long to send messages from mountain to mountain.

As metals developed, horns were made out of them—especially brass. A cup-shaped or funnel-shaped mouthpiece was added. The long tube was curled to make it more portable and easier to play in bands and orchestras. In 1815 a piston valve piece was added which opened and closed holes leading to extra pieces of tubing attached to the horn. Newer, rotary valves are a modern invention that have an easier and faster action.

The early hunting horns, ancestors of the French horn, had their tubing coiled in a circle like a garden hose so that the player could carry it over his shoulder while "riding to the hounds" on horseback. Some of the French horns were the French hunting horn in D, the French hunting horn in F that was curled up, the French inventions horn that had the extra tubing in the center, and the English inventions horn that was curled up to make it look like a snake.

Thinking Up

Dreams

Jot down a dream soon after you have it so you'll remember it better, or record your dreams regularly in your general journal. Tell the dream to a partner or group until you have it well in mind, listen to what they have to say about it, then write it as a story or poem. You don't have to stick completely to the original but can change it or add to it.

Read your dream to a group and talk about whether others have had similar dreams. Or include in a booklet of stories or poems by you or others. If the dream features dialog, write it as a script and arrange to perform it.

Penny World

Susan Hoagland

One night I dreamed a strange dream. I dreamed that I went to Penny World.

Penny World is a place where everything costs just a penny. Of course the bigger things like cars and houses cost about three or four pennies. When I went to this new place I didn't know everything cost just a penny so I brought a few dollars in pennies. When I got there everyone thought I was the richest person in the world. I could buy anything I wanted. And I did! I had the best time of my life. But it was a fantasy, like they have on Fantasy Island. My fun in Penny World only lasted a few minutes while I was sleeping, but it seemed like a day in Penny World. I dream a lot about Penny World now, because it is so nice.

Dream Call

Felicia Sze

A regular night,
Dozing off to sleep,
Finding myself in
An imaginary land.

Walking down
A country road
With a
Cool evening breeze
Blowing my hair
To the West.

Taking a left,
Or right it might be,
Into a forest
In this wonderland.

The forest was a beach
For a sparkling pond.
It seems as though
It called to me.

I jumped in the water
And woke with a start
To find that
I was back home again!

I remembered that dream
Forever more
Because in later years
I was inspired by it.

For, you see,
I am an artist,
And all my paintings
Are of that pond.

It inspired me.
It cheered me up.
And that's why
It was calling to me.

Story Drawn from Journal

Take some idea for a story that you jotted down in your journal or some real event mentioned there, fill it out, and finish it off as a story. That is, imagine more to it so that you develop the original kernel to a fitting ending.

Berries

Lisa Hoff

Listen, child, to the tale I tell, for it is a tale of berries.

Once there was a little girl. An ordinary girl like the one who might live next door. She was ordinary beside the fact that she lived in the forest. She was brought up by a vixen, but the fox was hunted down and shot. So now she lived alone, She hadn't a name, I fear, but the vixen called her Mistuglia, so we will call her Mish.

Now, then, Mish was eating some berries to her heart's content. (They were strawberries. Remember that.) These berries (unknown to Mish) were magic. All she wanted to do now was kill things like babies (poor babies) and birds (poor birds) and chipmunks and squirrels (poor chipmunks and squirrels) and rob peasants (poor peasants).

So one day she stopped a cart with food in it. She asked for a ride and got it. The people got down to help her get up, but she swung up and drove away. Mish went too fast for the people and got away. The people went to the king without any taxes. Meanwhile, Mish had a ball eating the food, but she only ate a whole raw chicken (poor chickens). She walked through the woods (away from the cave) and came across a blueberry bush. So she ate to her heart's content. (Remember they were blueberries.) These, too, were magical (unknown to Mish), and she got over her desire to kill.

Word-Chain Story

When someone says, "Start!" write down the first word that comes into your mind, then write down whatever word the first one makes you think of, and continue making a word chain, drawing a line from one word to the next. When the person says "Stop!" take the last word, put it with the first word, and make up a story based on them. (In the following example, "shirt" was the first word and "cute" the last.)

Cute Shirt

Wendy Ramsbottom

Cute Shirt was a person, believe it or not it. Cute Shirt was two feet tall with brown eyes and brown hair. He was the cutest person I have ever seen. Actually he wasn't a person. He was a baby gorilla. He would never grow taller than two feet. The kids at school called him C.S. for short. (Otherwise known as Cool Shrimp.)

The kids at school were mean to C.S. because of his height. They called him names so often that one day he ran away. He was so scared, he did not know what to do away from school. (School was his home because his parents ran away in love and forgot about him.) After two days of C.S. being gone the principals sent out a search for C.S. Everybody looked for days.

C.S. kept running so no one could find him. He was in the forest now. C.S. finally stopped. He was panting out of breath. He stopped and dug an underground hole for his home. Then one day C.S. got sick and died.

Story Starter

Get an unfinished sentence or an intriguing sentence from someone else and take it from there to invent a story starting with this sentence. If some classmates use the same story starter, you can compare stories afterwards. Make a booklet of stories started with the same sentence, which you can make the title of the booklet.

Example: "Her three curious eyes stared at me...."

Horrible Beginning

Kristen Cline

Her three curious eyes stared at me in a questioning way. I didn't know what she was or where she came from, but I did know I had to get her out of my bedroom. I inched toward her very slowly and then the chase began. I chased her around my bedroom 5 or 6 times then I heard a knock at my door. I knew it had to be my mom. I quickly shoved the three-eyed whatever into the closet. My mom opened the door and walked in. "Hi, Mom," I said while guarding the closet door.

"I wanted to tell you," said my mom, "that it's time for your eye appointment now and for goodness sake please let your little sister out of the closet."

Jokes

Write down some jokes that you have heard. Make up a new joke or two. Alone or with others, put together a book of jokes and exchange it with another person or group who did the same thing.

Jenny Ng and Kaati Brehm

What do you get when you cross a lion and a parakeet?
I don't know, but when it talks you'd better listen.

Mike Kraft and Eric Zinowski

What looks just like half a peanut?
The other half.

David Hendrick and David Rutcosky

Why did the Cyclops have to close the school?
Because he only had one pupil.

What did the stamp say to the postcard?
Stick to me and we'll go places.

Shannone Gabrys and Jenny Dean

Why should you never tell secrets in a corn yard?
They are all ears.

John Wall and Jim Nurss

What is it called when one giraffe comes one way and another
giraffe comes another?
A giraffic jam!

Why did the turkey cross the road?
Because it was the chicken's day off!

What did Tarzan say when he saw the elephants wearing sunglasses?
Nothing. He didn't recognize them!

Do you see elephants in cherry trees?
No.
Good hiders, aren't they!

Why do ducks have flat feet?
To put out fires!
And why do elephants have flat feet?
To put out flaming ducks!

What do witches use on their hair?
Scare spray!

What is black and white and red all over?
A penguin with a sunburn.

Riddles

*Write a Who-Am-I? or What-Am-I? poem by imagining
an object or creature describing itself—what it has and
does. No names. Just hint. Try several.*

   *Read them to others and let them guess. Make a book
or bulletin board of riddles.*

Who Am I?
Greg Aimonette

I am an amateur mime who is furry, quick, eats carrots, and has a burden of a family in my den.

(rabbit)

Who Am I?
Lori Gannon

When I move, I never make a sound.
I bake in the sun as I move across the ground.
I shed my skin, and hatch my kin,
And have a small family.
Some of us carry poison, some of us do not.
Some of us are pets, and *some of us are not!*

(snake)

Peck Around
Robert Wojnarowski

White as snow,
Orange like candle glow.
May be voiceless
But is noiseless.
Can swim a lot of ways,
But can't fly even two days.
Has a bill over his neck,
But can't sound a peck.
Has a pouch
Just like a king-sized "ouch!"
You he may touch
But can't do very much.

(pelican)

Keynotes
Carly Jacobs

It's notes you can't take. It's keys you can fit into any keyhole. But if you push on one it'll fit into the keyhole of the mind. It can make you think of places you've been.

(piano)

What Am I?

Ron Jackson

People use me
for memory.
When they look
at me, they look
at the past.
They can hang me
or sell me.
What am I?

(photograph)

Change

Bryan Hudrock

You can have
many things
with me,
big or small.
Sometimes
I can be
changed
into four things,
ten things,
twenty things,
or even
one hundred things.
People love me
always
and if
I was human,
I'd love me too.
I'll give you
a hint.
I'm green.
What am I?

(money)

Torment
Greg Ayotte

Starts small,
then grows big.
Grey as
an elephant,
White as
the snow.
Lasts for
a minute
but soon
is gone.
Tormenting everything
along the way,
Traveling nonstop
from town to town.
Then it's still
and no more
is heard.

(tornado)

Tail and Head
Cheryl Smith

Tail and head
have I both.
Dull or shiny
can I be.
Flip, flop,
one I'll be.
Which one
Will go?
Nobody knows.
What am I?

(penny)

Yarns

Think of one-sentence exaggerations that begin with "I know. . . ." or "I saw. . . ." "I saw a man so small and so weak that it took him a lifetime to write a lowercase letter" (Karen Ury). Write a number of these with a partner or two, look them over, pick the best to illustrate, and post it up.

We Have Yarns of . . .

Karen Ury

A man so small and so weak that it took him a lifetime to write one lowercase letter!

A map so big it is twice as big as the earth!

A two-day-old baby's smile so wide it took seven years to cross it!

A man who earned so many medals that you couldn't see him!

A test so long it took a teacher a lifetime to correct it!

A puddle so deep that the moon is totally covered with water when set inside!

A bear's roar so loud and shattering that all the planets in the universe fall out of orbit!

More Yarns

The lady had on so much makeup she looked like a Clinique cosmetic store.

Marie Pugliese

This girl was so ugly even the devil would not marry her.

Melissa Pollack

This child was so big the planets could be used for his marbles.

David Savlin

This man was so skinny he had to run around in the shower just to get wet.

Matt Goldman

This girl I knew was so small she could ride down the Mississippi on a cheerio.

Danny Israelite

The man was so small his best friends were bacteria.

Kenny Fisher

A lady's hair was so tangled that she couldn't comb it with a rake.

Nasutsa Mabwa

One man was so ugly he turned Medusa to stone.

John Adair

There once was a bird so big that when he chirped he blew the sun out.

Jeremy Herrick

Make It Famous

Think of some event that ought to be made famous, and imagine an appropriate monument to mark the spot. Now write a commemoration to go on the monument saying what happened there. You can commemorate an important local event or just something someone you know did. This could be humorous. If you want, draw a picture of the monument to go with the words or for the words to go on.

Post it up, pass it around, or collect it with others into a "history" book.

The Wright Brothers' Flight
(Kitty Hawk, North Carolina)
In Memory of Orville and Wilbur Wright

Katie LaJeunesse

Orville and Wilbur had a happy day,
When they got in their plane and flew away.
They had worked all day and worked all night,
Until they got their plane just right.
They started up on Kill Devil Hill,
And this all give them quite a thrill.
They shouted and laughed and sang with glee,
As they both went down in history.

Being Something Else

Imagine you are an object and make up a story told from that object's point of view about some predicament or typical situation it got into. (How about a kitchen blender or a yo-yo?) Or do the same thing for an animal or plant. Try to feel and talk as it would. You might agree with partners to pretend to be the same thing and compare your stories afterwards, post up together, or make into a booklet titled for that object or creature.

Teddy

Janet Rosenbaum

I hate being a teddy bear. My name is Teddy. How ordinary! And to top it off I'm a baby's teddy.

She drools on me and chews on me. I'm sick of it. Then after I'm chewed on and drooled on I am thrown in the washing machine. I get very dizzy.

I've been thinking about how I could not be drooled on or chewed on, but nothing would work. I've thought of biting back, but I don't have any teeth. I thought of jumping out of the baby's reach and running off, but then people would think they were going crazy. Finally I found the perfect solution. What I would do is go to another house. I'd do it this afternoon.

* * *

Here I am in the house next door sitting in their living room. In comes a young lady. With her is a younger lady about two years old. Oh no!

Sammy's Surprise
Karyn Christoff

Hello, my name is Sammy the pup. I am all white. I had been sitting in this store window for days.

I really wanted to get bought soon. Someone walked in the store. I hoped she would buy me. She walked to the salesman. She started picking me up and started to take me somewhere. We walked in one direction for a couple of minutes.

Suddenly I was dropped on a basement floor. The lady left me with a bowl of water and some puppy food. Every day she came and gave me water and food then left.

After two days I started to get worried. I thought I might get a mean owner. Will she ever let me play with anyone?

The next day the lady didn't come to feed me. I really got worried. Are they going to keep me here forever?

The lady came and picked me up. I was brought upstairs and put in a sock.

A little girl pulled me out. I didn't know it was my new owner but I was glad I was out of the basement. The girl said as she picked me up, "I love him. I will have to write a thank-you letter to Santa."

I went to a room upstairs with the girl. The girl sat at a desk while I sat on her bed.

She started to write a letter. Soon she was finished with it. I played with her. I loved my new home and owner.

Tennis Shoes
John Epple

Hi. I'm a pair of shoes. My name is Adida. My master's name is John Epple. He takes good care of me except sometimes he writes on me and pokes me with pencils and pens. Boy, does that hurt. Have you ever been poked with a pencil? It hurts, doesn't it?

Did you know that once he was sticking me with his pencil on the sponge part in between the sole and the shoe? Well, his lead broke and that piece of lead is still in me to this very day.

Sometimes my master doesn't think of me and he'll run through a puddle of mud or water. But sometimes he really takes good care of me. Like the time he could have walked through the creek but he decided to take the bridge.

Well, I got to go now. I think John is taking me to a track meet and I'm in it.

So here I am at the track. I hope he doesn't wear me out real fast because that hurts more than being poked with a pencil. Well, I hope I win. Wish me luck. 'Bye! Woosh!!!!

My Life as a Pretzel

Kent Chen

My life began in a wheat field on a farm. I grew and grew until I was tall and ready to be harvested in the fall.

Then they cut me and loaded me on a big truck. From there I was delivered to a large factory.

When I got there they pounded me and pounded me until I was nothing but flour.

After that they mixed me with other ingredients such as eggs, milk and so on. I was pretty sticky when that was all over.

They cut me into one slightly long, thin strand.

They twisted me up superbly. In fact, my arms crossed, my feet touched the top of my head and my hands prevented me from seeing.

When the twisting was done they put me on a conveyor belt that sent me to the salting room. All of a sudden they (by the way, if you didn't know who they were, they are the factory workers) started pelting small, white pebbles at me!

After I left the salting room on the conveyor belt I was sent to a huge oven where I got a stroke of luck! I got a free oventan! Do you know how much an oventan costs? I got one free! I was what you might call baked brown when I was done.

Then the conveyor belt brought me to the packaging section where I was on the very bottom of a pretzel bag.

When the packaging was all done I was sent to a store by truck. By the time I got to the store it was midnight and I was asleep. When I woke up I was in the back of the shelf.

Two days later I was bought by a lady. She brought me home to her cereal cabinet.

Then she had a party and a boy dropped me on the floor for about half an hour when a baby drooled over me and in that same minute a dog ate me! Now that's what I call sick!

Fill-In Comics

Clip some comic strips out of a newspaper, cut out the dialog balloons, and paste the strips over blank paper. Trade with a partner who has done the same thing (so you won't know what the dialog was). Make up and write in new dialog to go with the pictures. Title each strip. Pass around, post up, make a book.

The Elephant and the Trainer

Donald Ruesch

Frank Schaffer Publications. Used with permission.

The Lion and the Hunter

Joe Fiorita

Frank Schaffer Publications. Used with permission.

Photo Story

Cut out several photos from magazines, sift through them a number of times, think about the story possibilities of each, then choose one you want to make up a story about. If you do this with partners, you can exchange and have a greater variety to choose from. A photo of a place may suggest a setting for a certain action; a story of people talking, some characters and dialog; an action shot, some plot. Write what the picture seems to say to you about what is going on or what the circumstances are. From such hints make up the rest. Pair stories and photos side by side on a bulletin board or in a booklet. Or surround each photo with several versions if partners have chosen the same photo.

Zwulon Zelikowsky

The Garbage Picker

Derek Schueneman

A can is filled with all sorts of mush and goo, chewed up bubble gum, egg shells, rotten onions and burnt spinach with moldy coleslaw. A girl is rummaging through the garbage to look for the quarter she had dropped in the can. She gets down to the bottom of the can. The horrible smell of raw meat, garlic, onions and grape gum fill the air. Finally she takes up half an egg shell, and there is her quarter shining in the sunlight. She then puts it in her pocket and skips home.

Laurence Cameron

Land of Destruction

Deron Brownlee

I am the grass. I am small and green with dirt-bound roots. Big furry things keep picking and eating my friends.

Every time I look around I hear crunch, munch, splat, and ptooey. These darn furry things can't even clean up after themselves. They step on you not saying a word, no "Sorry" or "Thank you, you were very tasty." All they think about is eat, eat, eat, walk a while, eat a while. When people come, and they say, "Let's rest," the furry things use the bathroom. People say it's good for the grass. I say it's disgusting, and another thing—oh my God, I'm about to get eaten up.

Burp!!!!!

Tall Tale

Make up an outlandish yarn by telling something that you or someone else is supposed to have done. Make it realistic enough to intrigue your audience, but exaggerate so much that you pull their leg too. Tall tales are like boasts or wild claims but done for fun.

*Make a **Tall Tales** booklet with others. These are good also to read aloud or retell from memory.*

Tall Tom
Jeff Watts

Tom Turkey was a big turkey. Now I don't mean an ordinary big turkey. NO, SIR! I mean an extraordinary gigantic big turkey. In fact, Tom Turkey was so big that his right toe was big enough to feed 4,000 hungry men.

Now you may think that the first person on the moon was an astronaut. Well, you're wrong if you do because Tom Turkey told me so. You see, one day for the first time in his life Tom stood up. Now I don't mean just stood up. Uh-uh. He stretched way up with no bends in his body. In fact, Tom stretched so high that his head bumped into the moon, and that's when he saw the man on the moon. When Tom came down he described the man on the moon. He said he was green with big ears and looked very friendly.

But sometimes Tom's size got him into trouble. I remember one Thanksgiving when someone noticed Tom while he was taking a bath in the Atlantic. Now that person happened to be a turkey shop owner. And as you can imagine, being a turkey shop owner, he got pretty excited. So he got out his rowboat and started rowing. Well, across the country in Spain, a Spanish turkey shop owner saw Tom and he too started rowing.

Pretty soon Tom was surrounded by over 200 turkey shop owners. Being pretty scared Tom knew he needed to get away, unless he wanted to be dinner for everyone on the east side of the earth. So Tom leaped. Not only did he leap, but he jumped and with that one leap Tom went around the earth ten times. When his right foot landed it formed the Grand Canyon. Tom was tired now because of his huge leap so when he leaped again he only went around five times. Well, while he was on his fourth time around, a strange thing happened.

Tom grew smaller! Well, now Tom was only as big as a whale so he lost altitude and fell.

Tom landed in Loch Ness Lake in Scotland and seeing that he was safe, he decided to go to sleep.

When Tom woke up he stood up and saw that it was night. So Tom went back underwater, but as he was submerging he didn't notice a man fishing behind him.

Fortunately for Tom the man didn't see all of Tom, just his rear and his shadow. Seeing this, the man jumped out of his boat and swam quickly toward shore.

When Tom woke up, to his surprise he found that he was surrounded again. "Here we go again," said Tom as he took another leap. This time, Tom went around 20 times and on his 19th time around, Tom suddenly grew again. This gave Tom some extra spring and that was all he needed to break through the earth's atmosphere. Now Tom was **going so-o-o-o fast that when he broke through the earth's atmosphere he** kept going, and going, and going until he hit the invisible wall of the universe. Well, Tom was so-o-o-o big that he broke right through the wall. When he did, he made a gigantic hole, which is now called a black hole.

From that day on, Tom was never seen again, but personally, I think that Tom turned into what we think of now as "the dog star."

Race up the Mississippi

Albert Law

A long time ago before steamships arrived, Mike Fink's keelboat, the *Champion,* was the fastest boat around. He raced other boats and was always the winner of the race. After he had won all the boats he could race, Mike said something that caused him a lot of trouble. Mike said, "My boat, the *Champion,* can go faster than Paul Bunyan can cut trees."

Paul heard this and he got very angry. He walked up to Mike and yelled, "You think your boat can go faster than I can cut trees?! You must be crazy!" Paul yelled so loudly that he started a windstorm on the Great Lakes. Mike yelled back, "Of course it can! I'll even challenge you to a race!" Mike broke Paul's watch because Mike yelled so loud. "It's a deal!" Paul shouted.

Before the race, each person got a week to practice. Paul chopped down trees so fast that he cleared all the trees in Arizona in one week. Meanwhile, Mike was practicing on the Mississippi. He rowed so fast that one day, because Mike had to stop, the *Champion* hit a bank—but it didn't stop. The keelboat made a big ditch which is now the Ohio River.

On the day of the race, Mike had to row up the Mississippi. Paul had to cut trees alongside the river. The race was like a seesaw. First, Paul discovered that because his ax was so hot he could just tap a tree and the trunk would burn up and the tree would fall. So Paul got ahead. Then Mike broke his oars so the men hung on to the back of the boat and started kicking. When the men kicked, the water splashed so high that it touched the clouds. The clouds soaked up the water and it started raining. That put out Paul's ax and Mike got the lead. After it stopped raining, Paul heated his ax again and got the lead. Then the *Champion* shot across the water and tied Paul as they crossed the finish line.

After the race, Paul said, "Mike, you might do well as a lumber shipper for me." Mike replied, "I was thinking the same thing."

A Space Place

Imagine some place in space inhabited by people. What does it look like? What kinds of things does it have? How are needs met there? Tell all about your place—where it is and how it is set up. Include illustrations if you want. Give a name to your colony or space station. You might go further and make up a story that happened in your space place.

Exchange with others. Include in a book of stories, or post up with other Space Places.

Star Base #1

Jennifer Hoebeke

My space colony is located on the planet Mars.

The people live and work in big bubbles. They are white on the outside and yellow inside. The living bubble can hold 30 people and several pets. The air, climate, and gravity are like earth's and are controlled by a power plant located outside the colony.

The communication module is above where the people work and go to school. This is located in a separate bubble from the living quarters. The colony can communicate with other planets and space ships by radio and television. There is also a solar collector on the other side of the communication module. Solar power is used to run the power plant, which supplies electricity and controls the climate of the colony.

Transportation to and from the colony is by space ship. Transportation within the colony is by space cars or by walking through tubes that connect the bubbles.

My space colony is ruled by a queen. The queen's rules are not to use bad language and not to disobey your parents. People who break the rules are put in jail for a month.

The second bubble is divided into a factory and school. Here, children and adults are educated like earth people and also learn about living in space colonies.

Food is supplied by a garden in the third bubble. This bubble is divided into several floors. The top floor is the garden, the other floors have medical, dental, recreational and shopping services. Other food and supplies not grown or made in the colony are brought by space ships.

Colony X7P847

Bradley Thompson

Colony X7P847 is on Mercury. It is made of superstrength future metals and silver. Gravity is controlled by an invisible dome covering the entire colony. This dome not only holds out the heat of the sun but includes a cooling system which is run by computers. The air is filtered through the swimming pool, which purifies it for breathing.

Twelve families live on X7P847. Each family has two animals—one cat and one dog. All homes are in the central living complex. All houses are circular, having three floors with eight rooms. Kitchens are small with all cooking done on microwave ovens. Each house has two bathrooms. Most homes have three sleeping areas with beds that fold out of the wall for extra playing areas. Other rooms are usually living room, dining room, library and den. The den has a big T.V. screen for watching programs in 3D. The library contains the family computer.

Communication is handled in two houses on top of the living complex. These houses don't have furniture. They have computers, computer panels, speakers, big-screen T.V.'s, recording facilities, microphones and software library. Radio and T.V. programs are beamed in from Sealland on the planet Venus. Educational programs are also beamed in. Each student attends school on his own computer in his own library. One teacher gives out the program reels for the day. Preschool through college is handled in this way.

Sidewalks move between buildings. All sidewalks begin or end at the living complex. They move at two miles an hour. Movement from colony to colony and from X7P847 to other planets is in invisible mini-pods. The space pods go at light speed.

Some vegetables and fruit are grown in the garden. However, most supplies are brought from other planets. Water comes from Neptune, metal comes from Pluto, meat comes from Earth.

The southwest building is an office building. The doctor, dentist, eye doctor, tailor, wood carver and others have their offices here.

The government is a galactic spaceboard. The spaceboard rules all planets in the Milky Way from Europa (a moon of Jupiter). The president of the Milky Way is Caroline Kennedy. Samantha Thompson is the governor of Mercury. The police force and fire department are housed in the northwest building.

X7P847 is an out-of-this-world place to live.

Zardon, Planet of the Gods

Sandy Smillie

Introduction

The tiny vessel drifted slowly—silently—through the vast expanse of unclaimed darkness, a tired craft of forgotten purpose. In the faint light of distant suns could be seen the words printed with such pride so long ago: F.S.S.* Excelsior. It was within this broken-down hulk that the crew was forced to work. . . .

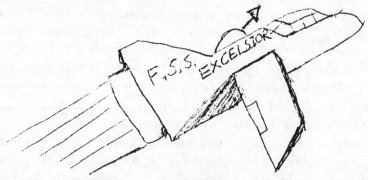

*Federation Star Ship

Chapter

1

"Everybody up here. Now!"

Yet despite their inferior working conditions they were tolerant. In a cramped storage area. Lt. William Presscott and Medical Officer Joseph Payne sat wearily playing a game that Payne had "whipped up" out of junk he found around the ship. In her quarters, Navigational Officer Kristen Alman sat on her bed reading *The Titantic* for the third time straight.

Lt. Jack Morstein and Foreman Mike Peterson sat at the bridge gazing into space. Peterson was still day-dreaming when Morstein got up and started toward the eating area. Peterson snapped out of it soon after. He cleared his head and looked at the control panel. He jumped out of his seat and ran to the Tele-Com system. He yelled excitedly into the microphone, "Everybody up here. Now!"

Morstein was still eating a nutrient bar when he casually strolled in. Presscott ran into Morstein on the way to his post. Morstein choked and coughed on the bar, then sputtered, "Hey, watch it!" He again stumbled around as Alman rammed him on the way to her station. "Yer not safe on this hunk of trash!" said Morstein, kicking a wall.

"What's wrong, Cap?" asked Presscott, not paying any notice to Morstein's remark.

"We have a case of gravitational pull!" exclaimed Peterson.

"What?!" said Morstein, not believing what he heard. "Out here in all this?"

"Yep," said Peterson.

Payne got to the bridge soon and said, "Permission to report to post . . . Sir!" snapping into military form. It was a joke between the two friends, but under the circumstances it wasn't funny.

Alman, who had been trying to pull the Excelsior out of the gravity field, said to anyone who would listen or was listening, "Bad news, there's no way to pull out except one. We would have to eject some of our fuel cannisters then blow them up. Then maybe . . . just maybe it'll blow us out of the field." She paused to let her words sink in. "On the other hand it could blow us down *to* the planet instead of away."

The team sat and wondered what the planet looked like, what things lived there and if it was inhabitable for humans. They had tried to scan the surface, but there was an overcast. Peterson finally said reluctantly, "Okay, let's try it before we get too close and can't pull out." So they set to work. Morstein and Alman went into the fuel room and detached half of the cannisters. They depressurized the fuel room, then opened the affectionately called "back door." The small cannisters drifted out of the ship slowly but surely. The crew fastened down to their chairs, then Peterson fired up the thrusters.

The ship rocked as the explosion sounded and echoed through the entire ship. It felt as though they were falling instead of rising. "It didn't work! We're falling toward the planet!" exclaimed Alman.

They fell for what seemed an eternity. Right before they hit, Presscott had the good sense to turn on the power shields. They hit the ground a split second later. Then nothing.

Chapter

2

"Hey, where's Payne?"

When they woke up, the controls and computers were on fire. Alman put out the fires while the others recovered. After the fires were extinguished Alman checked the damage to the controls and found something she didn't want. "We need a new micro-turbine and a new gyro-cube."

"Great. Okay, Alman, check the atmosphere and land form, oh, and soil content," commanded Peterson. She walked over to the robot arm's controls, struggled with a lever, pushed a few buttons, flicked a few switches, then finally gave up. She walked back to the others and said, "No use, the testing arm must have been crushed, can't get it to work. Only info I could get was from the star-chart. This dreaded planet we're on is Zardon. And guess what. We're almost the first people here."

"What do you mean *almost?*" asked Morstein.

"The last people here . . . um . . . died," said Alman.

"Is there any way we can get the ship fixed up . . . soon?" asked Presscott.

"Not unless we get the right tools," replied Alman.

"Well, now we'll have to . . . hey, where's Payne?" asked Peterson. They searched the ship from bow to stern and found no trace of Payne.

"Hey, everybody, get over here!" yelled Morstein excitedly. He had yelled from the scout-pod room, and the crew followed his voice. They all rushed in.

"What's up?" asked Presscott.

"One pod's missing, and guess who took it," said Morstein.

"Payne, that little . . ." said Peterson half to himself.

"And the man wins a cigar!" said Morstein sarcastically. Suddenly the bay door opened and a scout-pod cruised in. The door opened and Payne walked out, mouth wide open.

"It's beautiful out there, it's like Eden," he said, astonished. They all ran outside and understood why Payne was so dumbfounded. Trees of gold and grass of jade dazzled the plains around them.

"Look down there, it's a city, and look over there at that mountain," said Presscott in awe.

"Well, I'll be a monkey's uncle," said Morstein.

"Let's go to the city. If there are people here we should know," suggested Alman.

"Okay, let's go," said Peterson, signaling the team to start down the hill. When they were half-way down they heard a strange low rumble.

"What was that?" asked Alman. The answer came rumbling out of a concealed cave. The animal had three heads—a lion's, a goat's, and a dragon's. Its body was horrible. The forequarters of a lion, hindquarters of a goat, and it's tail was the long, scaly tail of a dragon. Out of the dragon's mouth came raging fire.

"A chimera from Greek mythology," said Payne to himself.

"Well, looky what I found," said Morstein, picking up a rusty sword.

"A lot of good that's gonna do. It'll break the first time you hit the thing," said Presscott.

Morstein took a swing at the chimera with all his might. A gaping wound appeared where the sword hit. But instead of blood, sparks and flames bubbled out. "It's a robot," said Morstein, starting to run down toward the hill. The fake chimera touched its tail to the wound. It healed instantaneously.

Peterson picked up the sword Morstein had dropped and signaled for the team to follow Morstein. They ran down the hill at top speed, tripping at times. They finally made it down and, boy, were they glad.

"Made it!" panted Alman. A lightning bolt hit the sky with so much force the sky screamed in the form of thunder. "A storm's moving in," stated Alman.

"That ain't no storm," said Morstein pointing to the sky. A chariot pulled by three swans and Pegasus, the winged horse, flared across the sky. It hung in air above the ragged party, then finally landed next to them with the grace of the swans it was pulled by. Animals came from the forest and stood by the gleaming chariot. They didn't seem afraid of the god-like figure that rode in the chariot, almost as if they knew him.

"I am god of gods. . . . I am Zeus," said the lordly figure in a booming voice. The group bowed deeply.

"Ohhh my god," said Morstein, stumbling backwards.

"Yes?" said Zeus again in his booming voice.

"No, I didn't mean you, I mean no offense, I just . . . ouch!" said Morstein fumbling around. Alman had kicked him in the shin and told him to shut up.

"I need your help. As you have seen, the creatures on this planet are robots, as you call them. I, Zeus, am the only *free* living being on this planet. *You* must help me defeat these impostors before they take over other planets, like yours for example. The other creatures that were on this planet are in the underworld, my captured brother's realm. That brother's name is Hades. We must also free my brother Poseidon. He is held captive in his own palace beneath the sea," explained Zeus.

They gathered on the chariot without any questions. A lightning bolt formed in Zeus's hand. He threw it above the swans' heads. They took off with a jolt. They flew for a long time, so long that Alman fell asleep. They landed in about a hour with a bang. "We're here," stated Zeus.

"Great, we're here . . . uh . . . where's here?" asked Morstein. They found themselves under water. They were scared half to death, but their fear ceased when they discovered they could breathe.

"We are at Poseidon's palace. Here we're unnoticed, but when we enter the castle itself we will be attacked by the robot sea nymphs. I am going to give you each weapons of the gods. To you," said Zeus pointing to Alman, "I give Athena's tiara. It will give you the power to change shapes. To Morstein I give Hades' helmet and a sword. The helmet will let you turn invisible. To Payne I give Hermes' sandals and a sword. The sandals will let you fly. To Presscott I give Ares' sword of speed. And to Peterson I give the power to make lightning. Ready? Attack!" yelled Zeus.

They ran into the castle, and just as Zeus had foretold, the sea nymphs attacked them. Morstein was the first to react. He turned invisible and attacked from behind and sliced through three on the first swing. Alman changed into a panther and pounced on two. Payne flew up into the air and arched his sword into the nearest nymph. Peterson, meanwhile, was in the middle of a group of nymphs. He twirled around, sword out. He must have killed off 30 or so by the time he stopped. Zeus and Peterson had killed enough to fill a graveyard and then some when they heard a heart-stopping war cry. It was Poseidon! He threw his trident into the middle of the nymphs. It lit up blue-green and shot rays of the same color at each and every nymph. The rays melted the robots into a pond of liquid metal. "Victory! But how did you escape?" asked Zeus.

"Your battle disrupted every nymph in the palace," said Poseidon, "including the guards to my cell. That was the chance I needed. I broke down the door and retrieved my trident. The rest you know." They jumped down a hole that Poseidon created with his trident. They fell, compared to their other journeys, quickly. They landed on a blanket of soft moss. There was a huge river in front of them and a large island beyond it. On the island were thousands of robots battling one man. "Hades!" yelled Poseidon to his brother. Hades looked up and a grim smile rose on his face. Alman changed into a boat. They paddled over to the island and attacked the robots. Zeus made a cage around Hades out of lightning bolts. Alman turned into a large hawk and picked up Hades from the cage. Hades let go of the claw when they were over the robots. As he fell he grew to the size of a giant. He fell full force on the robots, then shrank to normal size. All the robots had been crushed into spare parts. But more and more robots were coming into the cavern through the same hole the party came through. Zeus threw a lightning bolt at the ceiling, hoping to cave it in.

"Didn't work!" cursed Zeus.

"That's because you didn't focus all your energy into a structure," said Payne.

"He means put all your power in one thing then use that," said Morstein to the puzzled gods. They took Payne's advice. Peterson and Zeus made a hollow lightning bolt, then put the magic weapons and items in it. Zeus hurled the lightning bolt at the ceiling of the cavern. The ceiling began to cave in. The party escaped from the cavern and up a passage. When they reached the surface Morstein asked Hades, "How did you get free?"

The grim figure replied, "The whole underworld is my realm, and what those robots didn't know was I'm strongest when I'm down there. I simply broke free."

The ground about 20 or 30 feet away from the small band began to crumble, and to their amazement all the robots were still trying to get to the underworld. Therefore, they were over the crumbling cavern below. A snap of thunder sounded and the ground finally collapsed along with the robots. From the tunnel the group had come out of they heard a banging. Suddenly, animals and satyrs and nymphs sprang from the tunnel. They were the animals that usually live on the planet.

"Because you have been so brave I will give you each a wish and one group wish," said Zeus.

"I'll take a ruby," said Morstein greedily. A large ruby appeared in his hands.

"I wish for a new medical lab for the ship," Payne requested. His wish was granted.

"I would like a new rec. area," wished Presscott. His wish was granted.

"I request a new book, preferably a long one," Alman said. A book of mysteries appeared in front of her. "Thank you."

"I only wish for a reminder of this adventure," said Peterson. A small-scale chimera appeared in his hand. "Very funny." They all agreed on having the new micro-turbine and the new gyro-cube installed when they got to the ship. They said their goodbyes then started toward the ship. When they reached the top of the hill they saw that the ship had disappeared and a new one appeared where the old one had been. They entered the dream-ship and looked about. Peterson was looking around the cockpit when he found a note. It read, "No charge—Zeus." Peterson smiled, folded the note and put it in his pocket. Still smiling he said to the crew "Let's get out of here."

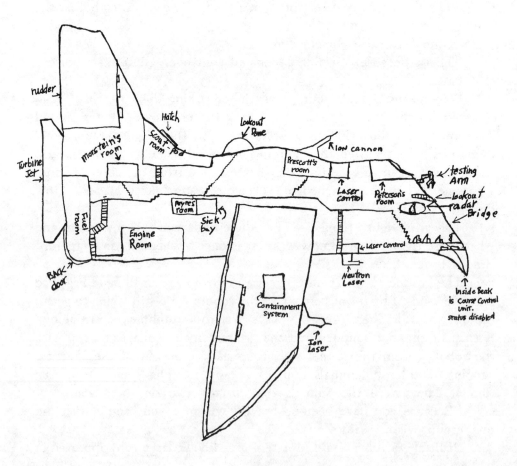

Making Up from the Real

Think of a real place or situation or activity that you know and make up a story based on it. Imagine an action in that place. Go beyond the real activity or situation, which is just your starting point. Or think of a character like some person you know and build a plot around his or her traits or habits.

The Four Time Warps

Aaron Karlin

On day at Camp MacLean I was walking to the nurse's cabin. I went in for medicine. When I got in, the nurse gave me my medicine, and I left. I went in my cabin only to find that all the people looked like the nurse! One of them pointed a laser gun at me. "I must be in another dimension," I said to myself. "I went through a time warp when I was walking back to my cabin," I thought.

"You're all clones," I yelled.

"Come with us, we're gonna make more clones from your body." I tried to run but they caught me. One shot me with a stun ray.

The next thing I knew was that I was locked in a kind of animal cage. Then a clone came and took me into a cloning room. I saw 50 bodies of pure 100 percent human flesh. I screamed and ran out of the room through the halls, out the door, and into the woods.

I saw a gigantic flea and it started chasing me. I ran as fast as I could. I hid behind a rock. I looked back and saw the flea was no longer behind me, but the rock I hid behind wasn't a rock after all. It was a Brontosaurus' head.

"I'm going through a time warp again," I screamed. It picked me up and flung me into the water. Splash! I went falling into the water. A Mososaur came up and almost bit my leg off. I luckily got to shore quick enough.

I ran again hoping that I would go through another time warp so I could go back to my own time. I did go through another time warp, but it took me to the future. There were no cars at all, only monorails and spaceships. It was really weird. Everything was rocket-powered, even the houses. A spaceship came down and tried to pick me up. I started to run, but this time the spaceship got me. It brought me to the king. The king said, "You may live here in peace or you can be put in jail, if you don't want to live here."

"I don't want to live here," I yelled. Two guards held my hands and brought me to jail. Before they could put me in the cell I used some karate I learned in 4th grade. I ran away and went through another time warp again.

This time I got back to camp. I told my friends what happened, but they all said it was hogwash. I told Mrs. Baldwin, but she told me to lie down. When I did I had a dream of the same thing happening over and over again. I never went back to Camp MacLean.

Crack of the Stone
Jenny Marx

It was our first night at Camp MacLean. Mrs. Friedberg came into our cabin and said, "O.K. everybody, go to sleep," and she turned off the light. I was just about to go to sleep when suddenly everything went black. Not that it wasn't dark, it was just that everything but me disappeared! Up ahead I saw a pale green light. It seemed to be beckoning to me. I decided not to come because I might get hurt, but then, a strong wind started pushing me towards the light.

"I told you you shouldn't have used the wind power, Parshaka."

"But, Jenna, she was resisting!"

"I think she's awake now."

I opened my eyes to find myself lying on a misty ground. Two young women were looking at me worriedly. "Are you all right?" asked one of them.

"I—I'm f-f-fine. Where am I?"

"You are in the land of Mistic. My name is Jenna. We need your help," Jenna whispered.

"We had to get you through Parshakow holla morbaka," said the other woman, who was probably Parshaka.

"What is Parshakow holla morbaka?" I asked in a weak voice.

"In your language, it means 'the green light.' We speak Narkaugo-goan."

"You s-said you needed my help. What for?" I questioned.

"Come, come," said a creature in the distance.

"Who is he?"

"Moranako. He is a wise creature," Jenna said.

As we crept towards the creature, he said, "Come, do not be afraid, I am here to help." When we got there, he said, "On a planet not far from here, there are creatures called Molasks. They have brightly colored wings, scaly tails, and three eyes. They are under the power of Master Klarganposter, a villain. Klargan is very powerful and has all the nice Molasks in a statue formation. We need those Molasks back, for in five hours, the statues will be burned. We need your help to save them."

"But I can't help," I cried.

"But you can," said Moranako. "You have more feeling than we do."

"How, what do I do?" I asked timidly.

"That, we do not know," Moranako sighed. "Jenna is going to come with you, so she will try to help you in time of need. Be off!"

The First Hour

What happened just now was just, well, amazing! I was holding Jenna's hand, and suddenly I was swept off my feet. I could feel myself flying like a bird. I landed softly, and here I am!

"What should we do now?" Jenna asked me.

"Me? How should I know? You tell me," I said.

"Let's go over there," Jenna sighed, pointing to a patch of bright light in the distance. We tiptoed towards the light. Suddenly, we were sucked into the light. It blinded both of us for a minute. When we opened our eyes, we saw that we were inside a huge room. The walls were a bright yellow. In the center of the room, there was a chair. It was a golden chair. It reflected the bright yellow light of the room, and we had to shield our eyes to see. Sitting in the chair was an old man. He had a cruel look on his face.

"Yes? What can I do for you?" he asked slyly.

"Where are you keeping the Molasks?" asked Jenny fiercely, but timidly.

"You have come to help them, I suppose? Well, you can just get out of here!" he said calmly. We looked around for a door, but there were so many, we did not know where to go. "GO!" he screamed. We rushed out the nearest door before he could say anything else.

We found ourselves in a room with blue walls and a pink ceiling. There was a door at the far end of it. We went to the door and opened it. The next room was a strange one. It was black with grey squiggles on the walls. At the far end, there were two doors. One was grey and one was black. We decided to go into the grey one. As soon as we entered the next room, we were frozen solid!

The 2nd Hour

"Mmmp!" I tried to talk. Crraack! My mouth was free. I tried to crack the stone around me but I couldn't do it. Jenna was standing next to me. "Crack the stone on your mouth," I whispered. She did. We looked around. There were many statues surrounding us. "The Molasks," Jenna cried.

"How can we help them?" I asked.

"Well, we'll just have to think of something," Jenna exclaimed.

We thought and thought and thought. Finally, I said, "Remember when Moranako told me that I had a lot of feeling. Do you think that has anything to do with it?" I asked slowly.

"Hmmmmm, maybe, I don't know," Jenna said thoughtfully. We thought some more. "We need to find out how Klargan made the power so that everything that entered this room would change into stone," Jenna said.

"But first we have to find out how to get out of here," I said.

The 3rd Hour

"I hate these stupid old statues!" I exclaimed. Another layer of stone covered me. I thought that if you can hate the statues and they form, could you love them and they disappear? I decided to try it. "Statues, your grey color is so bright, your protection so warm, I love you for that." There was a crack. Then all the stone around me shattered to the floor!

"Love the statue! Love the statue!" I cried to everyone. Everyone freed themselves. All of the little Molasks started to dance and sing.

"Wait, stop. The evil Klargan is coming!" cried a Molask.

"We've got to hate him!" I whispered. The door flew open.

"What is going on in here?" he roared.

"We hate you."

"You are ugly."

"You are rotten."

"Your evil deeds."

"Your casting spells."

"Klarganposter, WE HATE YOU!!!!"

Klargan was frozen. He had turned into a statue!

The 4th Hour and Back!

We noticed a pale green door that seemed to give off a light. "Parshakow holla morbaka," I squealed. "Come on," Jenna yelled. We raced through the door and found ourselves in Mistic. There was a great party. We feasted until dawn. We sang and danced. By then, I began to wonder how I was going to get back to Camp MacLean. I walked over to Moranako and asked him. The next thing I knew was a "Goodbye!" and I was back in my bunk bed. The next day, I had a fun one. We built our terra and painted rocks and acorns. That night I was tired. I was just about to go to sleep when I saw a pale green light. I smiled and walked toward it.

The Marlene Crandel Project

Meredith Wunning

I raced into the lunchroom, almost bursting with my excitement. I looked around for my friends. I found them and sat down. Diane Simpson and Kate Bartell were into a long conversation, but I interrupted them anyway. This *couldn't* wait!

"I have this really great idea!" I said to everyone.

They all stopped to listen. They were used to my really great ideas.

"How about you tell us what it is before we die of curiosity," Diane said sarcastically.

"Well, Mr. Holter is having his science class do a paper on whether or not people's personalities can really change."

"It sounds stupid," Kate said irritably.

"I'm not through," I yelled in reply. "I thought we could try it to see if it was possible."

"Yeah," Amy giggled. "Maybe we could change someone into thinking they are a frog."

"Shut up! I mean change someone dull into someone popular, like Marlene Crandel," I said as an afterthought.

Everyone at the table groaned.

"This isn't a bad idea," Sara announced suddenly. "We all have Holter for Science at some time during the day. We'll all have to do the paper anyway, so let's do it together."

"Raise your hand if you want to," I said, smiling at Sara for helping me to get the others interested.

Amy Pierpont raised her hand, followed quickly by her shadow of a friend, Chris Morgan. Finally Diane and Kate agreed. The only one left was Andrea Cornell.

"Well, Andrea?" Sara coaxed.

"I guess so," she replied doubtfully.

"Great!" I yelled. "It's all set!"

"Not so fast!" Diane said. "Tell us the rest of your brilliant plan."

"Well, we try to boost her self-confidence. Help her pick out a new wardrobe, get her a new hairstyle, invite her over to our houses, things like that," I answered.

Unfortunately, I was elected to be the first to start "boosting her self-confidence."

"Uh, hi Marlene," I said. I was standing at her locker. She was so startled she dropped her books in the hall. We gathered up her stuff as quickly as we could so it wouldn't get kicked across the hall.

"I'm sorry I surprised you," I apologized.

"It's okay," she said shortly.

"Well, I was wondering if you could come over to my house after school?" I said, wondering if she could tell I was uncomfortable.

"Really?" she asked suspiciously.

"Really," I told her.

"Well, I guess so, but I have to call my mom," she replied. "Okay. Here's a quarter," I said, handing her the quarter. Marlene ran over to the phone booth. In a few minutes she returned smiling.

"I can come," she told me happily.

"Great, let's go!"

We ran outside. My mother was waiting for me outside and looked surprised when Marlene got in the car too.

"Mom, this is Marlene," I said.

"Hello, Mrs. James," Marlene said to my mother.

"Hello, Marlene. I haven't seen you around before."

"She's sort of a new friend," I said quickly.

When we got home, Marlene and I went up to my room and played records and talked until 6:30, when Marlene had to go. The reason she's so unpopular is because she's smart and shy. She can't help that she has red hair, freckles, and green eyes. Actually, she's not that bad. She's really nice, and I wish more people knew it. I'm really glad I didn't give up on this project even though everyone else did.

The next few days flew by. I was really having fun. I hardly gave the paper a second thought until Friday night, when I decided to sit down and write it. Actually, it was pretty good, but I felt a little guilty about using Marlene as a human guinea pig.

On Saturday Marlene came over for pizza. When she got here we went upstairs to watch TV in my room. I went downstairs to get the pizza when it was delivered and left Marlene in my room. When I went upstairs again, I found Marlene reading my science class paper.

"Uh-oh! How do I get myself into these things?" I felt sick.

"Hi," Marlene said, still reading.

"I'm really sorry I used you like that," I told her. "I really like you now that I know you."

"Don't be sorry," she said. "I used you too."

"What!" I exclaimed.

"I used you for my science report too," she said calmly. "I wanted to see if I could turn a stuck-up, popular person into a person who liked everybody."

I felt awful. Like for two weeks I had no privacy. I was thinking of something terrible to say to her until I realized I did the same thing to her.

Marlene gathered her stuff up. "It doesn't feel good when you find out your good friend isn't as nice as you thought, does it," she said bitterly.

Now Marlene is back to being a loner at school, and I'm back to my regular self. I feel kind of sorry for her, but if she wanted people to like her they would.

When I told Sara what happened, she wanted to make "that dirty rat pay," but I talked her out of it.

I wonder if Marlene feels bad about us not being friends. I know I do. Now I live by the Golden Rule — "Do unto others as you would want others to do unto you."*

*I got an "A" on my science paper.

Scruffy's Surprise
Kathryn Ann Rauch

Chapter I

"Go fetch, Scruffy, go fetch!" yelled Paula Rauch as she threw a stick to the golden retriever.

"You'll never get Scruffy to fetch that way!" said her twin sister Kathy.

"Why not?" retorted Paula. "We can do it. I know we can!"

Paula and Kathy stood watching with their brown hair flapping in the breeze as Scruffy ran into the water after a jumping fish.

It was a nice sunny May in Endicott. Over the rolling pasture, the twins ran to tell their mom that Scruffy caught a fish.

The ten-year-old twins burst through the screen door of the cheerful house.

"Mom's out in the stable," said Julie, their 16-year-old sister. "Don't forget, it's your turn to set the table, and dinner is almost ready."

"Mom said we didn't have to because we are going to Jenny Boshard's for her birthday sleep-over party," said Kathy. "We are also going to eat supper at her house."

"Well, then," said Julie, "you had better start getting ready!"

Just then Scruffy ran in holding her head up proudly with the dead sunfish in her mouth.

Chapter II

"Yech! What is that thing?" yelled Julie.

"Oh, it's just an old sunfish," said Paula as she tossed it into the garbage can in the closet.

"Come on Scruffy, let's go upstairs," said Kathy.

The twins and Scruffy ran upstairs to the room they shared. The yellow room was filled with their favorite animal pictures. Several were of horses and the rest divided between dogs and cats.

"Beat ya," said Kathy as she plopped on one of the two twin beds. Scruffy scampered up beside her.

"We have to decide what to wear," declared Paula. "Let's go in our new blue outfits."

Quickly the girls got the things they needed together. Paula wrapped the stuffed animals the girls got Jenny for her birthday.

Jenny Boshard was the twins' best friend—next to each other, of course.

Last month, when they saw the mother horse and her colt in the store, they knew it was the perfect gift for Jenny. She loved horses almost as much as the twins did.

After Kathy packed the presents safely in the overnight bag, the girls ran down the stairs. Scruffy followed. She didn't want to be left alone.

Chapter III

"Hey Mom, Scruffy caught a fish!" said the twins excitedly as they ran into the kitchen where Mrs. Rauch and Julie were talking.

"I know, I can smell it. You had better take the garbage out on your way to Jenny's," advised their black-haired mother.

Just then Erinn Greene rode into the yard on her horse, Princeton. "Come on, you two, saddle up your horses and let's go!"

After the girls said goodbye to their mom, they ran off to the barn and saddled their horses, Sunny and Nero.

"Let's take the shortcut," said Paula as they headed for the forest.

"Let's not," said Erinn. "My mom doesn't allow me to cross the river."

"Don't be a spoil-sport," said Paula. "Hurry up, Scruffy! Let's take the mountain route. It isn't as long that way," said Kathy.

When they were almost to Jenny's house, Erinn broke the silence by saying, "Guess what Jenny got for her birthday . . . a VCR! We are going to watch *Peanuts* all night."

Just then Kathy yelled, "Watch out!" They looked up to see a rockslide coming straight toward them. They urged the horses faster and just missed being buried.

"Scruffy!" screamed Kathy.

Chapter IV

The girls hopped off their horses and ran to the place they had last seen Scruffy. They searched through the rocks for the missing dog. Once Errin thought she saw him, but it was a hat.

Finally, after what seemed like hours, Paula yelled, "I found her. She looks hurt. Erinn, since your dad is a vet, see if Scruffy is okay."

Scruffy lay trapped by the rocks. She whimpered and looked pleadingly at the girls.

"Come on, we have to get these rocks off of her," said Kathy.

They pulled the stones away, uncovering the dog.

Erinn said, "We should get Scruffy to my dad right away!" Very carefully, they picked up Scruffy and placed her on Nero. Scruffy was whimpering loudly.

They rode on to Jenny Boshard's house because it was the closest. Erinn called her dad and told him about the accident. He said he would come right over.

Mrs. Boshard made a comfortable bed for Scruffy. The ten girls crowded around the bed and spoke softly to Scruffy while Kathy petted her gently.

Chapter V

Dr. Greene came a few minutes later, as he promised. He examined Scruffy and said she had a fractured leg. After the twins called home, Dr. Greene asked if he could take Scruffy to the hospital to place a cast on the leg.

With tears in their eyes, Paula and Kathy agreed to let Dr. Greene take Scruffy. Sadly they watched him take Scruffy out to the car. Mr. Rauch was going to meet Dr. Greene at the hospital. The twins and Julie were going to go over in the morning after Scruffy had rested.

After a while Mrs. Boshard came out onto the porch. "Come inside, girls, you won't help Scruffy by standing there," she said. "We are going to eat now."

Even though the girls didn't really feel hungry, they went in to the table. "Oh, boy! Spaghetti, my favorite!" they cried in unison.

Chapter VI

In the morning the girls rode Nero and Sunny home. This time they went the long way by the road. The party had been fun even though the girls felt sad when they thought about Scruffy.

When the girls got home they were excited about going to see Scruffy. When they got to the hospital, Dr. Greene came out to meet them. "Scruffy is much better," he said. "The fracture wasn't bad and will heal quickly. I expect she will be able to go home in a few days. Oh, by the way, did you know Scruffy is pregnant?"

"Oh boy! Can we keep the puppies?"

"Yuck! What will we do with them?"

"Hold it, kids. The puppies won't be born for about four weeks."

Mr. Rauch looked at Dr. Greene, who nodded, then continued. "Let's go inside and see her."

Chapter VII

(Four weeks later)

Kathy couldn't sleep, so she went downstairs to get a drink. As she went down the dark staircase, she heard little barks.

"Mom! Dad! Paula! Julie! Scruffy had her puppies!"

They ran down the stairs to the family room, where Kathy was about to pet one of the puppies. "Better not," advised Mrs. Rauch. "Scruffy might not like it. Jim," she said to her husband, "why don't you call John Greene? He may want to check them."

Paula and Kathy looked at each other and smiled. Now they had three more dogs to teach to fetch.

Sara 'n' Dipity

Laura Francis

Sara ran out of the house with her cheek smudged with jelly, her hat stuffed in her pocket and her coat buttoned crooked, just in time to catch the school bus.

Sara Johnston is a bright student, but there are two things Sara hates about herself—being short and being clumsy. She is four feet seven inches short and wishes she were tall and graceful. Sara resembles a dwarf in a giant's world. It seems every time she turns around she bumps into someone or something.

Lunchtime with Sara is often a series of bangs, booms, and bonks. She tries being careful, but it's a hard task for Sara. The other day as she was chatting with her friends and buying a cookie she backed into Mr. Rob, the science teacher. He reached out to catch himself from the fall and threw his tray of chicken, which came crashing down on top of him. He looked amazed that a little thing like Sara could cause such a disaster. She was so upset that when she sat down at her usual spot on the lunch bench next to her friends, her orange drink did a forward roll onto Mary's french fries. Everyone grabbed napkins to catch the flowing orange spill before it plunged over the edge and made a bigger mess. Sara ran for more napkins, and when she came back she plopped herself down into a tray that had been put there on the bench to get out of the way of the run-away drink on the table. So it was now fifteen minutes into lunch period, and Sara had terrorized the science teacher, flooded her friend's french fries and squashed a tray of food, the tracks of which were all over her jeans. Although she hadn't had a bite to eat yet, Sara was too mad at herself now to eat anything.

So she went to Mr. Dipity's "office" to ask him how to get the catsup out of her pants. Mr. Dipity, the janitor, is Sara's good friend because whenever she spills something he helps her clean up the mess. He knows just what to use to make spots and messes disappear. His "office" is a large closet, and he is usually near there at lunchtime.

As he was helping her remove the spots from her jeans, she told him about her next big problem—art.

"Today is our last day to work on our art assignment, and Mrs. Dume has given us a really dumb one this time," she moaned.

"Oh, how so?" Mr. Dipity asked as he rubbed more cleaning fluid on a catsup spot.

"She wants us to create an emotion. What kind of assignment is that? In math, I can add or subtract, multiply or divide, and get an answer. In social studies and science we learn facts. In reading we do vocabulary and spelling words. But in art we have to create an emotion!" she exclaimed in disgust.

"Sara, you're excellent at creating commotion. You surely can create an emotion." Mr. Dipity smiled as they erased the last trace of lunch from her clothes.

When she got to art class she took out her clean canvas, which only had her name on it so far. She started telling the kids at her table about her disasters at lunch. They were laughing and enjoying her tale. As Sara flung her arms wide to demonstrate how Mr. Rob reacted, her hand knocked over the red paint onto her canvas and the floor. One of her friends called her a "clumsy little kid," which made her really angry, and her face turned as red as the paint. She was so mad she threw her canvas in the trash and stomped out of art as the bell rang with no assignment to turn in. She left the school not knowing she left a trail of red paint footsteps that started at the art room and faded to the bus door. She was too mad to see anything, so she didn't notice the footsteps or Mr. Dipity standing in the doorway of his "office" shaking his head and smiling.

The next day Sara was worried throughout the morning and lunch about art. She knew art would be a disaster because she had no painting to hand in. As she was slowly walking down the hallway to art she could hear Mrs. Dume saying, "Class, this is exactly what I meant when I made this assignment. Here is the creation of the emotion *anger* by a potentially great modern artist, Sara Johnston!"

Sara walked in as her name was announced and saw her trashed canvas at the front of the room. She could hardly believe it, and in seconds she realized who saved it from the trash.

When Mrs. Dume asked Sara what she would title her art she replied "Sara 'n' Dipity" because this was a happy accident.

Pearls of Wisdom

Sridhar Prasad

I am now an old man, an invalid steadily journeying towards the only known destiny of all. As I lie here, my mind can focus on only one thing. Before I tell you, you must know the background.

Being the only son of a merchant who belittled the word "well-to-do," I was considerably proud of my place in feudalism. To ensure my standing in the future, I enrolled myself in the pursuit of learning.

I was still engrossed in my study when my father told me that I was to practice as a merchant. I was utterly aghast at this intelligence. However, I consoled myself with grand visions of arriving ostentatiously at the market in a chauffeured limousine. Alas, it was not to be! From behind his newspaper, I was told that I would be given a cycle as my means of transportation to the market. I could not see myself pedalling through dusty, narrow streets defiled with cow dung. I was about to protest vehemently, when I remembered my father telling me once, "My son, I will never ask you to do something unless I myself have also done it." This, however, provided little consolation other than the feeling that my father must have also suffered a similar humiliation. Soon, this warm feeling too was dispelled, for I recalled that my father enjoyed all forms of exercise, and so, bereft of all consolation, I was left to mourn my lot in privacy.

The next morning, I shamefacedly made my way to the market. My head was bent low, my back arched double, and my face was all but concealed with a scarf and a hat. My excuse, a lame one, was that I was cold. I had taken this stance of course, to preserve my face from recognition. Yet, even with such camouflage, I was still ridiculed by urchins, loafers, and vagabonds—many of whom asked me with a visible smirk why I was bundled thus on a beautiful day. I could merely spurn them with my foot and pedal on.

When I came to the bazaar, however, I found that which would compensate for the entire journey. I saw fruit vendors carrying litters full of painstakingly arrayed pyramids of fruit. The air was perfumed with the tantalizing aroma of colorful, sticky sweets, which bespoke of long, blistering hours over a hot fire.

There was also entertainment in characters like the animal trainer with his menageries, who "enchanted" them, or so he said. The bazaar was overpopulated with idlers and vagabonds who came for fun, making mischief or playing pranks on those bogus magicians, or simply to watch the excitement, the latter of which I could hardly blame them for. Here a woman haggling with a vendor, there an apprentice half-dragging a customer to his master's shop, and still elsewhere a young urchin receiving a sound tongue-lashing from an irate marketwoman.

I, however, was to keep in mind that I was not a market-goer, but a colleague to these scattered members of a guild. My father bought the products of these poor but skillful craftsmen and sold them to a discriminating public, without either party becoming aware of the process. When my father revealed his secret to the master craftsmen, the look of deep gratitude in their eyes was fathomless. They promised to offer him nothing but the best of their skills, and he in turn gave his solemn word not only to deal with them fairly but to educate their offspring at the expense of his own purse. It was a perfect arrangement that worked exceedingly well, with the increasingly flourishing trade ample evidence.

When the craftsmen saw me, the scion of their patron, and the customers noticed the heir-apparent of their supplier, they readily flocked to my shop. Unfortunately, their reasons were not purely in commerce. For several days I was uncomfortably aware of the fact that I was under surveillance, and bits of gossip gleaned from careless tongues did nothing to lessen my apprehension.

My duties included a survey of the various smithies, weavers, and tailors who supplied goods to my father to ensure that all were indeed working smoothly, and, if not, to determine if their excuse was valid. Many were the hours when I watched tailors patiently measure a piece of silk and jewelers painstakingly fashion the most intricate patterns from beaten gold filaments. Their attention to every trivial detail was in itself an education to me, and I never ceased to marvel at their utter dedication to perfection. Ah, to catch a gleam of satisfaction in the eye of a master craftsman when lovingly inspecting his completed creation— a profound experience I deeply cherished.

My trip home was no less uneventful than the hours preceding it. I was often forced to ride in ditches, hindered by enormous masses of people slowly wending their way to the temple, carrying a precious portion of their meager earnings as offerings for the appeasement of the gods. I privately believed that this practice was largely encouraged by the bogus so-called intellectuals, who spurred the illiterate rustics into superstitious fear for their own personal and ill-gotten gain. I also crossed paths with many an odd person, such as the nameless hawker-girl with an inflammable temper, who wreaked her vengeance at my refusal to buy her wares by subjecting me to the fury of her cruel-clawed raptor. To this day, I bear on my body scars of that grievous encounter.

And thus I could go on recounting countless tales of my adventures of the bicycle days—some infuriating, some amusing, but all of them colorful. I soon became accustomed to my routine and having enjoyed the benefits of the vigor and exercise of my daily rides, quickly became a staunch if boring advocate of cycling myself.

There was, however, one particular alley which I disliked to pass from the very first day I started out on this venture. It was the dwelling place for beggars with shriveled bodies and uncared-for wounds. I would always cycle through this region with averted eyes and bated breath and with as much speed as I could muster, my sole goal being to put the distasteful scene behind me as quickly as I could physically manage.

One monsoon day, it began to rain on the way and by the time I approached the alley, the sky seemed to open, drenching my inadequately clad body to the bone. I attempted to cycle through the alley in vain, and it then occurred to me that any continuation of this ridiculous folly would soon reward me with an ignominious end in some flooded ditch. Close inspection revealed that these paupers' domicile was no less sturdily built than those fanciful shops in the bazaar. I repeatedly shouted for shelter, but none would come out onto the now deserted streets, and risk the fury of the lashing torrents.

As I commenced to despair of ever returning to my own abode alive, one of the paupers held open the door to his housing and ordered me to come in. For one frozen moment, I reflected on the miserable situation that prompted me, the scion of the bazaar's monopolizer, to seek shelter in the home of a slum-dwelling pauper. Finally, I entered. I muttered a barely audible word of gratitude and proceeded to inspect my new dim surroundings with an equal measure of revulsion and curiosity. I was strangely surprised by the scene that assailed my sight. The single room that I now occupied seemed to comprise the entire house, and while its furnishings were minimal and threadbare, every nook and corner bore sparkling evidence of thorough cleanliness. And the shriveled beggar revealed himself to be a quiet, small man who was offering me a straw mat to make myself comfortable on the scrubbed floor with no less dignity than that of my father's affluent friends who conducted me to their costly couches. As I was desperately attempting to accustom myself to the overwhelming feelings of severed pride and shame that threatened to choke me, I spied another occupant in the far end of the dwelling.

She was a young beggar girl, about my age, who was silently absorbed in the task of fashioning appetizing bread from the most meager ingredients. A deep calm emanated from her, and her beauty was as radiant as the moon reflected by the sea. Presently, she served her father and me, and under their combined urgings, I partook of the delectable nourishment, unhappily aware that I must be dangerously diminishing their normal share of the meal. Her father then retired, ordering his offspring to entertain me.

I bluntly asked the girl how she could exist so peacefully amidst all the squalor of such a slum. To this she replied, "It is better to be barefoot and capable of enjoying life's immense joys, than to be blessed with filled coffers and unable to enjoy God's wonderful creations." I begged her to enlighten me further, and she proceeded to explain about the days when she too believed that riches held the solution to all problems and had once run off to serve in a rich man's house. There she realized that death was no stranger to a millionaire than to a beggar, that suffering springs as much for a sick rich man as for a poor hungry man and that pain can hurt as much from the careless vanity of a spoiled child as from the deprived look of a starving child.

I sat stunned amidst the shambles of my crumbled pride, while she told me that she was now happy with her status in life. She chopped wood and took time to listen to the birds or she drew water from the well and let the warmth of the sun caress her. She picked flowers and hummed under her breath or walked through the rain, tasting the drops. She breathed luxuriously of the freshly wet earth or marveled at the miracle of a star-studded night sky. She taught me, in short, to be grateful to be alive and enjoy each gift that the Almighty Creator showers ceaselessly on every keen perceiver.

By now, the rain had ceased, and I reluctantly took leave of my wonderful hosts and stepped out onto the rain-washed streets with a light step and a song in my heart.

Since that memorable day when a most astonishing friendship was forever forged, I have never ceased to visit my friends at every available opportunity. Over the years, I have secretly lavished vast amounts of gifts on them, but the peace or the status of their home has never changed, and each time she has remained the benefactor and I the recipient. In time, the quality of her neighborhood improved, and I know that the mysterious cause of the change could be none other than her accomplishments with my resources.

As I lie here, I know that my time will soon be up and I will rest happily, secure in the knowledge that I have finally found "the philosophy of existence" which proved to be the pearls of wisdom from the lips of my friend.

Story for Younger Children

Think of the kind of stories you used to like to hear before you learned to read or when you were just learning to read. Make up a story that you can actually read to preschoolers or children in first or second grade. Illustrate it if you want. Rewrite if their response indicates how it might be improved. Keep reading it to other younger children, or give it to some child or class.

The Knight and His
Unicorn vs. the Dragon
Ari Lindner and Gabe Morgan

Once upon a time there lived a Knight in shining armor.

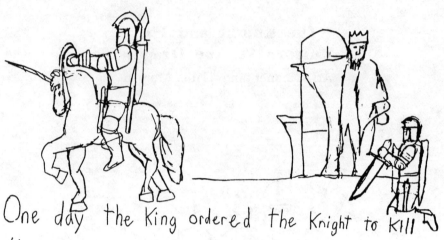

One day the king ordered the knight to kill the nasty, mean, chromatic dragon. It lived in the Black Forest. On his black, silky unicorn he set off.

With sword in hand he entered the forest.

He saw a sign that said, "Beware of Dragon."

He said to himself, "Oh, boy, "

He looked around and saw a dark cave. So he went slowly and carefully into the dark, gloomy cave.

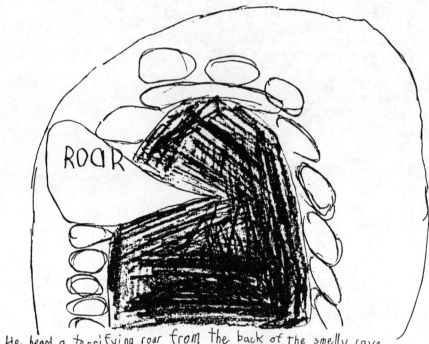

He heard a terrifying roar from the back of the smelly cave.

He walked closer and closer, more carefully and slowly, to the sound.

When suddenly he saw a big, smelly, nasty, mean, ugly, scaly, green, chromatic dragon.

He raised his sword, Seeing this, the dragon lashed out his spiked tail and knocked the knight off his unicorn.

Then the dragon threw a fire ball at the knight, but luckily the unicorn shot a ray out of his horn.

Seeing that he was beaten, the dragon zoomed away. Then the knight jumped on his unicorn and galloped swiftly after the dragon.

They caught up with the dragon and the unicorn stabbed the dragon with his horn.

Then the knight took his sword and, with one mighty swing, he killed the dragon.

For killing the dragon, the king gave him the princess, and they lived happily ever After

Tiger and His Amazing Car
Chad Kingsley and Arlando Palmer

One night Tiger went out in his amazing car to pick up his girlfriend.

Then Tiger saw a hotrod car.

It was going about 80 miles per hour.

Then He Saw another hotrod Car that had a shiny silk Stripe on it.

The Two hotrods wanted
to crash into Tiger.

Quickly Tiger made a spinout
and turned a switch on them that made
slippery oil come out of the back of
the Car.

After getting out of the oil, the two hotrod cars chased Tiger, but he shot smoke at them and got away.

Then the two hotrod cars called two other hotrod cars on their radio.

The four hotrod cars cornered
Tiger in his car.

Quickly Tiger pushed the ejection
seat that made him go straight up into the
air.

Then automatically Tiger's car jumped over
two hotrod cars and came to meet Tiger.

Tiger shot at
the brick walls
and got away.

Then Tiger went to pick up his girlfriend.

The end.

Illustrated Storybook

Make a storybook like those that are sold for your age in book stores or that appear in children's magazines. Alone or with a partner, make up a story and try it out first by telling it to a small group. Let them ask questions and give responses, then write a draft of the story and try that out by letting a small group hear or read it. Make whatever changes you need. Illustrate key actions or scenes, make a nice cover, and bind the pages together as a book.

Pass it around or read and show it to others. Maybe you can even get it published with help from your teacher or other adults.

French Fried Frog Legs
David Hall

    Puff-Puf my pet frog was in a terrible situation.
He was going to be turned into frog legs! My mom
wanted to cook him and eat him for dinner that night.

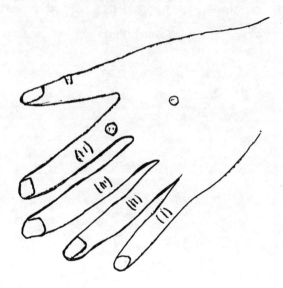

Even if Puff-Puf gave me warts I still liked him.

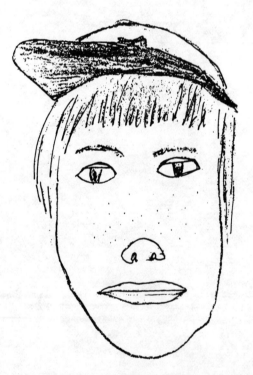

I had to think of something to stop my mom from
cooking Puff-Puf. Then I finally thought of something and that was to find another frog for Mom to
cook.

After school I found a frog behind a bush and I
        brought it home.

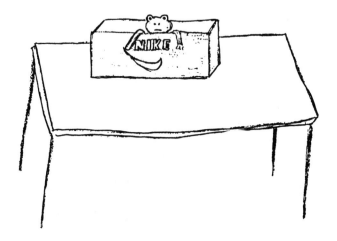

I took Puff-Puf out of his box and put him in the
closet and I put the new frog in Puff-Puf's box so Mom
would think the new frog was Puff-Puf.

After that I went outside to play football with my
friends.

Right when I was about to score a touchdown, my
mom called me to come in.

When I got home I saw my mom and dad dressing up in
their rooms and the frogs still were where I left them.

I asked my mom why we weren't eating frog legs.
She said, "Your dad didn't want to see a frog being
hurt, so we're going to eat at Pizza Hut." After she
said that I felt so relieved because no one got hurt
I started to laugh.

Soon I took Puff-Puf out of the closet and put him
with the other frog.

The Lonely Ant

Mary Rapsey

Once upon a time there was an ant named Fred.

He had a problem.

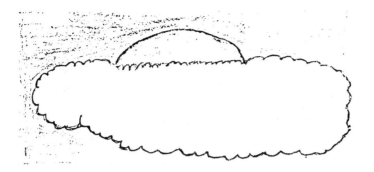

He was all by himself. He could not find ants
anywhere. He thought he should get some sleep so
he could get up early in the morning to find some
ants to play with.

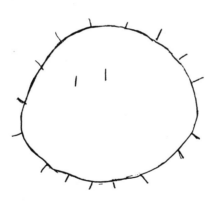

The next morning Fred woke up bright and
early.

Fred walked a little way up the road. He
found a little house. He got up closer and
went inside.

Fred saw an old woman cooking.

Then Fred sneaked into another room. Right before
his eyes he saw an anteater!

So he ran out of the house.

He went by a tree. Fred said to himself,
"I think I'm going to take a nap for awhile
under this tree."

While Fred was asleep, the old lady let the
anteater go outside while she went shopping.

The anteater sniffed the whole yard. The
anteater got over to the tree and ate him.

A couple of hours later Fred woke up and saw
another ant.

Fred said, "Where am I?"

The ant said, "You are inside an anteater. Come
over here and meet all of my friends."

All of the ants liked him very much. Day after
day, week after week, they were still inside of the
anteater. They had fun times inside the anteater.

One day as the old lady was cooking, the
anteater was watching. The lady loved lots of
salt and pepper. She had bought a big bag of
each. As she picked up the bag of pepper, it
broke.

The anteater went to see what it was and
sniffed it.

He started sneezing. One by one all of the ants
flew out. He didn't know he had eaten that many!

Now Fred had someone to play with and they lived

happily ever after.

Twice-Told Tales

*Do your own version of a famous fairy tale, short story,
nursery rhyme, or story poem. Make it enough like the
original to be recognized but different enough to be funny
to compare. You can make fun of the original by doing a
comic imitation of it—a parody—or you can just modern-
ize it in today's terms and language. With partners make
a book titled something like RERUN CLASSICS (or RE-
TREATED, THREADBARE CLASSICS).*

Goldy and the Three Val Bears
Molly Buren and Debbie Rubin

One day Goldy was going for a walk to find a really jammin house
that she could explore. Now there were three val bears who lived in a

real jammin house just west of the big oak tree in the forest. They were invited to a Police concert so they left for the concert.

Now Goldy found their house, opened the door, and went in. Suddenly she saw some pizza on the table. She took the biggest piece and bit into it but soon spit it out. "Ouch," she said, "this piece is too hot." Then she bit into the next piece and soon spit it out. "Brrr," she said, "this one is too cold." Then Goldy bit into the next one and it was just right so she ate it up. Then she went into the living room and turned on a stereo. "Oh," she said, "this is too loud!" Then she went to another stereo. "Sick, this music is too slow!" Then she went to the last stereo. "Oh jammin! This is just right." So she listened to the music for a while.

When she got bored she went upstairs. She saw a waterbed and lay down on it and said, "This doesn't have enough water in it." So she tried the next one. When she lay down on it, it popped and she said, "This one has too much water in it." So she tried the last bed and said, "Oooo, this is jammin good!" So she fell asleep.

About two hours later the val bears came home. They found their pizza all eaten up. They went into the living room and found their stereos were broken. The Mama bear said, "Grody to the Max!" The baby bear said, "Gag me with a spoon!" and they all went upstairs to find a punk girl on Baby Bear's bed. They threw her out of the house and the next day got a new waterbed for Mama Bear (because Goldy popped it).

Now to this day Goldy has stopped exploring houses and got a job as a waitress in a real jammin restaurant.

The Mouse Ran up the Clock
Ari Lindner and Andrew Turek

Hickory, dickory, dock. The tiny rodent hurtled up the old timepiece. The old timepiece chimed at the one-o-clock mark. The tiny rodent hurtled down.

Hickory, dickory, dock.

Little Ms. Muppet

Erjan Fortson

Little Ms. Muppet
    Sat on her puppet
Eating Cream of Wheat and Toast.
    Along came a bear
and began to stare.
    And said, "How does she eat that stuff?"

The Tell-Tale Maple Syrup

Andy Bragen

It was the tree, oh yes, it was the tree. The tree was a normal maple tree in all respects except it had one humongus leaf which seemed to always stare at me. I had to kill that tree.

You may fancy me mad, but you should have seen how I thought my plan over, not like a madman. I was going to kill that tree while its leaf was not blowing in the wind.

I had nothing against that tree except its leaf that haunted me day and night. I was going to cut down the tree and stick it in a hole which I had dug.

As you can see, I am not mad. I am not a madman, but I had to get rid of that tree.

I went out at exactly midnight with my axe in hand, but the leaf was blowing in the wind. This was true for the next five nights after that. I had my chance on the seventh night. I had to get my job done quickly because my friends, Bob and Harry, the environmentalists, were coming over for poker in about thirty minutes.

When my friends arrived from their league bowling, we talked about what we had done all week while chewing on carrots sautéed in maple syrup.

Then it was time for poker. Harry dealt the cards and I received four jacks and a king of hearts. We were playing five-card draw.

At that moment my wife walked in carrying some popcorn for us. She was wearing a grey flannel skirt which went down to her knees and a red turtleneck blouse which she adored. On the blouse was a flower and two leaves which she had picked off the maple tree earlier that day. I trembled under my breath.

The king of hearts had a knife in its head. When it was my turn to discard I hastily got rid of it. I picked up the queen of hearts. She was holding a flower and two leaves.

Then I heard it, the gurgling of the maple syrup in my stomach. At first it was not very loud, then it started getting louder and louder until it sounded like a tremor.

They must have heard it, my poker friends must have. I yelled in a hoarse voice that sounded much like a whisper, "I admit it, I killed the maple tree." I dragged them to where I buried the tree. I dug it up and yelled in the same way as before, "You see it, so do what you please with me."

The Magic Pill
Matt Rich

A few years ago Laura's mother died of cancer. Six months later her father remarried. Her stepmother had two children—a spoiled boy, Chuck, and a girl, Lisa. Chuck and Lisa wouldn't let Laura use their car. Laura's father, who was in Japan, wrote that he would talk to Lisa about the problem when he got home. Laura's stepmother was also selfish, for she had taken away Laura's miniskirt and designer clothes and given them to Lisa. At school Laura had to wear out-of-date clothes, and nobody liked her.

Laura hated the world so much she made a long-lasting sleeping pill with her brother's chemistry set and took the pill. Laura's stepmother was so glad to not have to remind her to do her homework or to pack her lunch that she let Laura sleep for three years.

Laura's science teacher, who in the meantime had become a millionaire by perfecting the microchip, wondered why Laura hadn't come to class for three years and came to visit her.

"Where have you been, Laura?" asked the science teacher. Hearing his voice made Laura feel guilty for not doing her last homework assignment, so she woke right up.

She sat up straight and said, "Stepmother, come here right now!"

The stepmother yelled, "How dare you call me by that name. You call me Mother!"

"You are not my mother," said Laura.

The science teacher said, "How would you like to have a career selling microchips with me?"

Laura said, "Fine, as long as we can go to Japan to sell them."

Mix Media

Choose something you have read and rewrite it in another form. Turn a news story into a poem, a poem into a short story or play, an informative article into a story, a play into a ballad, and so on. Make all the changes you want. The idea is to play with the original piece to make your own creation. Take the main story line or idea and see what you can do with it in another form.

Pair off a copy of the original with your version of it when you present it to others.

Lord Randall Dies of Poisoning
Ben Sander

Yesterday at 4 o'clock P.M. Lord Randall, a prominent business-man, died of food poisoning. Suspects are being held in the case, Randall's mother and his sweetheart, Lady Singapore. Earlier today I talked to the Lord's mother. She said that the Lord had come in and asked to go to bed. Then she learned that Lord Randall had been poisoned by his sweetheart. However, Lady Singapore has denied everything. She says that Randall asked to have lunch with her, and she agreed. So, she boiled some eels in a broth for lunch, and then Randall left.

New evidence has been discovered in the case, though. The sheriff found Lord Randall's hounds dead of food poisoning. They were found near Lady Singapore's cottage. It appears Lady Singapore was angry at Randall for leaving her (he left to go on a hunting trip) and poisoned him.

Campbell Missing
Rebecca Morss

Good George Campbell went out for a ride last Saturday wearing his good knee-high boots and his fancy riding clothes and never came back. His horse, still with its embroidered saddle, came back, though, carrying a note. It reads:

My meadow lies green and my corn is unshorn.
My barn is unbuilt and my babe is unborn.
I am in some woods.
                    HELP!

Unfortunately for the people searching, there are many woods. Meanwhile, his old mother is wild with despair and his good wife is tearing out her hair. If you have any information or would like to help search please contact Mrs. Campbell.

Fictional Journal

Tell a story through a journal you make up as if one of the characters in your story is keeping it. All the reader sees is this character's journal. So everything has to come through it. Indicate where the entries begin and end. Write in the style this character would use. What series of events is this person writing about from day to day or time to time in his or her journal?

Present this to others as you might any other story. Reading aloud might be especially good if you or someone else wants to act the voice of such a character.

Dr. Halim Dhanidina's Scientific
Journal of Observation on Triceratops.
Date Begun: 24038/6
Date Completed: 24038/7
Halim Dhanidina

The Plan

It is about 5:00 in the evening. I am working on a plan. The plan is something most scientists have laughed at. It is to go back in time!

I will do this by building a time machine. I had been working for years and years, and today, I finalized it! I would very much like to share the blueprints with the world, but I am too impatient.

The fuel it will run on is very rare, so unfortunately, I can only go back for 24 hours. Back, back, into the dinosaur age I will go. A lonely, unknown, and exotic place, and I will be the first of my time to reach it.

The very sound of it sends chills down my spine. I have to go now if I'm going to make my 9:00 A.M. deadline. Professor Dhanidina signing off.

I have finally completed my master creation, the time machine! In just a few minutes I will be in the realm of the dinosaurus.

I'm not going back just to observe all the dinosaurus. I'm going to see the one dinosaur that grabbed my interest like a magnet, the Triceratops.

Now, I must not waste time. I can't put it off any later. I am leaving now, and for the sake of God, it will be a safe trip.

The Encounter

I have landed. The air is breathable. The weather is pretty cool, about 62 degrees. I have landed on a grassy hill. There are trees to my right and hills in the background. Night is falling. Only a few of the sun's rays break through the mist. Cool icy mist and fog are creeping closer and closer on their little cat feet.

What is that? Could it be . . .? Yes, it is the Triceratops. It is a big fat herbivore. It has two long horns on its head and one on its nose. It has short stubby legs and a short stubby tail. Its skin is rough and thick. It has a big-boned shield above its neck. Its skull looks hard and very protective.

It is feeding on the wet grass and plants below him. It is gumming and grinding most of its food, because its teeth don't look sharp. He is taking lots of time to fill his big stomach. It looks like it's going to doze off but not here. It is the beginning of night and the meat-eaters are coming out to feed.

It looks like he's headed towards his home. I had better follow him so I can watch him in the morning.

At last we are at his home. It is like a large burrow. It is made of twigs and hay.

I am tired so I will make myself comfortable just outside his home. Professor Dhanidina signing off.

The Courtship

I had just woken up a while ago. What . . .! What's that . . .! Oh no, the Triceratops is gone! There are his footprints. I think I'll mold one of them for my collector's bag. When I come back it should be dried up. Professor Dhanidina signing off.

When is this search going to end? I have been traveling for hours. Huh ...? Could that be ...? Yes, it's him. And there's another Triceratops. They seem to be courting in a strange way. It must be mating season.

First, the male takes a few steps to the right. Then, the female faces him and does the same. Then the male takes a few steps to the left, and the female does the same. Then the female takes the lead and bobs her head up and down and the male does the same.

I would guess that the mocking of each move is done so each of them can test the other's loyalty.

Now I've got the mold. It is large and heavy. It will make a good souvenir. Professor Dhanidina signing off.

Leaving Time

Now that I've got everything I had better leave. The weather is warm. The air is clear. In all it's a beautiful day. I say in regret, good-bye, Dinosaur Age. A tear touches my eyes as I write. Professor Dhanidina signing off.

Fictional Correspondence

Make up an exchange of letters as a way to tell a story. Why are these particular people writing to each other? Date the letters. Try to make the style of each correspondent's letters fit his or her personality. The correspondents may be telling each other about events happening where they are, but the letters themselves can be events— requests, threats, suggestions, congratulations, flattery, thanks, etc.

Your Move

Elizabeth Pontikes

Dec. 25

Dear Daphnie

Hi! Are you having a good time in Arizona? I hope we're still BEST FRIENDS! Oh, yea! Merry Christmas! Do you know that the people who moved into your house next door are ALL BOYS! I'm lonely without you, but I have my other friends from school. I hope you're making new friends too! Is your new school nice? I hope the cafeteria food is better than here!

I guess I STILL have not got used to you being away. Yesterday I almost stopped at your house to pick you up when I was going to the park! I hope you still like me even though we live far away!

　　　　Sincerely,
　　　　　Samantha Anchor

Jan. 2

Dear Samantha,

I am enjoying Arizona very much. It's much better than back there with you. I have a new next-door neighbor and she's much nicer than you! You are the dumbest person I know! My new next-door neighbor is also my new best friend. I know, I know. I acted dumb last year too. But I've matured! So now either you shape up or ship out of the slot as "my best friend" or even one of my friends, for that matter.

Anyway, I'm glad you told me to have a Merry Christmas. I guess I should say the same for you, so Merry Christmas! I'm sure your dumb self and family had a great time. You always do with your dumb games! I really don't believe I liked them last year. Anyway, I've got better things to do than this! Write back if you want; it doesn't matter to me!

　　　　Sincerely,
　　　　　Daphnie Crets

Feb. 5

TO Daphnie,

I don't care if you don't like me anymore and think I'm dumb. I've got better things to do than bow at your feet and I'm not going to shape up, 'cause I don't have to do anything to my personality. I'm fine and millions of people like me!

I really wasn't going to write this letter, but I want to get the last word. I don't care about your "new best friend," and you're a snot. If

you were still at this school everyone would hate you, especially me!
                    FROM
                Samantha Anchor
P.S. It took me so long to write this because I was hurt!
P.P.S. You'd better apologize or I'll never be your friend!
P.P.P.S. IF YOU DO I WILL!

                                        Feb. 7

Dearest Samantha,

    I'm very sorry for what I said in the other letter. I know I was
acting like a jerk, but it must be that terrible girl who lives next door.
She is such a brainwasher! You're still my best friend. I guess I'm doing
this because yesterday she just ignored me. People warned me about her,
but I didn't listen.

    I said you were dumb because when I explained you to my neighbor
she said you sounded dumb. She said I matured, but I think I just got
snotty. You said you'd forgive me if I say I'm sorry, so I guess you have.
Guess what? I got into the chorus at school! Isn't that great? Oh no! My
mom's calling me. Got to go!
                    S.W.A.K.
                Sincerely,
                    Daphnie
P.S. I wrote to you the minute your letter came!
P.P.S. The cafeteria food here is worse than at our old school!

                                        Feb. 10

Dear Daphnie,

    I'm glad we're still friends. We can still be best friends even if you
move to Japan! My mom said I could visit you for spring break, but I
have to be here for Easter. Leslie, Sarah, Amy, Nancy, Rachel, Jennifer,
Jessica and Alex, your best friends say hello. All your other friends say
hello too, and of course me, your very best friend, says hello.

    What's your schedule for after school? Mine is Monday, piano
lessons; Tuesday, I'm free; Wednesday, I'm free; Thursday, Jazz; Friday,
I'm free; Saturday, I'm free; and Sunday; I have church from 10:00-
11:00.
                Sincerely,
                    Samantha
P.S. Call me tonight and we can make arrangements for spring vacation.

Feb. 16

Dear Samantha,

I'm glad we made arrangements for spring break. I can't wait to see you again. Did you get your hair cut? If it's in a new style, I can't wait! I'm making new friends at this school, but none are like you. You're the nicest person I know! I hope you're having a good time there too!

Guess what I got on my report? An A+! Isn't that great! I gotta go!

Sincerely,

Daphnie

P.S. TRY TO UNCODE THE MESSAGE:

I an'tc aiwt tunil prsign cavatoni hewn oyu omce veor!

March 1

Dear Daphnie,

I wish you would move back here! I don't know how I lived through the year this far without you!

Ask your parents to come back, or live with us! Really, but wouldn't that be fun? I wish you would come back, but I guess that is impossible. I couldn't write until now because my schedule's so full! I know, I know, I wrote you my schedule before, but my mom added on tennis and ballet in addition to jazz and violin. How am I supposed to write with all that? Anyway, gotta go.!

Sincerely,

Samantha

P.S. I can't wait until spring vacation when you come over! That's the code!

Mar. 12

Dear Samantha,

Your dream has come true. I'm moving back! I know, I don't believe it either, but it's true! I just found out yesterday, so I threw away the other letter I had written to you and started writing this one. That is, in case you're wondering why it's so late.

Anyway, we're moving back in June. People say they miss daddy's business back there and profits aren't as good here as they were there. That's why we're moving back. Don't ask me why we came here in the first place. I think it was to see how the business would work out somewhere else. They sure found that out!

I guess I will miss my new friends, but my very best friends are back there. I'm so excited!

Sincerely,

Daphnie

The Challengers

Josh Gisselquist and Bryon Rickerson

Dear Bryon "The Animal" Steele,

How's life? I'm fine. But I wanna wrestle you. I'm gonna whip you so bad you aren't gonna know what in the world hit you! You are shakin' in your boots right now, huh, Bryon "The Wimp" Steele? I'm not a liar. I'm not afraid of you, but you're afraid of me!

To wrap it all up, Bryon "The Wimp" Steele, YOU ARE DEAD!!

Your foe,

Junkyard Josh

Dear Junkyard Josh,

I received your letter, you dip! I think you're crazy to ask me to wrestle you, dude. I'm gonna teach you a lesson if I wrestle you. But I'm not for your wife's sake because I'm sure she doesn't want you to die, fool. I hope you have enough courage to say sorry about calling me Bryon "The Wimp" Steele. This is a fact that you're a liar and I'm not 'cause you're a DEAD MAN!

Your foe,

Bryon "The Animal" Steele

P.S. I'm not shakin' in my boots. You are!

Dear Bryon "The Animal" Steele,

You're not concerned about my wife, you're just freaked out that I have challenged you! Maybe you'll beat me, but I doubt it!

Let's compromise. I'll challenge you to CAGE wrestling. Now you are DEAD!

I'll waste you so hard, Bryon "The Wimp" Steele.

Your *Super* foe,

Junkyard Josh

P.S. I don't have a wife.

Dear Junkyard Josh,

After I slaughter you no grave robber is gonna want to dig up your chains that you got from a cereal box, you blimp. I'm gonna make you eat the metal on the floor in the ring. I know the reason you don't have a wife—'cause you look like a dog. I say you were stupid to challenge me especially in cage, but I accept, fool. Anyway, my philosophy is, fools die.

Your Super Duper foe,

Bryon "The Animal" Steele

Get the Limo Ready

Amanda Barnes

7/3

Dear Mike J. (Slick Dad) HaHa Joke,

How's Alf? Are you still dating? You little devil you! I hope you know who this is. Well, it's your good old 10-year-old kid A.J.B. at good old Camp Mahagahime. Do ya miss me? Well, I miss you! LOTS! I hope you don't mind, I'm bragging about your cool show, and they're crawling all over me. They are all in love with you. So you better W/B so I can show them your writing.

XXXOOOXOXO

Amanda, your daughter

P.S. Say Hi to Alf for me.

7/5

Dear Amanda (Cool Kid) HaHa Joke,

Alf is fine, and yes I'm still dating. Well, I hope *you* know who this is. Well, it's your good old 32-year-old pop. I miss you *lots*. I hope you're having fun. No I don't mind, of course I don't mind. Let them crawl. Show them this letter. Well.

XXOOXOXO

Dad (Michael J. Fox)

P.S. Alf says Hi!

7/7

To Dad (Awesome Dad) HaHa Joke,

As you know I'm coming back on the 15th. When I'm back I know you won't be able to have as much fun but, THAT'S THE FUN OF IT! I showed them the letter and boy did they crawl! I think they read it and touched it about 100 times. Dad, they are waiting for you to come pick me up. I told them NO limo ride! Except for ten, O.K.? Well...

XOOXOXOOX

Amanda

A.J.B.

(Cool Kid) HaHa Joke

P.S. Marci and Pam, Jody, Robyn, etc. say hi cutesy!

7/9

To Amanda (Sly Kid) HaHa Joke,

Tell Marci and Pam, Jody, Robyn, etc. I said hi. I'm looking forward to your coming back in a few days. I better do MY FUN fast.

Yes, ten people can get a spin in it, but no more! Let them touch this one 109 times. Do ya like my handwriting? Well, love ya, bye.
XOXOXOOOXX
Dad (Michael J. Fox)
P.S. Alf ate a stack of paper.

7/13

TO Dad (Sweet Dad) HaHa Joke,
Since I'm coming back on the 15th, by the time you get this you won't be able to W/B. I'll see ya later (in a few days). Oh, and ya! I let them touch it 109 times. Everybody including me *loves* your handwriting. Well, see ya in a few days. Love ya *lots!*
XOOXXXOXOXOXO
A.J.B.
P.S. Get the limo ready!

The Quarrel

Heather Graham and Shannon Rigney

Dear Mom,
Why couldn't I go to the zoo Saturday? I wasn't busy! I didn't lie that Laurie drew on the wall, and you accused me!! Why would I draw on the wall! I'm 11 remember! Don't say I talk like a baby anymore because I don't!
Heather
P.S. My next letter will be on your bed! Hope you find this one on mine!

Heather—
I thought you were doing you're homework on Saturday, and I told you when you were done you could have Ashley over.
The reason I accused you instead of Laurie is Laurie was supposed to be taking a nap, but if she really did do it, fine, I made a mistake. Don't you make mistakes sometimes?
Mom
P.S. My next letter will be next to your cereal bowl.

Mom,

I never said I was going to do housework! You never said I could have Ashley over! We're not even friends anymore! Laurie wasn't taking a nap. She was playing with her crayons! You always make mistakes!

Your X daughter,
Heather!

P.S. The next letter will be in your purse!

Heather—

Maybe I misunderstood you when you said housework instead of homework.

I thought I said you could have Ashley over. That's just another example of your not listening! It's not my fault you have fights with *everyone* you know!

Maybe Laurie *was* playing with her crayons, but she was *supposed* to be taking a nap!

Mom

P.S. My next letter will be in your lunchbox.

Mom,

You always misunderstand, Mom! I think you should go to a hearing doctor! You never said I could have Ashley over either! I listen very well too! You never put Laurie in her bed! I want to run away! You're mean!

Your X daughter,

P.S. My next letter will be under your placemat!

Heather—

I'm not the one who needs a hearing aid, you are!

I always put Laurie in her bed! When she starts crying *you're* the one who takes her out!

And another thing, if you want to run away, I'll pack your bags, make your lunch, and open the door!

Mom

P.S. Please stop signing your letters, "Your X daughter" because wherever you go and whatever you do you'll always be my daughter.
P.S.S. My next letter will be in your back-pack.

Mom—

Really, Mom, I think you're an old lady! Let's see you answer that! I bet you can't! Well, you didn't put Laurie in her bed this time! I'm not going to take care of your pet (Laurie) and never have! There, I proved

it, you don't like me!!
> X person in family

P.S. My next letter will be under your pillow.

Heather—

When you said I couldn't answer that dumb remark listen to this, I think you're a little baby and you're getting *very* silly over nothing! So poo on you! Laurie is *not* my pet and I never said you were taking care of her anyway! I love you just as much as I love her. There, *I* proved I *do* love you!

> Mom

P.S. Don't sign your letters "X person in family" either.
P.S.S. My next letter will be in your desk in your room.

Mom

You can't call me a baby. I'm in the 6th grade, and 6th graders aren't babies! You get very *silly* over nothing! So poo on you too! Laurie is your pet so don't say she isn't! I would never take care of her, so there! You didn't prove anything.

> From
> Heather

P.S. My next letter will be in your room desk.

Dear Heather,

You're right, I can't call you a baby without a good reason. I guess I just wanted to get back at you. And, you're right about another thing, I *am* getting very silly over nothing.

But one thing you're not right about is Laurie. She is not my pet. *She* probably thinks I love you more than I love her when I do things with your and not with her.

> Love,
> Mom

P.S. Please don't write any more letters, I'm getting writer's cramp!

Dear Mom,

I agree Laurie is not your pet. I'm sorry about all the things I said, and I love you very much! You can hate me if you like! I'm sorry! I love you! I hope we never get in a big fight again!

> Love,
> Heather!

P.S. I won't write back any more!

Limerick

Read some limericks until you get a feeling for their daffy subjects, tumbling rhythm, and special rhyme scheme. Sing them to a tune that fits all limericks, like the one below. Drum the rhythm with your hands as you read or listen. Now try your luck at it. Let your imagination go. Test out results by trying to sing them to the limericks tune. Try them out also on others and change wording to improve if needed.

Perform these with funny voices, record, illustrate, post up, and collect in limericks booklets.

Limericks

Todd Kilbaugh

There once was a maiden named Ada
Who came from the Isle of Grenada.
She was shot in the head,
Said, "I wish I was dead."
Now there isn't a girl named Ada.

Todd Kilbaugh

A haunted house stood on a hill-a.
They said it would make you quite ill-a.
You'd pay to get in
And pray to get out
Making Halloween night a big thrill-a.

Tori Landau

There once were two kids who had braces.
The girl cried that it ruined their nice faces.
The dentist he hovered
After mothers discovered
The kids kissed and got tangled in braces.

Tori Landau

There once were two Girl-Scoutish meanies
Who really were Brownies in beanies.
Forced children to tears
And got twenty years
And all that they ate were burnt weenies.

Tariehk Geter

Tariehk went to camp at MacLean.
His toothpaste became a great pain.
It burst in his pocket
About like a rocket
And now there's a very bad stain.

David Palladino

There was an old lady of Tire
Who started to sweat and perspire.
She got such a chill
that she thought she was ill,
The little old lady of Tire.

Greg Gibson

One day a man had to bullfight.
He wasn't too smart or too bright.
He said he was zealous,
But he really was jealous
of the bull, with all of its might.

Karen Chambers, Beth Grossman, and Maria Pugliese

There once was a pig from Iran
Who loved to eat food from a can.
He opened some soup
And out jumped a troop
Of army men getting a tan.

Song

Write new words to a familiar tune. Just try out different words until some begin to fit that make a kind of sense or nonsense. Then follow out whatever the idea is until you have a new set of words. If you agree on a tune with partners, you can each write your own words and compare later and make a booklet giving the tune. Teach your song to a small group and sing it for others.

The next step is to make up both the words and the tune, starting with either. If you have in mind first a nice line or phrase of words, you can try to vocalize it until a melody begins to come also. Use each to draw out the other until you have a whole song.

First Snow
Gina Galassini

Cold, shimmery, white, sunlight shines like silver.
It's the first snow
in my eyes.

Winter Today

Edythe Johnson's Fourth Grade Class

Cold and bright,
Trees screech.
Vapor hangs like a low cloud.
I shiver.

Return to Go

Ruth Feightner's Fourth Grade Class

(To the tune of "I've Been Working on the Railroad.")

I've been cleaning up my bedroom,
Found Monopoly—
Wrinkled Property and Chance Cards
And hundred dollar bills . . .
Markers, dice, hotels, and houses.
Also, found the board.
Cannot find the yellow Chest cards.
      No Game!
      Your friend,
      Rob

Three Lyrics

(All set to the tune of "Red River Valley.")

We must go now for father is calling.
We are building a mill in St. Rig.
We must go where there's new timber falling,
For the trees here are no longer big.

Gina Galassini

From this valley Mom says we are going.
I will miss the bright skies and sweet spring,
For they say I am taking the best part,
But I never could do such a thing.

Janne Rylander

I am leaving tomorrow forever.
I will wander awhile till I tire.
When I sit down to eat my good supper,
I will see your bright eyes in the fire.

Denise Lynn

Story Poem

Tell a story as a poem. The events can be made up or based on truth. You might first want to read some story poems or listen to some ballads and other folk songs that tell a story. Think about which line length, rhyme scheme, and other patterns might help your story. Consider a refrain that repeats at the end of each verse. Take advantage of the features of poetry—richer language, rhythms, comparisons, sound play, and images. Is the person telling the story one of the people in the story?

Make a collection of story poems with others or include in your autobiography or memoirs. Illustrate and post for display.

The Goldfish Fred

Robyn Harms

I walked home from school with my good friend Jen.
On the way to my house I found a shiny new gem.
It was in the shape of a little cupcake.
When I got to my fishbowl I started to shake,
For what I saw in the bowl was a fish not awake.
So I ran up the stairs with a great thought of fear
That when I got to the top my brother would sneer.
So I went to his room and he didn't glance
Although I was shakin' like I had ants in my pants.
So I called his name. I thought he would leer, but instead he looked up
    and said, "May I help you, my dear?"
"Yes," I said as I sat on his bed, and out of my mouth all the news fled.
I told about my fish named Fred and how he looked like he was dead,
Didn't move and didn't tread, and that is what filled me with dread that
    poor Fred was probably dead.
I tore down the steps with the greatest of fear, so that when I tripped on
    my ball I flew through the air.
The only thought that went through my head was a picture of poor Fred
    floating around dead.
How could this happen? How could this be? That poor Fred looked as
    stiff, as stiff as a tree?
I ran to the bowl and shook it like mad, I just couldn't believe it, I was
    feeling so sad.
"Fred, Fred," I called as I shook. "Open your eyes and give me a look!"
Then what a surprise, Fred opened his eyes.
He moved his tail and started to wiggle. I was so happy I started to
    giggle.
I closed my eyes to make sure it was real! When I opened them again
    Fred was swimming like a seal.
I called my mom and I called my dad and told them, "This is the best
    surprise I've ever had."
"Hooray!" they said. "We are glad. We'd hate to see our daughter
    sad."
My mother said, "Let's celebrate and I will bake a great big cake."
I wanted to give something to my good friend Fred to celebrate that he
    wasn't dead.
I ran to my brother's room and looked on his bed, and what I saw was
    Fred's new gem.
It was so shiny, it was so red, it was the perfect gift for Fred.

I dropped it in the bowl. A splash it did make, and when he saw it Fred
    started to shake.
"Oh wow!" thought the fish. "I got my best wish."
Something that sparkles, something that shines, makes life for a fish
    simply divine.
Fred thought, "I guess it was mean to pretend I was dead. I broke the
    girl's heart and filled it with dread, but when I stopped playing
    dead, she said, 'This is the best day I've ever had.'"

The Disastrous 18th Hole

Bill Vincent

The 18th hole is on it's way,
And I am in for a horrible day.
I sat my goose-pimpled sphere on the ground,
Hoping to hit it over the sound.
I approached the tee with a swagger,
Hoping I wouldn't start to stagger.
The ball went firing through the air,
But suddenly it lost its flair.
All of a sudden the ball fell down,
And goose pimples just flew everywhere.
I looked around and all I could say was,
I am in for a horrible day.
The ball hit the water with such a splash,
I flew back like a racing flash.
I got up trying to feel proud,
But inside I wanted to yell out very loud.
Everyone thinks the 18th hole is such a breeze,
But I just stood there shaking my knees.
Golf is a terribly frustrating game, you never play two days exactly the
    same,
But something always makes you come back.
That something is a super golf crack,
But that first shot of the day can always make you say:
I am in for a horrible day,
I AM IN FOR A HORRIBLE DAY.

Moving Day

Justin Schultz

It was moving day and every time a package went by I broke down and
     started to cry.
One went by, then two, and three.
My dresser, my bed, my clothes, and me!
I could not stand it!
The movers were like bandits.
Next went the kitchen.
My heart needed stitchin'.
Next went the dining room with all of its dishes.
It practically shattered all of my wishes.
Next went the family room with TV and Atari.
I felt just like I was on a safari.
Now goes the hallway.
I wonder how they got it through the doorway.
Next went the basement with all my toys.
My cousin said, "It's awful because they're all for boys."
Now goes the bathroom with all the towels.
I do think my cat uttered some howls.
Because every time a package went by
I broke down and started to cry.
Finally, as the truck drove away,
I knew it was time to start a new day.

Duolog

Make up a conversation between two people that runs for several minutes if actually spoken aloud. Write the name of a speaker in the left margin, put a colon after it, then write down what he or she says. Do the same thing each time one of them speaks. Give the duolog a title that catches the main action or relationship. If the place and physical action can not be made clear in their speech without awkwardness, state these briefly between parentheses at the appropriate points. (Looking at a play script will show you a standard form.)

Your duolog can have any point. It might show the personalities of the people or their relationship. Or it might develop serious ideas or be a funny give-and-take.

Direct two people in a rehearsal of your script so that they can do a good reading of it for the class or another group. Make changes if rehearsals show need for improvement. Include in a collection of plays that others can read or perform.

The Sisters' Massacre

Kristy Rank

MOLLY: Let's bring the puppies to the park.

MAGGIE: I don't want to. I'm going to Kristy's house.

MOLLY: Well, I can't carry both puppies at a time.

MAGGIE: Well, I can't live my whole life around what you want me to do!

MOLLY: Then I'm calling Mom.

MAGGIE: No you aren't.

MOLLY: Why not?

MAGGIE: Because I won't let you.

MOLLY: Yes you will, because I'll lock myself in your room. Here I go.

MAGGIE: I'm the oldest here and you'll listen to what I say.

MOLLY: No I won't. You'll listen to what I say because I don't think the youngest should be bossed around by someone older except their parents.

MAGGIE: Oh yeah?

MOLLY: Yeah.

MAGGIE: I don't care what you do because I'm still going to Kristy's.

MOLLY: And I'm still calling Mom.

MAGGIE: Good, you do that.

MOLLY: OK, *I* will.—Mom, Maggie won't bring the puppies to the park. Maggie, Mom wants to talk to you.

MAGGIE: Oh, thanks. Now I have to call Kristy and say I can't play.

MOLLY: OK, that's great!

MAGGIE: Great. Now Kristy hates me.

MOLLY: I know. You can call Kristy and ask if she wants to go with us.

MAGGIE: OK, I will call her.

MOLLY: Is she coming?

MAGGIE: Yes.

MOLLY: Come on, let's get the dogs and go over to her.

MAGGIE: OK.

MOLLY: You're my best sister.

MAGGIE: And you're mine.

Math Problem

Beth Taylor

KATHERINE: Do you think math is fun?

ELIZABETH: Yes.

KATHERINE: Man, I think math stinks!

ELIZABETH: Why?

KATHERINE: It's hard and disgusting, and I hate math and nothing is going to change that.

ELIZABETH: Oh Katherine, you're just getting discouraged because you hate division.

KATHERINE: No, I have hated math all along, and another reason I hate math is because you are always ahead of me.

ELIZABETH: Katherine, I am not always ahead of you.

KATHERINE: Yes you are, all the time. I'm never ahead of you, not once this year.

ELIZABETH: Remember when you were ahead of me in Spectrum?

KATHERINE: Yeah, well.

ELIZABETH: I think you should give math one more chance.

KATHERINE: Yeah, maybe you're right. Maybe I should give math one more chance.

ELIZABETH: We can work together in division.

Duolog Between Book Characters

Imagine that a character from one book you have read has a conversation with a character from another. Name the characters and the books at the beginning. If they're well known, other people will get more from your duolog. Write down, in the playscript form described for **Duolog,** *what you think they might say to each other, considering what each is like and what they experienced in their original stories.*

Rehearse as a reading, revise if needed, and perform. Include in a play collection, or place somewhere special for readers of those books.

Duolog Between the Cowardly Lion from *The Wizard of Oz* and Aslan from *The Lion, the Witch, and the Wardrobe*

Ranee Chaturantabut

COWARDLY LION: Hello, your majesty. I am honored to be in your presence. I have come here to talk to you about a problem I have.

ASLAN: And what might that problem be?

COWARDLY LION: Well, I am always scared. And what I want more than anything else is courage. I am asking you because you are the King of Narnia, the most wonderful place I have known. You are also very brave and courageous.

ASLAN: I'd be delighted to help you.

COWARDLY LION: I would like to tell you that I really admire the time when Narnians were being ruled by wicked and evil people and that you allowed yourself to be killed, and how you led all the Narnians to a beautiful new paradise.

ASLAN: Why, thank you.

COWARDLY LION: Can you please tell me what your secret is for being so brave?

ASLAN: I have no secret. Courage comes from being confident in yourself and thinking positive. Face up to your problems. Don't hide from them.

COWARDLY LION: Do you really think I can be as brave as you?

ASLAN: Of course.

COWARDLY LION: How can I ever thank you?

ASLAN: You can thank me by coming and visiting me again someday.

COWARDLY LION: I'd be happy to. Now I feel like a brand new lion, as brave and courageous as the king of the jungle should be. Goodbye, Aslan.

ASLAN: Farewell, my friend.

Duolog Between Gilly from *The Great Gilly* and Jenny from *Jenny*

Heather Hocking

GILLY: Hey! Get out of here, stop picking those berries!

JENNY: Do you live in my jungle?

GILLY: *Your* jungle? Huh, I found it first! It's a vacant lot! No, I don't live here!

JENNY: What's wrong with you?

GILLY: Do you want to fight about it?

JENNY: I'm just trying to make friends!

GILLY: Friends, I have enough friends!

JENNY: Want to see my puppy?

GILLY: Why would I, I hate puppies!

JENNY: Want to meet my little brother?

GILLY: I hate little kids, too!

JENNY: Do you have a brother?

GILLY: No, not a *real* one!

JENNY: What do you mean? Is it a robot?

GILLY: I'm a foster child, stupid!

JENNY: Let's ask my mom if we can have a popsicle.

GILLY: I hate popsicles, too!

JENNY: What *do* you like?

GILLY: Nothing, not even you!

JENNY: Oh, come on! I'm trying my hardest to make friends!

GILLY: Well, I'm not!

JENNY: Do you have any money with you? We could go shopping at the mall.

GILLY: What kid would carry money around with 'em? Besides, I hate shopping!

JENNY: What would you like to do then?

GILLY: What I would like to do is go home to my *real* mother!

JENNY: Well, you're not going to get home without a friend's help! Come on, let's go get ice cream.

GILLY: Well, I guess you're right. I *do* like ice cream. Let's go!

Play Script

Write a script for live performance or videotaping that has several characters and takes place in no more than one to three scenes. (Each scene is a different time and perhaps different place also.) Remember that the story and the point of the story have to come across in what the characters say and do before our eyes. There is no storyteller to inform the audience of what it cannot see and hear for itself. Stage directions can say only how to stage the play; that is, describe physical setting and action. Directions for filming indicate angles and distance of shots and other instructions for the camera.

Arrange with your teacher or other adults to perform live or to film. Rewrite as needed during rehearsals. A performance can be a rehearsed reading only, in the manner of Readers Theater, which avoids memorization of lines and full staging.

Madman on the Loose

Sarah Kane and Susan Berris

CHARACTERS: Jamie, Hillery, Katie, Mikey, John Smith, Mr. & Mrs. Hemsted, Police Chief, Carol Marin, and Ron Majors

TIME: 5:00 P.M.

SETTING: The Hemsted house

AT RISE:
  RIGHT: Jamie and Hillery getting out of car.
  LEFT: Katie and Mikey playing.
  CENTER: Hemsted's house.
  BACK: Mrs. Hemsted.

Scene 1

HILLERY: *(Getting out of car.)* Hi, Katie! Hi, Mikey!

KATIE AND MIKEY: *(Waving.)* Hi.

MRS. HEMSTED: *(Motioning with hand.)* Come on in. I'll show you around the house.

JAMIE AND HILLERY: *(Walking toward front door.)* Okay.

MRS. HEMSTED: *(Pointing to food.)* Give them macaroni and hot dogs for dinner and they can have cereal and orange juice for breakfast.

HILLERY: *(Questioning.)* Where are we going to sleep?

MRS. HEMSTED: *(Tisking.)* Oh, I'm so forgetful! You'll be sleeping upstairs in the guest room. Unless, of course, you want to sleep in different rooms.

JAMIE: *(Looking at Hillery.)* That's okay. We'll sleep together. Is that okay with you, Hillery?

HILLERY: *(Shaking her head yes.)* That's fine with me.

MRS. HEMSTED: *(Looking at watch.)* We should be going soon. I guess that wraps it up.

MR. HEMSTED: *(Walking into kitchen.)* Hi, girls. *(Looking at Mrs. Hemsted.)* Are you ready to go, Hon?

MRS. HEMSTED: *(Walking out of kitchen.)* Yes, I think I have everything I need. Do you girls think you'll be all right?

JAMIE: *(Following Mrs. Hemsted.)* Yeah, we'll be fine. What time will you be home tomorrow?

MRS. HEMSTED: *(Putting suitcase in trunk.)* Probably around 4:00 or 4:30. Come on dear, we'll miss our flight. *(Kissing Katie and Mikey.)* Goodbye, children. Be good for Jamie and Hillery.

Scene 2

TIME: 6:00 P.M.

SETTING: Inside Hemsteds' house.

AT RISE:
  RIGHT: Jamie and Hillery sitting on couch.
  LEFT: Katie and Mikey playing school.
  CENTER: TV

HILLERY: *(Turning channels.)* I wish there was something good on TV.

JAMIE: *(Rolling eyes.)* Let's just watch the news. There's nothing else on.

MIKEY: *(Whining.)* I wanna watch Sesame Street!

KATIE: *(Bribing.)* Come on, Mikey! Let's finish playing school!

MIKEY: *(Agreeing.)* Oh, all right.

HILLERY: *(Questioning.)* Do you guys want to eat soon?

KATIE AND MIKEY: *(Looking up.)* Yeah, we're hungry.

JAMIE: *(Getting up.)* I'll go make dinner now. Hillery, do you know where they keep their hot dog buns?

HILLERY: *(Quickly.)* They're in the cupboard next to the sink, but wait! Come here, hurry.

JAMIE: *(Rushing in.)* What?

HILLERY: *(Pointing to TV.)* Look at the special news brief!

JAMIE: *(Nervously.)* Oh, my gosh! We better lock up the house! There's a madman loose in this town!!

MIKEY: *(Starting to cry.)* I'm scared!

KATIE: *(Reassuring him.)* Don't worry, Mikey, we'll be okay.

MIKEY: *(Calming down.)* Can we sleep in with you tonight?

HILLERY: *(Hugging Mikey.)* Sure, you can. Jamie, you better start dinner.

JAMIE: *(Getting up.)* Okay, do you want to help?

HILLERY: *(Sitting back down on the couch.)* If you really need me, just give a call; I think I'll stay with the kids right now.

JAMIE: *(Walking to kitchen.)* Good idea.

HILLERY: *(Looking at Jamie.)* It's really easy to make macaroni and cheese and hot dogs, but I'm always here for ya!

Scene 3

TIME: 8:00 P.M.

SETTING: Hemsteds' kitchen.

AT RISE:

> RIGHT: Katie and Mikey
>
> LEFT: Sink.
>
> CENTER: Jamie and Hillery clearing table.

JAMIE: *(Scraping leftovers in the garbage.)* Bedtime, guys! Go get your pajamas on and brush your teeth and we'll be up as soon as we finish the dishes.

KATIE: *(Heading towards stairs.)* Should we set our sleeping bags in your room?

HILLERY: *(Putting dishes away.)* I think you guys will be okay in your own room!

MIKEY: *(Sticking out lower lip.)* Yeah!

JAMIE: *(Looking up from doing dishes.)* Hillery's right, kids. You'll be fine. Now scoot up to bed!

HILLERY: *(Walking towards stairs.)* I'll tuck them in. You finish the dishes.

JAMIE: *(Picking up dish and putting it away.)* Okay. After you tuck them in come down and we can watch MTV.

HILLERY: *(Starting to walk up stairs.)* I'll hurry.

Scene 4

TIME: 9:00 P.M.
SETTING: Family room.
AT RISE:
    RIGHT: Front door.
    LEFT: Jamie sitting on couch. She is waiting for Hillery.
    CENTER: TV

HILLERY: *(Coming down stairs.)* Sorry I took so long, but Mikey refused to brush his teeth.

JAMIE: *(Switching channels.)* That's okay, I was trying to find something good on TV. Oh, look! The video True Blue is on!

HILLERY: *(Sitting down by Jamie.)* Good. Keep this station on.

JAMIE: *(Listening closely.)* What is that?

HILLERY: *(Worried voice.)* It's the doorbell. Who could it be at this hour?

JAMIE: *(Hiding fear.)* Oh, don't worry. I'll get it.

HILLERY: *(Tears coming to eyes.)* What if it is the madman?

JAMIE: *(Tisking.)* Oh, don't be silly! *(Opening door)* AHHHHHHHHHH! HELP! *(Slamming door.)* It's him!

JOHN SMITH: *(Thrusting door open.)* No wait, there's been a mix up. Let me in and I'll explain. Don't worry, I won't hurt you! I'm not really the madman!

HILLERY: *(Biting lip.)* You're not? Then who are you and what do you want?

JOHN SMITH: *(Walking back and forth.)* No, you see they mistook me for the real madman because I was at the scene of the crime. Please help me.

JAMIE: *(Backing off.)* How do we know if you're telling the truth?

JOHN SMITH: *(Walking towards her.)* Please believe me. I wouldn't hurt anyone.

HILLERY: *(Unsure.)* If this is true, then you have nothing to hide. Why don't we go down to the police station right now and settle this right away. You wouldn't run away from something that you didn't do?

JOHN SMITH: *(Thoughtfully.)* You're right. Honesty is the best policy. I'm not going to run any more. I'll be on my way, now. Thanks. I'll turn myself in. You girls don't need to go with me.

GIRLS: Good Luck. *(Slamming door and leaning on it after closing it and letting out sigh of relief.)* Whew! That was close! Call the police!

Scene 5

TIME: 10:00
SETTING: Living Room.
AT RISE:
    RIGHT: Girls on sofa.
    LEFT: Police Chief on chair.
    CENTER: News team packing equipment.

POLICE CHIEF: It was a good thing that you girls called me even though John Smith did turn himself in. You did the right thing. As it turned out he was innocent. We cleared him of all charges.

JAMIE: We were so scared.

HILLERY: *(Wide-eyed.)* I almost had a heart attack.

POLICE CHIEF: I think that you two were very brave. I'm just glad you're okay now. But remember never to open the door to strangers. Always ask who is there. And if you don't know the person don't open the door!

GIRLS: *(Together.)* We won't!

Scene 6

TIME: 10:00 P.M.
SETTING: Guest bedroom.
AT RISE:
    RIGHT: Jamie in bed.
    LEFT: Hillery in bed.
    CENTER: TV

JAMIE: It will be so exciting seeing ourselves on the news!

HILLERY: Yes, but I wouldn't want to go through that again, ever!

JAMIE: I think the news is on now. Turn on the TV, please.

TV: *(Carol Marin smiles.)* Good evening. This is the 10 o'clock news. We have a special report tonight. Here is Ron Majors with the story.

TV: *(Ron Majors serious.)* Thank you, Carol. A man named John Smith turned himself into the police tonight in a case of mistaken identity. They had been searching for him as a suspect involved in a crime. He frightened two young girls, Hillery and Jamie, who were babysitting at the Hemsted House. *(Shows picture of girls.)* The girls apparently let him in the house, then urged him to go to the police. As it turned out, he was just an innocent bystander. He has been cleared of all charges and the girls are safe. That is our story for tonight. Thank you and goodnight.

JAMIE: *(Turning off the TV.)* Well, what are you going to tell the Hemsteds?

HILLERY: *(Smiling.)* Nobody would ever believe this!

The Field Trip

Irene Rahder's Fourth Grade Class
(authors listed at end)

The "Field Trip" was assigned as a typical follow-up to a class field trip, but instead of reporting on what they saw and did, the students were asked to write what they *heard* on the bus. Each wrote as much of what he or she could remember; then they divided themselves into groups according to where they had been sitting on the bus and read their papers aloud to each other. As they read, they remembered more, put in bits from other groups nearby, and rearranged the order of their conversations. One person from each group then read the group-script to the whole class. We were surprised how many threads of conversation ran through the many voices.

We intended to rework the various sketches into a play. We put short bits of the revised script onto note cards, trying to stop each card with a natural "punch line" and then arranged the cards into a beginning, just snatches of talk, and a sort of end. The cards read aloud very easily and we thought it was going to be easy to stage the bus ride. It wasn't.

We had planned for the setting to be half of a bus (a cutaway) with the driver to the right, a row of double seats with a window behind each, and the teacher in the back, or left. The kids would sit two to a seat, and as each group talked, the other groups would "freeze" so the audience would know where to look. It didn't work that way. Nine year old kids don't "freeze" very well, we found out; if they're on stage they are ON STAGE. So, we solved the problem by video, taping the play so the audience *had* to look where the lines were being spoken.

There were advantages to taping: the broken scenes were more easily memorized because they were so short; we could force the viewer's attention to "zoom" to something important (like Mr. Brate's hearing-aid and Marty's constant complaining about hunger); and we could use sound effects to open and close.

Irene Rahder, Elmwood School, Naperville, Illinois

(Takes place inside a school bus. We see half of it with driver at right. He has a mirror above the steering wheel. The teacher sits somewhere near back. Other groups are together but may be in any order. Sound of gears grinding as bus starts. Horn honks occasionally.)

(All together.)

1: How ya doin'?

2: Oh, fine.

3: The Cubs won yesterday.

4: Ha. They stink.

5: You stink!

BUS DRIVER: Everybody sit down. *(Hubbub continues.)*

SOME GIRLS: "Boys go to Mars to bet behind bars."

SOME BOYS: "Girls go to Mercury to get in the nursery."

1: What day you free?

2: Monday, Thursday and Friday.

1: Meet you Thursday at four.

6: You aren't so tough.

7: Shut up.

8: I don't have to.

9: Gimme that.

8: No.

BUS DRIVER: Hey, you turkeys, sit down and be quiet!

6: Gobble, gobble.

* * *

MARTY: I want to sit by Mrs. Rahder.

TRICIA: No, I'm going to.

MARTY: Please!

TRICIA: No, they're all the same seats.

MARTY: But TRICIA! *(Gives up.)* Kendra, get in.

KENDRA: I want to sit by the aisle.

MARTY: No, I'm going to.

KENDRA: But MARTY!

MARTY: Get in, Kendra.

BUS DRIVER: Everybody SIT DOWN!

MATT: Let's finish Dungeons and Dragons.

STEVE: OK, you go down the secret door and there you find some treasure and some equipment guarded by three hobgoblins each with 20 hit points. What do you want to do—flee or fight?

MIKE S.: Hey, we're there awready!

JOHN: No we're not. *(Disgusted.)* There's a stop sign.

* * *

JULIE: How about sitting here, Jennifer?

JENNIFER: That's fine with me.

MICHELLE: I'm right in back of you guys.

JULIE: Gosh, Michelle! Good for you! ... Hey, Jennifer, can I use your Snoopy Radio?

JENNIFER: Yeah, sure.

JULIE: Thanks. *(Fiddles with controls.)* Mr. Brate, can you get WLS?

MR. BRATE: I'll try. *(Puts on earphones. Never takes them off ... snaps fingers occasionally.)*

EVERYBODY: Yoo-hoo. Mr. Brate has a hearing aid!

* * *

JOHN: Can I play with you? *(To D & D players.)*

STEVE: Sure, we have one more room to go, then you can.

JOHN: Schmidt, can you teach me how to play?

MIKE S.: Sure, I'll make you a fighter.

TIM: *(Butting in.)* Hi, somebody gonna fight?

STEVE: *(And others.)* G-E-E-T-T-T out of here!

TIM: *(And others.)* Yeah, yeah.

BUS DRIVER: Be quiet, you kids.

* * *

LESLIE: I bet the sewage plant will stink.

LEELIE: P-You! Boy, are you right! I smell it already!

LESLIE: Are we near the sewage plant, Mrs. Rahder?

MRS. RAHDER: No, we are a long way from there.

LEELIE: Uh-Oh!

* * *

MARTY: Oh barf. This place stinks.

KENDRA: I know it.

MARTY: I can't wait for lunch.

KENDRA: PLEASE!

PATTI: I brought a book so we can read.

KRISTY: Good.

PATTI: I also brought a pencil and a piece of paper.

KRISTY: Why?

PATTI: I don't know.

* * *

AMEE: I really liked *Tales of a Fourth Grade Nothing.*

MICHELLE: Fudge is so cute the way he always says, "Pee-tah, Pee-tah."

AMEE: My mom uses pita bread to put stuff in.
MICHELLE: I hate stuffing.

* * *

AMEE: Hey, Jenny, my dad fixed my Barbie pool.
JENNIFER: He did?
AMEE: Yes, do you want to play after school?
JENNIFER: Sure.
AMEE: Jenny, I forgot, I can't play today, because—.
JENNIFER: *(Interrupting.)* Good, because I can't either, then.

* * *

AMEE: *(Who is a very dark Indian.)* Scoot over.
TIM: No.
PATTI: Let burnt french fry sit down.
TIM: *(Chants.)* Amee's a burnt french fry.
AMEE: I'd rather be a burnt french fry than a raw one.

* * *

MICHELLE: I'm going to keep my lunch with me when I leave.
AMEE: Good idea.
PATTI: I've got a big pocket.
KRISTY: So do I. I'm going to stuff my lunch in there. *(Puts lunch in back pocket.)*
PATTI: It makes a big hump in the back. I have mine in the side pocket.
KRISTY: You're smushing your lunch!
PATTI: I think I will take it out—.
KRISTY: I think I will too—.
PATTI: *(To teacher.)* Look what me and Kristy did to our lunches!
MRS. R.: "Look what *Kristy and I* did to our lunches."
AMEE: Oh—did you ruin yours, too?

* * *

BRIAN: I feel sick.
TIM: Hey, Michelle, Brian wants to sit by you!

* * *

MATT B.: *(Reading a sign.)* I love New York.
JOHN: I hate New York.
MATT: You've never even been there, I bet.
JOHN: Why don't you—.
MIKE S.: All of you shut up or you'll hate Chicago.
MATT and JOHN: OK. OK.

* * *

BRIAN: Will we be back to school in time for music?

MRS. R.: No, I don't think we can be. We'll probably miss it.

BRIAN: *(Not meaning it.)* Oh, I *love* music. Did you hear that, Tim? *(Screws face up to cry.)* We're gonna miss music!

TIM: Darn! That's not fair. Do you think we could have a makeup?

(Both boys snicker.)

MRS. R.: That's not very nice.

BRIAN: *(Innocently.)* What did *we* do?

* * *

TRICIA: Mrs. Rahder, I know a place we could go for a field trip.

MRS. R.: Where?

TRICIA: There's a bicycle tour of Chicago's famous buildings that would be fun.

MRS. R.: Can you imagine us getting 30 bikes off the bus and going to Chicago?

TRICIA: Well, maybe Downers Grove?

* * *

(Leelie and Leslie scream.)

MRS. R.: *(Yelling.)* Leelie, Leslie! Be quiet! *(Laughter continues.)*

TRICIA: Leelie! Leslie! Be quiet, Mrs. Rahder said.

MRS. R.: Chris, lean over the seat and tell them to be quiet.

CHRIS: Leelie, Leslie be quiet.

LEELIE: Sez who!

CHRIS: Sez Mrs. Rahder.

LEELIE: Leslie, Mrs. Rahder said for you to be quiet.

* * *

KENDRA: Did you see "V"?

MARTY: *(Squeals.)* That was gross when he ate the guinea pig .... *(Both Marty and Kendra scream and cover mouths.)*

MRS. R.: Talk quieter, girls.

MARTY: And the MOUSE! *(Both scream louder, roll eyes.)*

MRS. R.: GIRLS!

* * *

TRICIA: Mrs. Rahder, is that the Dial Soap plant?

MRS. RAHDER: I don't know. I've never been here.

TRICIA: It's got to be. Look how clean everything is.

* * *

OLIVER: Can I sit by the window now?

MIKE K.: No.

OLIVER: Aw, come on. Let me sit by the window.

MIKE K.: I said No.

OLIVER: But I've never sat by a bus window.

MIKE K.: Ever?

OLIVER: Not ever.

MIKE K.: OK. You can sit by the window. *(To himself.)* I don't get to sit by the window that much either. . . . *(Loudly.)* Mrs. Rahder, going back can I sit by the window?

MRS. R.: MAY I sit by the window.

MIKE K.: *(Depressed.)* Sure. . . I guess so. . . .

* * *

HANS: Let's pretend this is a STUKA.

GEORGE: The STUKA had puny guns.

HANS: Well, what do you want to be?

GEORGE: This feels more like a B-29.

HANS: Right. And this is a secret mission. . . .

GEORGE: Roger. *(Talks into pretend mike.)* Enemy fighters at 10 o'clock.

HANS: *(Laughing.)* Those are cows!

* * *

KRISTY: I think we're here.

PATTI: I don't think so. It's just an old farm.

KRISTY: Hey, look! There's smoke coming out of the barn!

PATTI: Maybe it's a smoke house.

* * *

LEELIE: I'm volunteering to work at the Settlement this summer.

LESLIE: Why are you doing that?

LEELIE: It'll look good on my resume when I look for a job.

LESLIE: Leelie! You're just ten years old!

LEELIE: Yeah, but I like to plan ahead.

MARTY: When do we eat?

* * *

HANS: *(Looking at barn smoke.)* There's a fire on the ground. Impossible to land here. Try to get a message to headquarters. Find out what happened down there.

GEORGE: *(Listens to pretend earphones.)* There has been a heavy raid . . .

many enemy bombers ... airfield is destroyed. We are to fly on
until our gas is gone.
HANS: Wilco!

* * *

TIM: Do ya wanna hear a joke?
JENNIFER: Not really.
TIM: Well, here it is anyways: "What kind of flowers like to be kissed?"
JULIE: I don't know and I don't care.
TIM: Tulips. TWO LIPS. Get it, get it? Ha, ha, ha. Do you wanna hear
another one?
EVERYONE: No. PLEASE. NO!

* * *

BRIAN: Matt!
MATT: What?
BRIAN: There's a bulldozer stuck in the mud.
MATT: Where? (Looks around.) Oh, you're foolin' me.
BRIAN: Monkeys always look!
MATT: Apes always tell them to!

* * *

STEVE: It's hot in here. I'm gonna open the window.
CHRIS: Be careful. The sign says "KEEP ARM INSIDE BUS"
IRWIN: He could put the other one out.

* * *

MARTY: Can we have something out of our lunch?

* * *

MIKE N.: Look at that barn!
OLIVER: It's on fire.
MIKE: No, it's just smoking.
OLIVER: OK, it's smoking.
MIKE K.: No, it IS on fire. Driver! That barn is on fire!
BUS DRIVER: YOU KIDS QUIET DOWN.
OLIVER: (Giggling.) Maybe this is the non-smoking section.

* * *

CHRIS: Are you counting water towers?
IRWIN: No.
CHRIS: 'Cause there are four there if you are. That makes seven so far.
IRWIN: Well, I'm not and there have only been six.

CHRIS: I thought you weren't counting?
IRWIN: Who cares?

* * *

LESLIE: Did I tell you I went to Red Lobster last night?
LEELIE: Lucky duck.
LESLIE: No, I had the shrimp lovers' platter. *(Both laugh.)*
MARTY: *(Groans.)* I can hardly wait til lunch.

* * *

JULIE: Marty has on her Valley Girl shirt.
JENNIFER: Fer shur, fer shur.
JULIE: I like her boing-boing curls.
MICHELLE: *(Leans over them to call.)* Annie!
JULIE: Cover your mouth, Michelle.
MR. BRATE: Why do you say that? *(Taking off ear phones to adjust dial.)*
JULIE: Because her name is Pachuta—like a sneeze.
JENNIFER: Get it? Pa-pa-pa CHU ta! *(Pretends to sneeze.)*
MICHELLE: That's not nice.
JULIE and JENNIFER: Cover your mouth!

* * *

HANS: We've been hit. Engine number 3 is out. I'll feather the prop.
    You look for a place to set her down.
GEORGE: You forget, we can't land . . . we have "The Fat Man" aboard.
HANS: That's the secret bomb! Never call it by that name.
GEORGE: OK. let's use the code name "Little Boy."
HANS: It's going to be rough today. *(Bus hits bump.)* What did I tell you.

    (Both laugh.)

* * *

LESLIE: What's your favorite saying?
LEELIE: "I love it when a plan comes together." . . . Mrs. Rahder
    (Yelling.) do you have a favorite saying?
MRS. R.: Keep it down, girls!
LEELIE: *(Looks at Leslie.)* THAT'S a *saying?*

* * *

JENNIFER: *(Listening to one ear of earphone.)* Oh, my favorite song just
    ended.
JULIE: *(Not meaning it.)* Ohhhhh, tooo bad. What kind of pop do you
    have?

KENDRA: I have Coke.

MARTY: I have Pepsi.

JENNIFER: *(Loud enough for Mrs. Rahder to hear.)* Me and Leslie don't got no pop.

MRS. R.: *(From back of bus.)* "Leslie *and I* don't *have any* pop."

JENNIFER: I knew that would get her. *(Jumps up and down.)*

DRIVER: You kids SIT DOWN.

MARTY: I'm so hungry.

* * *

BRIAN: *(Shouting.)* Why are we slowing down?

TIM: Brian—would you SPEAK UP! *(Both fall into seat laughing.)*

* * *

JULIE: *(To audience.)* Don't you just LOVE field trips?

Written by:	Steve Lyon	Marty Hammes
Tricia Ekey	Kendra Jiannino	Matt Becker
Mike Schmidt	John Novotny	Julie Lause
Jennifer Flory	Michelle Pachuta	Tim Higgens
Leslie Esposito	Leelie Selassie	Patti Forsythe
Kristy Kitzmiller	Amee Shaw	Brian Hurd
Chris Gray	Oliver Herbert	Mike Kuchyt
Hans Aichlmayr	George Bennett	Irwin Lee

Radio Script

Radio is for sound only. So a radio script indicates only voices and sound effects. "Stage directions" can tell only how words are voiced and what sounds are made and when. But a narrator may be used to give background and to bridge between scenes if necessary. Listen to some plays on the radio or on recordings of old radio plays. Think of a story that can be got across mainly through voices, and write such a script. Rehearse, tape-record, and play for others.

The Key of Gagiheb
Jenny Marx

I

DEEP-VOICED NARRATOR: Dear Joanne,

Nothing much has happened since you moved away last week, except that we are going to an art museum pretty soon, and I don't call a field trip much. The teacher said that we should really pay attention to the different paintings, because they are supposed to be very strange and exciting. She also told us to bring one dollar and forty cents for the two bus trips. The bus fares are getting expensive!

I hope I can visit you soon!

Your BORED best friend,

Mary

TEACHER: All right class! I want you all to line up by the door; then you may board the bus, quietly!

MARY-NARRATOR: We all boarded the bus with much scuffling and shoving and squeezed into the small seats. I was squished against a wall, not very comfortable, but at least I could look out the window.

At first, there was nothing much to look at, just tall buildings and billboards. After a while, we were on a highway, with many fields and barns on the right side and huge trucks on the left.

Finally, after what seemed like fifty light-years, we arrived.

TEACHER: Everyone come outside and line up by the entrance. Let's go!

MARY-N: The museum was made up of narrow passages, with hundreds of pictures hanging on the walls. Each painting was very different, very strange, but not very exciting. Some were designs, and a lot were just blotches of color.

Then I came across a pure, white canvas. No, wait, there were little blue lines swirling around on the white surface, so ... so ... inviting ... these are exciting, these pictures, especially this one! Very exciting ... exciting ... exciting....

DANDYPANDIES: What's so exciting?

What's so inviting?

Is a Percipliting

Biting

You?

But that's not inviting!

MARY-N: I found myself lying on a patch of yellow grass, in the center of a circle made of . . . little men and women! They were short and fat, with brightly colored clothes and pink cheeks, rosy from the exercise. You see, they had joined hands, and were singing, galloping around me.

MARY: Where am I?

DANDYPANDIES: You are in the lands
        of strange beings of many brands!
        You are in the lands
        where you get many helping hands,
        like us!

        We are called the Dandypandies,
        and we like to sing,
        With our sweet voices,
        we entertain the King
        of Karmen!

II

MARY: *(Laugh.)* What am I doing here?

DANDYPANDIES: You are here to visit the King.
        You are here to listen to us sing!
        But mostly you are here
        to go on a mission that makes us all tremble with fear!

MARY: I have to visit the king?

WOMEN DANDYPANDIES: You may ride our peoplecar, men!

MARY-N: The little men jumped on a raft with a sail on it.

MARY: What should I do?

WOMEN DANDYPANDIES: Come with us to visit King Karmen!

MARY-N: I cautiously stepped on the raft; the women and children began
    to push the raft as they ran as fast as they could.

MARY: Did you say that I had to go on a mission?

DANDYPANDIES: Off to see the king, we're a-going!
        With our peoplecar's sail blowing!
        Without knowing
        where to go!

        So we will just have to
        follow our noses
        to the palace
        decorated with roses!

        Oh! No! Hang on to your hats!
        Here come the Pandicular Cats!

MARY: Pandicular Cats?

DANDYPANDIES: The Pandicular Cats are very mean!
>They come from the South.
>You have to be careful around one of them,
>Or you will be in its mouth!
>
>The Pandicular Cats are very big.
>And sulky, they like to pout.
>They gobble up food like a pig.
>You'd better watch out!

MARY-N: The peoplecar went faster and faster. The women and children suddenly jumped on it, and the men jumped off. Now the men were pushing.

III

MARY-N: The Pandicular Cats were indeed very large. They were dark grey ... with blue stripes! They were running very fast, but not fast enough to catch us.

>After a while, we turned on to a dirt road. Up ahead was a palace completely covered with roses! A large gate slammed behind us, leaving the giant cats behind.

>Suddenly, a huge door opened before us. The King of Karmen was in front of us.

>He was short and chubby, dressed in a long purple robe, and a big fur wrapped around his neck. On his head was a tall golden crown.

KING OF KARMEN: (Booming voice always.) Thank you, thank you, Dandypandies!

MARY-N: He beckoned for me to come with him into the palace. All of the Dandypandies waved at me, and I waved back. I followed the tall king down a long hallway decorated with pretty flowered wallpaper. At the end of the hall was a huge room full of rows and rows of files. He stopped at one and began writing on the file paper.

KING OF KARMEN: Hmmm ... name is Mary McCoo....

MARY: How did you know my name?

KING OF KARMEN: Age is twelve....

MARY: How ... how ... ?

KING OF KARMEN: Grade is seventh....

MARY: What? ... HOW ... ?

KING OF KARMEN: Birthday ... hummm ... October fourteenth....

MARY: HOW DID YOU KNOW?

KING OF KARMEN: Why ... a little bird told me ....
MARY: Don't give me that ... I—.
MARY-N: Then, I noticed a little bluebird on his shoulder!
MARY: How did it know?
KING OF KARMEN: A little bird told it so!
MARY-N: Another tiny bird flew on to the bluebird's shoulder!
MARY: (Sigh.) Why am I here?
KING OF KARMEN: Come with me....

IV

MARY-N: Once settled in a high-ceilinged room, with tall velvet chairs, the king began to tell me my mission.
KING OF KARMEN: We are asking you to go on this mission because everyone here has tried and failed. The mission is ... to retrieve the stolen Key of Gagiheb from the land of Carnipolis.
MARY: What is the Key of Gagiheb?
KING OF KARMEN: It unlocks a jeweled case that contains the secrets of my kingdom.
MARY: Why did they steal just the key?
MARY-N: The King of Karmen gave a sigh.
KING OF KARMEN: I am sorry that I yelled. I am just worried. I can explain in detail of your journey later. Let us go have dinner.
DANDYPANDIES: We are starving!
     May we start the carving?
MARY-N: All the Dandypandies were seated around an enormous table. In the center of the table was a huge feast, a huge ... colorful feast! There were mounds of orange mashed potatoes, piles of purple pasta, and glasses of green milk! In the very middle of all the food was a shiny blue turkey, with pink stuffing coming out one end. Next to each plate was a bowl of red butter and a basket of crusty rolls. Each person had different colored rolls. The King of Karmen told me to sit at one end of the table, and he sat at the other. My rolls were purple and pink!
KING OF KARMEN: (Laugh.) Yes, you may start the carving!
MARY-N: Knives clashed, and spoons waved in the air. Before I knew it, I had a full plate of food before me. I began to eat. After the delicious meal, the King of Karmen stood up.
KING OF KARMEN: Will you go on our mission?
MARY: (Shaky voice.) For the good of your Kingdom ... I guess so.
EVERYONE: HOORAY!!!!!

V

MARY-N: The King of Karmen explained to me where I was to go, what I was to bring, and little facts about the mission. In the meantime, the Dandypandies hurried around, packing my necessities into a large pink suitcase.

Once I had my suitcase, I began my journey. I got on to the peoplecar, and the Dandypandies gave it a big push. I steered it by shifting my weight in the direction I wanted to go. In about an hour, I was in a small forest. I stopped the peoplecar by standing up on it and jumped off. In the distance was a tall castle with two towers on both sides of it. I was to go up the one on the left.

First, I decided to eat. In my suitcase was a little golden case with a blue button on it. The King told me to push the button if I was hungry. So I did. The case changed into a tablecloth, and on it appeared a blue pizza, a large bowl of multi-colored salad, and a glass of lavender juice.

After I finished eating, I folded the tablecloth and put it with the dishes into my suitcase. I then took out a long rope and a hook. I decided to tie the rope to the hook and try to attach it to the left tower so I could climb up. Then I saw a line of guards marching back and forth. They were wearing green uniforms, so I decided to dress up as a guard and sneak my way up the left tower! I noticed a bush of bright green leaves nearby and a stream. I dipped the leaves into the stream, and then I covered my body with them. I left my suitcase and joined the guards.

After about fifteen minutes of marching, I followed the guards into the castle. A tall man with a long grey beard told us to take a one-hour break. I had one hour to get the Key of Gagiheb. I went up a long winding staircase which I hoped led up to the left tower. I entered a dark room with nothing in it but a guard and . . . the Key of Gagiheb! I saw a rope nearby, and I picked it up.

MARY: Look at that pretty bird!

MARY-N: I tied the rope around him tightly. I grabbed the jeweled key, slipped it into my pocket, and went back downstairs. I told the tall man that I was going outside for a breath of fresh air.

All the way back to the palace, I thought and sang, "I did it, I did it, I did it!"

DANDYPANDIES: HOORAY!

    HOORAY!

    MARY SAVED THE DAY!!

MARY-N: I laughed as the Dandypandies did a dance to celebrate my success. The King of Karmen did a little jig.

EVERYONE BUT MARY: Thank you, thank you,
>Mary McCoo!
>You saved the day!

>We did not have
>the Key of Gagiheb,
>until you came our way!
>DA/LI/DA/DI/DI/LI/DA/RE/ME/DO/FA/SO/LA/TI/BOO
>Oh Mary McCoo ... we thank you!

VI

JULIE: Mary ... Mary! We have to move on now!
MARY-N: It was Julie, a girl in my class! I was back in Illinois!
DEEP-VOICED NARRATOR: Dear Mary,
>I'm so sorry to hear that nothing much has happened to you. I
can't write a long letter, I have homework.
>I hope that something exciting happens soon!
>Your best friend,
>Joanne

Do-It-Yourself Folk Tale

Make up a story about people and objects from today's world that has some fantasy in the plot. That is, some of the events could not happen—so far as we know now! Your story can be an original modern folk or fairy tale, full of wondrous adventures. The plot thickens if you let certain key objects or figures stand for inner things like feelings, ideas, and ideals. In a fairy tale, for example, a ring may symbolize union and a sword power, or a certain person may represent jealousy.

Three Little Baseball Players

Todd Eldredge

Once upon a time there lived three little baseball fans—Bob, Matt, and the youngest one, whose name was Mike. All of the boys were good at baseball except for Mike. Mike was always getting three strikes because his brothers were mean and threw the ball really fast. Mike was sad because he could never get a hit.

One sunny day there came in the mail three White Sox tickets. Everybody was really excited, especially Mike. When Bob and Matt saw him excited they asked, "What are you so jumpy about? You're not coming, our friend is," and the boys went off to the game. Mike went into the woods to get away from his family.

When the boy was walking he heard a voice say, "Sit down on that big rock next to you and recite the word 'baseball' three times." A few minutes later he heard the same thing again, but even louder. It was the voice of his guardian baseball angel. Mike didn't know he had one, so this puzzled the boy. Still puzzled, he decided to sit on the rock and recite the word "baseball" three times. Mike heard a rumbling sound beneath his feet. A big hole opened up in the ground. He stared in and saw a treasure chest. He reached down and pulled the heavy chest out. He opened it up and saw thousands and thousands of baseball cards. He also saw a small package.

He tore open the package and found a book. On the front of the book it said, "Tips on How to Be a Better Baseball Player." He opened the book and started to read.

In about 30 minutes he read the book and was ready to play a game with his brothers. He went back home and waited for his brothers to return from the Sox game.

When they came back they saw Mike with the treasure chest and they said, "Where did you get that, little twirp?" Mike told them his story, and Bob and Matt said they would cremate him anyway.

So they started a baseball game. At the end it was 3,333 to 3. Mike won! After the game Matt and Bob were amazed and sorry for what they had done to him. They promised they would be kind to him. He forgave them and the family lived happily ever after.

Jack and the Space Shuttle

Christian Parker

Once upon a time, there was a boy named Jack. And Jack had a mother named Samantha. Samantha said to Jack, "We don't have any money! So will you go out and sell our old jalopy?"

"Okay, Mom." Jack said. So Jack set off to sell the car when a man came up to him and said, "I'll give you this micro-chip that will turn into a space shuttle overnight, if you give me your car."

"Okay, here are the keys," said Jack.

When Jack got home his mother said to him, "Stupid! That's what you are, stupid! I asked you to sell our car, not trade for this!" And she threw the micro-chip out the window.

The next day, when Jack woke up, he saw right outside his window a space shuttle.

So Jack began to get ready for blastoff. 10-9-8-7-6-5-4-3-2-1-0-ignition—blastoff!

Jack landed on Mars next to a space station. Jack rang the doorbell. A woman answered. She asked, "What do you want?"

Jack said, "I'm hungry and I would like to know if you have anything to eat."

"Okay, I'll give you a Mars bar," she said.

Just before Jack finished eating, the woman said, "It's my husband! Hide yourself!" A Marsman walked in and picked up a device. Then he said, "Fe fi fo fum, I detect an Earthmun! My nose tells me he's in the trash compactor!" Jack jumped out of the trash compactor and hid in the toilet. Just in time because he heard the trash compactor being turned on. "He's gone!" The Marsman said, "I'm going."

Just as soon as he left to go to sleep, the lady helped Jack out of the toilet. Then the lady said, "Since you may need these three things on Earth, I will give them to you. Here is an oil-making machine. Just add a Milk-Bone dog biscuit and out comes oil. Next, a coal-making machine. Just put in a rock and out comes coal. Last, a uranium-making machine. Add water but don't drop it within the first minute or BOOM it explodes. Also I have prepared your shuttle for takeoff."

All of a sudden there was a big roar and the Marsman said, "I know he's here, and I'm going to kill you for helping him." Then he slapped the woman and beat her, and then Jack threw oil on the Marsman. Then the Marsman chased Jack to his ship and followed him with a laser gun, but before he could fire it, he was hit by an asteroid. Jack made it back to Earth safely and lived happily ever after.

The Ancient Plague

Sarah Lieberman

The kingstock for breeding fire lizards comes from Grenden Forest. Grenden is the northwing. The Telem Forest, Crand and Quince are eastwing. It was founded in the peace years after the War over Batten Cove (2064). It survived the Ancient Destruction, another war that occurred from 2081 to 2092. It also survived the epidemic gas poisoning that almost destroyed the entire population in 3005. They called the almost indestructible poison ATLA 3.

Mirene lived in the northwing with her little sister, Nena, and her mother, Grenda. Her father, Midoz, lived in eastwing Crand. He was wing representative. Grenda owned six kingstock fire lizards, four silvers and two emeralds. She proudly presented the multi-colored eggs to the northwing council for shipment to eastwing settlements and the southern wilds for further breeding.

Mirene was 14 rounds old; Nena was 7; Grenda was 30; and Midoz was 47. Mirene's family lived on the edge of the Kraunt sector in a natural cave formation near the Erend Ocean. They picked reeds (for pipes) and played for the festival. The festival was a joyous occasion for everyone; even the lizards danced! Silver and emerald streaks whirred around Mira's (Mirene's) head, and the fire blazed until late at night.

The next morning Mira rose at dawn to wash clothes. At 14 rounds she already did most of the household chores, including all the cooking. At morn-break a shriek made Mira look up from her washing. The shining royal-blue message-lizard hovered protectively above her, trilling to awaken the council.

Mira had a strange ability no one knew about. She understood the strange piercing calls of the lizards. The message, she knew at once, was from southern—something or other about gas—but it wasn't important or the council would have set off the alert.

Mira was dressed in a wool tunic and a long full skirt.

"Mirene!"

Mira looked into her mother's piercing brown eyes.

"Krysia needs her travel cloak today; the message lizard doesn't!" Grenda snapped.

"Yes, Grenda. Is Nena awake?"

"Yes," Grenda snapped again. "Work!" Mira bent down to her washing.

"Yes, Grenda" meekly wobbled in the air for a moment. While Mira washed, Nena woke alongside her mother.

"Mira?" That was Nena. "We finished your skirt for the trip to Quince. It's rust-colored."

"Thank you, Grenda, Nena." The appropriate formality stuck in her throat. She walked to the stable to feed the plow-beasts, unaware of the royal-blue lizard above her head. Then it spoke.

"Mirene, daughter to Midoz, we honor you!" Mira cried out at this intrusion into her mind.

"Mirene?" It had a soothing musical voice. "Fear not, we protect you!" A delicate wail rose from the lizards on the sun perch. Mira sat down, afraid of fainting.

"Mirene." She shook her head. "Rise." She felt compelled to do so.

"Mirene, we protect you!" The wail grew stronger, penetrating every fiber in her body; it was louder, it was painful. Then it stopped. The lizards resettled themselves on the perch. Mira drifted to the stables, dazed though she was, and fed the plow-beasts. For the next few days Mira enjoyed chats with the lizards, even called some by name. One day as she was taking care of the children, Tren, an emerald lizard, began an awful crying. In a moment Mira was up.

"Tren, find Deet and meet me in Forlon!" Five minutes later Mirene was arguing with her headwoman to let her go. Finally, disheveled though she was after her fight with Liges, she appeared in Forlon. Tren and Deet cried greetings in a tired sort of way. Up all night worrying about the south, she soon learned. But why? The mental images they gave her were blurred, too blurred to understand. She saw a man in a mask in one of the clearer images. The lizards were in a flurry.

"Slow down, dears, I can't read your images so I can't help you." Deet chirped, but it was a scared chirp.

"Tren?" His eyes whirled.

"Get Liges, don't come back without her! Deet, get Renon!" Both trilled and flew into the clouds. In a moment the lizards were back, each dragging an annoyed headwoman. Liges was first to speak.

"Mirene! What do you mean by this! I shall tell your mother!"

"Tsk-tsk-tsk," Renon clicked softly in the background. Mirene silently cursed Liges.

"If you tell, Deet will peck your eyes out."

"And I am scared of a lizard?"

Mira turned, leaving the woman to her haughty looks.

"Renon." Mira tried to win the quieter woman to her side. "Please listen, close your eyes, try not to—."

"She is crazy!" Liges burst in.

"Try not to think about tiring things, I need your complete concentration." Mira surprised Liges by bursting in so forcefully.

"Renon, try to see the images I give you: a man wearing a mask spraying a—. Deet, give me stronger images," Mira snapped.

"Again, Renon, he is spraying a type of gas."

"Yes, I see it."

Mira smiled and then laughed. "I knew it!"

"That you can get lizard images," Mira replied.

"WHAT!" sputtered both Renon and Liges.

"The lizards speak with images, and a few people can hear them, like Renon and me. The lizards gave you images, I only relayed them to you!" Renon was bewildered, and Liges was raging with anger.

"For this you brought me here? For the useless discovery that lizards talk, I am missing my work? I insist that one of the lizards escort me home!" Deet fluttered out of Liges' grabbing range, and Tren too seemed to glare at her.

"Well? Come now, Mirene, I am your elder!"

"No! The lizards are who you ask, not I, and you have downed them!" Liges turned beet-red at this and stormed out. Renon looked like a scared lamb, then turned and strode off. Mira gave a giggly sort of a laugh, and the lizards cried out in an imitation of this.

"Now, Deet, try to tell Renon, yes the quiet one, tell her that she must tell the council that we are in danger." Deet chirped in reptilian, "O.K."

"Go!"

An hour later Mira was luxuriously rubbing soap-sand on her somewhat dirt-stained arms. "Hurray" was the first thought to race through her mind; she was ecstatic. They listened! She must remember to thank Renon. She was to appear before them to prove her point. Tren and Deet were chirruping in happiness to the lizards on the perch.

"Tren, come here so I can scrub you." The lizard hopped from perch to perch, being sure to get as sandy as possible. An hour later (centuries to Mira) she was called to the council heights. All went smoothly, and the council promised to look into the nature of the gas. That night her mother whispered to her that she was to pack for a trip to southern. "Me," she thought, "Why me?" A voice whispered that she must hurry, they would be late.

Southern Lands

(The rest of the story is from Mira's diary)

Date: 14 Septica #56 SOUTH

We discovered an ATLA pocket today at 4 Ante Meridian. Still being studied at 7 Post Meridian. The lizards smell them at a great distance. We still do not know why they are important; ignorance is not bliss.

Date: 17 Septica #57 SOUTH

We received a terrible message this morning, as follows: 9 Post Meridian first victims of sudden plague buried at Nontcha. Recorded as "Nanone" in tablets; only cure, poisonous gas ATLA 3. We were overjoyed, we finally had a use for the unknown gas!

Date: 19 Septica #59 SOUTH
More and more gas. We have discovered a new method of collecting the gas.

Date: 25 Septica #63 SOUTH
The plague has discovered my family, I am an orphan with no home now.

Date: 27 Septica #65 SOUTH
We just found out why the ancients called the lizards "fire lizards." They breathe fire! Like the mythical dragons. The first shipment of gas has been made to Nekkin, where the plague is the worst.

Date: 10 Octica #2 NORTH
Almost home, the plague is over and I am to be given my due as council woman. Grenda would be so happy.

Here is where the diary ends. Mira was a hero, but the lizards were not. She always thought they would be the crowning factor of her reign as head woman, but instead they were forgotten. Years later a scientist found the remains of one of these beautiful creatures and named them "flamers" because of the way they resemble a flame. . . .

Perhaps it will happen, perhaps not. . . .

Underwater Sam!

T. J. Fullington

One day Ma and Pa Suthurd were walking on the beach and they saw a bundle of seaweed. They went to see what it was. When they unwrapped the seaweed they found a little baby boy. They took the baby to their house because they had always wanted a baby boy. Ma told Pa the first thing they had to do is name the baby. They couldn't decide what to call the baby. Here are some of the names they thought of: John, Bill, Jeff, Shawn, Tim, Chris and Eugene. Pa settled it when he said, "Let's name him Sam." He got no objection from Ma. All she said was, "Come on, Sam, it's dinner time."

That summer Pa took Sam to the beach. Pa set Sam in the water to let him get used to it. Then Pa turned around to get his raft. When he turned back around Sam wasn't there. Pa was worried. He looked everywhere and couldn't find hide nor hair of Sam. All of a sudden Pa saw some bubbles. He reached down and grabbed an armful of Sam. Pa couldn't believe it. Sam had stayed underwater for at least three minutes, and he came up with a smile from ear to ear like he could have stayed under for two more minutes.

Pa was so amazed he decided to test Sam again. The next day Pa took Sam back to the beach and put him in the water. Sam went under and Pa started counting. After five minutes Pa was wondering if something happened to Sam. Pa saw some bubbles and reached down to grab Sam or what he thought to be Sam. Pa had a hurt finger from that lobster for a month. Pa didn't really mind because Sam stayed under for nine minutes.

When Pa's finger was better, he took Sam to the beach. Sam crawled into the water and went under. Pa started counting. After thirty minutes Pa was really worried, but he didn't reach under to get Sam, from recent experience. Just then Sam came up with a big smile from ear to ear.

The town found out about Sam's talent through the grapevine. By the time Sam was five years old he could stay under for two hours. Every time Pa and Sam went to the beach the town followed to see if Sam could break his own record. Each time he managed to stay under longer, and the crowd cheered for him. At age ten Sam could stay underwater for a day at a time. Sam was the town's hero.

Sam made many friends under the water. Some of his favorites were two dolphins and a seahorse. He also had a pet sea turtle that lived in a cave by the bay. The turtle was lazy and didn't move very much unless Sam came to visit. His best friend was a jellyfish named Allen.

One day Sam went to the beach without permission. Ma and Pa grounded him for one month. Sam decided to run away from home and live with his friends in the sea!

He packed his clothes and went to the beach. He jumped in the water and started to swim. The first friend he met was Allen, the jellyfish. Allen and Sam had a long talk. Allen talked Sam out of running away. Sam ran out of the water and to his house. He unpacked his clothes and dried off. Ma and Pa didn't know about Sam's plans, but they did wonder about the wet carpet.

One day a little man walked into town with a funny contraption on his back. The man called it scuba gear. The little man said it allowed you to breathe under water. He also said that no man could breathe under water longer than he could with his scuba gear. Of course Sam challenged the little man. The whole town was betting on Sam.

In a week the contest was to start. The week went by quickly. On the day of the game everybody was there. The schools let out. Even the frogs were at the beach. Sam and the man went down on June 1, '85. Most of the people left on the twenty-fifth day. On the thirty-second day they were both coming up at the same time when the little man stopped but Sam couldn't stop. Sam came up one second before the little man. Sam was so ashamed he dove into the water and didn't come back.

Most of the people thought he went off to an island with his friends from the sea, but I know what really happened. He turned into a fish and went to live in the ocean. If you ask me how I know, this is because I am Sam, the dolphin.

Whinny and the Black Ghost
Corinne Chee

It was night, and the stars were twinkling brightly against the darkening sky. Whinny, a little girl who lived in a clearing in the woods, quietly slipped outside to breathe the crisp, cold, fresh air.

Whinny lived with Mr. and Mrs. Robner, her "mom" and "dad," in a cozy log cabin. The Robners had found her when she was about two years old sleeping on the grass in front of their house. They had named her Whinny because the name just seemed to fit her. She liked the name, too.

One day, Mr. and Mrs. Robner had gone hunting with some friends. They had tried to persuade Whinny to come with them, but she was too stubborn. Deep down inside, though, she knew the real reason. She was afraid. Afraid of the woods after the sun was gone. Trying not to show her fear, she stoutly said she did not want to go. Already late, the Robners finally gave up and left her at home. Her mother and father had been gone for two days, and Whinny was beginning to get worried.

As she stepped out of the house, she knew something was different. She could feel it in her bones. Cautiously, she took a few steps forward. Nothing moved. Then, thinking it was her imagination, she sank down onto a rock and started gazing at the stars.

Alertly, she looked around again more carefully than before. She saw mysterious dim shapes of horse-like creatures with wings on their backs and a horn coming out of their foreheads, standing motionless in the pale moonlight. They were staring at her with steel blue eyes.

As the creatures started closing in on her she started screaming. The noise startled the creatures, but they still came steadily toward her.

Then she started running blindly around, trying to find a way to escape from their tight circle. Finding an opening, she ran screaming toward the woods. Suddenly, she stumbled and fell forward. Her head hit a rotting log. Then she became unconscious and fell into a deep sleep.

She was awakened at midnight by low, murmuring voices. For a moment, she couldn't quite figure out who or what was talking. Then she remembered. They were the creatures she had seen earlier. The fear she had felt earlier seemed to have gone away. Suddenly, the voices came to a halt. A dark, looming shadow appeared and seemed to cover the moon and stars. Then, a sharp, shrill voice pierced the air like a gun shot. It said in an echoing voice, "I am here." Then, as quickly as the ghost came, it faded and was gone.

One of the creatures then came and explained what had happened.

"When you were young, your grandmother gave you, and only you, a special gift. It was the gift of power that she would someday have to use to conquer the Black Ghost, the dark shadow which hovered over you just now. The Black Ghost also heard of your special power and decided to do away with you. We heard of his plan. So through the years we've been trying to hide you down on earth as a human until you were strong enough to fight him. Our powers were drained after we changed you into a human."

"You mean I was once like you?" Whinny gasped disbelievingly.

"Yes," the creature replied softly. "The Black Ghost will try to take you and turn you into a ghost like himself. You wouldn't want that to happen, would you?"

"No! I would never want that!" Whinny exclaimed.

"Then you must use your powers in full strength against the Ghost. You must be quick and alert, for the Black Ghost could easily capture you. Do you think you are ready to face the Ghost?"

"I—I am ready," Whinny whispered unsteadily.

"You must go at once and meet the Ghost. Perhaps it would be better if you went looking like one of us. Are you willing to fight as one of us?"

"Yes," she answered firmly.

"OK. Let's go quickly."

They saw the Black Ghost in the woods.

"It is time for you to change," the creature said.

All of the creatures gathered around Whinny with their eyes focused on her. The power that came through her eyes was making Whinny grow wings. Suddenly, the Black Ghost came swiftly toward them! The creatures began running.

The creature who had talked to her shouted, "You will have to fight him as you are!'' And with that, he was gone. Now she was alone with the Ghost, and he was drifting rapidly toward her!

Just then a thought came to her. "What do I do now?" she thought. She knew she had power but how was she to use it? She began getting frightened. As the Ghost came nearer, the air became cold and clammy. It became dark. Then blackness came over Whinny. It was unlike the night sky. It had an unfriendly feeling about it, and it seemed to be trying to pull Whinny away and control her.

Hurtling all her hatred and fear at the Ghost, she staggered back a few steps. Then, braced against a dead tree trunk, she forced all her powers to their fullest extent, directing them through her eyes with a piercing stare at the Ghost. The Black Ghost let out a shrill scream of defeat and disappeared into thin air.

Suddenly, the clouds broke away from the sky. The moon shone again more brightly than it ever had before. It was a sign of victory. The battle had been won.

Whinny, who was thoroughly worn, slumped into a heap and was soon fast asleep as the creatures came dancing out of the woods shouting for joy.

After Whinny had slept a while they gently woke her to ask her a few questions.

"Will you come and stay with us?" they all asked.

Whinny answered, "Yes, I'd love to, but can my mother and father come too?"

All the creatures gathered together and discussed this new idea. It wasn't long before they encircled her and solemnly nodded their approval.

Some folks wondered what happened to the happy little family that lived in the woods. Others noticed three new stars shining the brightest.

Myth

Read some myths, then invent a supernatural story that pretends to explain something true about nature or human nature. This could take place today or in a made-up time and place. Characters in myth stand for things in life, like growth or greed, and the plot connects these things in some relationship. So what the characters do with each other shows how these forces act on each other. Places and objects also may represent things in real life—

a swamp or a jewel, for example. Make your own myth to state or explain something about the world.

A simple kind of myth explains how something came to be the way it is, like how fire was first made, or how the tiger got his stripes. You might start with that type. Agree with partners to show or explain something with myth, then compare your myths afterwards. You might post or print these together.

Why Jupiter Has a Red Spot

Ben Sander

Long, long ago, when the only living creatures were the gods, the gods created the planets. The planets were alive, and they all had names. The gods chose the planet called Earth as their home, and they made it beautiful. This made the other planets hate Earth. To punish the planets for disliking the new Earth, the gods put the planets on long metal strings that circled the flaming star known as the Sun. This forced the planets to circle around the Sun in what we now call orbits.

Restricting the planets' movements only made them more hostile. In an effort to control the planets, Odin the All-Father appointed the planet called Saturn the "King of the Planets." He was given a crown that had the power to control the other planets. This made the planets angrier, especially the one named Jupiter. One day, when Jupiter passed Saturn in his orbit, Jupiter took part of the crown away from Saturn. Saturn did not notice, since he was asleep.

Jupiter gave some of the crown to the other planets, but kept most of it for himself. The parts of the crown are today called moons.

The added power from the parts of the crown gave the other planets the power to break their metal threads. The breaking of the threads woke Saturn up, and he controlled all of the planets except Jupiter, who was too big and powerful to be controlled. Jupiter raged toward Earth and woke the gods. Thor, the defender of the gods, hurled a thunderbolt at Jupiter and hit him. Jupiter started to bleed but was still charging Earth. Before he came within 50 miles of Earth, Odin turned him to stone, and Saturn put him back on his orbit. Then Odin turned all the planets except the Earth to stone. When Jupiter was turned to stone, his red blood was petrified on his surface. This is why Jupiter has a red spot.

How Pegasus Got Wings

Kristy Rank

Once there lived a herd of horses, and they wished they could fly, so one day they all went out to find someone that would give them some wings. First they saw a snake. They said, "Will you trade us your wings for our pasture?"

"I don't need a pasture to live in," he said. So the horses went off trying to find someone, but no one would trade their wings because they didn't have any. They searched for days. Days turned into months, but they still could not find anyone.

They were going to give up when they saw some birds. The horses said, "Will you trade your wings for our pasture?" But the bird said, "We don't need your pasture. We live in trees and are in the air most of the day, so why give you our wings?"

The horses walked off hoping to find someone to trade their wings. They got so hot and thirsty that they had to have a drink. All of a sudden one of the horses said, "Look! There is a lake where we can get a drink." They all charged over and drank and drank until they looked like blimps. Then one horse said, "Look, there is someone that has two pairs of wings. Maybe he will give us a pair of wings." The horses put their heads under water and said, "Will you give us a pair of your wings?"

The flying fish said, "Why sure! Here." Then all the fish gave a pair of their wings to the horses. After all the horses had a pair of wings they started to fly. One said, "Hey, this is fun!"

And that's how Pegasus got wings.

How the Turtle Got Its Shell

Todd Bluhm

One day the rabbit told a great joke. He laughed so hard he fell into the water and sank to the bottom. When he was at the botton of the sea a clam shell caught him and it stuck to him. He tried to get it off but he couldn't. And from then on the turtle had the shell stuck to his back. That is how the turtle got his shell.

The First Rivers

Karen Ury

Kaweloe was sitting on a mountainside watching his father trying to fish. His father was sad because the pools of water were drying up. His people's main source of food supply came from the water.

Most of the Chinook people had died from starvation. Kaweloe thought that if he could find the God of the Sun, he could ask him to heat the earth until it cracks.

So he set out over the hills and mountains and finally came to where the God of the Sun is.

He asked the god, "Oh mighty god, would you spare our people? Would you please heat the earth until it cracks?"

"What outcome do you want from this?" asked the god.

The boy answered, "I want fish and water to be plentiful." The boy continued, "I will make sure every person in our tribe always has food to eat as a gift of thanks to you, oh mighty god."

The god thought, "Okay. I agree with that."

So Kaweloe went back home. He told his father what he did.

His father was very proud and said, "You will become a great leader some day!"

That night Kaweloe woke to an immense heat wave. In the morning, the people awoke to find a crack that went along the edge of the village and branched out in many directions. All of its branches held lots of clear, blue water and lots of fat fish!

"Who has created this miracle?" wisemen of the village asked.

Someone said, "Kaweloe did."

Kaweloe modestly replied, "We must give thanks to the God of the Sun." The Chinook tribe had a celebration to give thanks. They called this body of water "revere," which translates from the Indian language to mean river.

How the Zebra Got Its Stripes

Jennifer Ng

One day a zebra was grazing with many other horses. The zebra's wife called for him because she couldn't tell the difference between her husband and the horses. Her husband didn't respond to her. She had an idea.

"Time for dinner, Honey!" she yelled.

This was the only way she could get her husband to come. As usual, he was sitting at the table.

When dinner was over, their children went to bed.

"Honey," Mrs. Zebra paused. "From now on, don't graze with the horses that look like you."

"But that's where all the tasty grass is!" he cried.

"I don't care if that's where all the tasty grass is."

"Yes sir," he said meanly and he marched upstairs.

Mrs. Zebra started to sew until she went to bed.

The next morning Mrs. Zebra couldn't find her husband.

"Children," Mrs. Zebra said nervously.

The children ignored her because they were watching Saturday morning cartoons.

"Children!" she said furiously.

"Huh?" the children answered.

"Do you know where your father is?"

"He went to the tasty grass where the horses are."

"Oh."

"He told us not to tell you."

When she got down where her husband was she said, "Time for dinner."

But no one came running.

"Oh gosh, why is it so hard to find my husband?" Mrs. Zebra said quietly.

All of a sudden she saw black stripes on herself. When she looked at where her husband was grazing, she saw her husband. She knew it was him because he too had black stripes on him. She walked straight up to him and said, "Hi Honey."

"How do you know it's me?" he asked.

"Because you look like me."

"Oh, no."

Mrs. Zebra dragged him home.

"Oh, Mommy," the little zebras cried. "I think we're sick. We have black stripes all over us."

"It's nothing. God just let us look different." This is how zebras got black stripes.

How the Snake Tempted
Two People to Eat the Apple

Michelle Rick

Once upon a time, on a planet called Zurelia, there lived a man called Mr. Griffith. He always felt isolated from other people on his planet. His salvation was carving dolls. People from far and wide comets came to see the man's magical dolls.

One day Mr. Griffith was sitting at his worktable when a man dressed in elegant velvet appeared riding down the road in a carriage covered with pearls and diamonds, pulled by some noble white horses. The man was surprised to see a man of nobility riding through a peasant town such as the one in which he lived. Normally these rich men avoided poor towns for fear that they might be robbed. Mr. Griffith was especially surprised when the carriage stopped in front of his house. He tried to ignore the arrival because he didn't want to seem too envious.

"Sir Griffith." The man bowed before him. "My name is Sir Henry. I am here speaking for the king. He wishes to see you as soon as possible. Are you willing?"

"Of course," replied Mr. Griffith, trying not to seem overanxious.

"Very well. You will be expected at once. It is requested that you bring two of your best dolls. The king shall crown them if they live up to his expectations. If you decide not to come, I and an army of men, if necessary, will drag you to the king's palace ourselves. After this we will hang you and take all your dolls to be displayed around the princess's bedroom."

"Never worry, Sir Henry, I shall be at the king's palace before daybreak tomorrow."

So Mr. Griffith packed his bags, grabbing his favorite dolls. One was a man and one was a woman. The woman had eyes of stone, lips of blood, and hair of silk threads from the spider in his work tower, in his house, in Drewry Lane.

The male doll was a shriveled up old man. He was leaning over his cane, all hunched over. His dry, wrinkled eyes peeped up through sagging eyelids. He always stood on Mr. Griffith's shelf, separated from the other dolls. He reminded Mr. Griffith of himself.

A slightly too weak pony soon emerged from its stall with Mr. Griffith on its back. He turned it toward the road and began his journey toward the castle.

He rode for a few hours, over the long stretch of road, looking through the foggy land for his destination's door. Suddenly the horse began to slow down. It started panting and whinnying softly. The man jumped off its back, knowing the horse was going to die.

He took no time to wait for it. He began running. If he did not find someone who would give him a ride to the palace he surely would not be there by daybreak.

He ran for such a long time that he could run no longer. He stopped before a large redwood tree and sat under its branches. He was so tired that he saw no point in running any longer and soon was in a deep slumber.

When he woke, the sun was flashing brilliant rays of light on his frail body. In the distance he could hear the hooves of at least one army of horses. Running would have been pointless because he was no match against the superiority of horses. So he waited. "Lord!" he cried, "What have I ever done to you to deserve this?"

Sir Henry was at the front of the lines of horses. He answered with a simple, "You betrayed the king."

The man was hung at noon.

The next day Sir Henry returned to his house to collect the dolls which would be placed at the princess's bedside.

The princess was overjoyed with the dolls. She felt that none of them should be ugly, so she began changing such works as the old man, the derelict, and the slave. She also disapproved of the lion so she burned it in her fireplace.

There was one flaw in the magic of these dolls, however, that she hadn't known about. If she happened to abuse or change them in any way, she would be cursed and changed into an evil snake and be sent to Earth for the rest of her life. This is what happened.

Meanwhile on the planet Zurelia the beautiful woman doll fell in love with the handsome man doll. Happily they escaped from the palace and went to Earth, where they planned to spend their life together. However, a snake who still felt betrayed tempted them to eat the apple.

Fable

Read some fables, then try your hand at some. A fable is a brief story that illustrates some general truth or advice. This "moral" is stated in a separate sentence at the end. The characters do not have to be animals, and fables can be modern.

There are several ways to go about making fables. You

can take some familiar saying and write a story to illustrate it. Or make a fable out of a true incident you've heard or read about that you think is a good example of something general. Or make up a moral, then invent a tale to illustrate it.

Fables are especially good to post on a bulletin board or make into a booklet. If several of you write fables to illustrate the same moral, cluster these around a little sign with the moral printed on it, or collect them in a booklet with the moral as title.

Fred and His Predicament

Jeff Stoyanoff, Michael Harasym, and Chris Lehman

One day Fred Turtle was walking down the street. Scattered insults came from all directions toward him. Fred felt terrible.

Fred went to a wise old owl. This owl was very peculiar. He had a long white beard. He also had five-inch spectacles. He stroked his beard constantly.

Good ol' Fred walked up to the owl and said, "I am a failure, I have nothing going for me." The session went on for hours. The turtle talked and talked. Finally, the turtle said, "What should I do?"

The owl went into his little black bag of things. He pulled out a book. He gave it to Fred and said, "Read." Fred read amazingly well. The owl was impressed.

Then the owl proceeded to place Fred in many life-endangering situations. Fred handled them all perfectly. The owl said, "I hope you realize what you are capable of doing, Fred."

Fred said, "I am *now*, and walked away happily.

Moral: Every cloud has a silver lining.

The Fly and the Frog

Jeremy Herrick

Once upon a time a fly was zipping around. He was going to and fro and fro and to and he saw a frog (from a distance). He thought that the frog looked gentle, so he went in for a closer look. The frog (of course) was very cunning and sneaky. He said in a comforting voice, "Come, fly, so that we may talk." So the fly went closer, and the frog opened his mouth and instead of words came a tongue, which snatched the fly's wing. The fly fell to the ground unable to fly. Then the frog snatched the fly himself.

Moral: You can't judge a book by its cover.

Friendship

Chrissy Mattson

Tiffany Fox skipped through Redwood Forest looking for berries as she went. As she skipped she met K.C. Fox. She asked K.C. if she wanted to come over and play. K.C. said, "I have some chores to do around the house, but I'll call you when I'm done at 3:00." "O.K.," replied Tiffany. Then she skipped off back home, picking berries as she skipped.

Tiffany waited until 4:00. Then she decided to go over to K.C.'s house. When she got there Jennifer Fox was over at K.C.'s house. Tiffany said, "You lied to me. You told me you had chores around the house."

"I only did because I didn't think you liked Jennifer," said K.C.

"I do," replied Tiffany. "You should have told me the truth. I don't want to be your friend anymore," said Tiffany.

"Me either," replied Jennifer. They both said goodbye and left.

The lesson is: Don't lie to a fox.

The Mole and the Skunk

Sara Dabrowski

A skunk had been teasing a mole because the mole was afraid of everything. The mole didn't like this one bit. He wanted to express this to the skunk, but he was too afraid.

One day the mole decided to ask his mother what he should do. His mother thought and then answered, "Only the great owl knows that," and turned back to her laundry.

When her son was gone, she called the owl and asked him not to eat her son and in return she would give him chocolate cake.

The mole was very happy with the news, so immediately he set off on his journey to find the great owl. He did know that owls ate moles, but he tried not to be afraid.

When he got there, the owl said, "You were very brave to come to me. You now know that you are not afraid of everything. I will not eat you."

The mole was overjoyed with what he had found out and rushed home.

Just after he arrived and told his mother what happened, Sam Skunk appeared at the door.

He started teasing him and then the mole said, "I don't care what you say because I know more than you. I went to the great owl for advice and I'm not afraid of everything anymore."

Sam was astonished by what he just heard and never bothered the mole again.

The lesson is: Sometimes courage is what you need.

Poem of Thought and Feeling

Think of some feelings or memories you may have about an experience or a person or place or object (or animal). Or make up some fantasies that express feelings you may have had about real things. Maybe these would make a good poem. The main things about the subject may stick in your mind or come to your mind as a picture or sound or smell. Try to capture more of this and see where it leads. Or a feeling or idea may stand out most. Start with whatever is strongest and let the poem build as you try to follow details or connections.

A poem does not have to rhyme, especially if you have to force it. You can play with sounds and rhythms and where you break the lines even if you don't rhyme. And you can make comparisons between what you are talking about and other things that are like them in some way. Choose your words thoughtfully, to get the effect you want.

Post your poems (perhaps with illustrations), collect

them into a pass-around book with others' poems, or
make a collection of just your own poems and print it up.
Try sending a poem or two to a local newspaper or
magazine.

Recipe for Witch's Brew

Jenny Wambach

1 pair of frog legs,
2 big bats,
3 old spider webs,
And 4 black cats.

1 cup of magic dust,
2 cups of water,
3 gray mice,
And 1 wizard's daughter.

Put all these things
In a big black pot,
Stir it around,
Till it's nice and hot.

Take a bowl,
Fill it with joy,
Take a spoon,
Then eat and enjoy.

A Lamp

Ryan Larsen

A scaly old dragon
With many different forms
Is hiding in houses, apartments,
    and dorms.
Its tail size is varied
From long to small,
And they're not sturdy.
If you hit them they'll fall.
When I give it a tap
In the right place
It'll blow out some fire
And light up a face.
But when I tap it again
The face shall not show.
The room will be dark.
It's night time, you know.

A Vacuum

Brett Walter

In the hall closet I saw a creature.
It was really quite a feature.
When it turned alive it made a big roar
As its long snout ate dirt off the floor.
When it looked like it was fed
I pulled out the plug and now it is dead.

On the Outside
Cheryle Turner

I am a bright person
    on the outside
Whom all of my family love
And if I were to change that person
They would not give me their love
And if I were to be like a tree
All of my family would change
    their image of me.

On the Inside
Cheryle Turner

I am an icicle on a frozen
    cliff
And a clumsy ballerina,
But if I were to tell you
    the personal things
My heart would sue you.

Wimpledozer
Torie Sewell

Wimpledozer is a lazy dog,
Lying on the floor.
The wimp of southern Naperville,
Never doing a chore.

He barks at wild Hawaiian shirts,
He's called "the fraidy cat."
And when he begs for chewsticks,
He's really quite a brat.

He didn't cost us anything
Our worthless little pet.
But he's the "bestest" dog
I bet I've ever met.

Snow
John Cote

Snow is beautiful.
    Snow is white.
It falls like crystals
    through the night.

It sweeps across
    the frozen lands.
It spreads and mounds
    like desert sands.

It looks so soft,
    but when it blows
It stings your hands
    and feet and nose.

At first it's like
    a cottony billow
As soft and fluffy
    as a downy pillow.

But then it turns
    to hard packed ice
Delighting sledders,
    who think that's nice!

The Watcher

Amy Billone

There is a window
Between the world and me
Through which I watch
And wait
Like a rock in a wild sea.
The surf of the crowd
Rises and swells.
Invisible to them
I listen to the tragic
Tale time tells.
I want to plunge in,
To flow with the tide,
But I am on the other side.

The Blues

Amy Billone

The Blues come
Deadly and Black.
They lock themselves in
And hide the key,
Then they cackle
Wickedly.
They pound inside
Like a tantrum,
Put a rock
In your throat,
Send tears rushing
Out of your eyes
Like waves tossing a boat.

My Eyes

Amy Billone

My eyes are like green stones,
The color of Evil and Envy.
My eyes are like green leaves,
The color of Birth and Growth.
My eyes are like swirling pools,
Endless and Deep.
My eyes are bad like Devils
And good like Angels.

Thinking Over

Directions to Make or Do Something

Explain step by step how to make something, so that some type of reader you have in mind can make the item from your directions. Include any information about materials, tools, or functioning of the item necessary to understand how one goes about making it. If you already know very well how to make this, just write the directions alone from memory and ask someone to try them out. Or explain step by step how to do some activity such as operate a certain machine, care for and feed certain animals, or get from one place to another.

Watch or find out the results and rewrite to clear up any problems the person had following your directions. Copy for those interested. With others make a how-to book.

A group may work out a way of making or doing something and write down the directions as they work them out. Discuss the wording and the organization of the directions as you go. After you've finished the item, read the directions over together to see if you want to change anything. (The last two examples below were done this way by a group.)

Sesame Seed Honey Balls

Melanie Mincy and Vicki Remington

¼ cup butter
½ cup sesame seeds
1 cup grated coconut

½ teaspoon vanilla
¼ cup honey

Melt butter in electric frying pan over low heat.
Stir in sesame seeds and coconut.
Stir the mixture over low heat for five minutes.
Turn off heat and add vanilla and honey. Put the candy in the refrigerator for one hour. When it is chilled, roll into balls. Keep candy refrigerated.
Makes about 3 dozen (36).

How to Play American Tic-Tac-Toe
Marjorie Young's Fifth Grade Class

This is a game for two players.

1. How to draw the board: draw two parallel lines about two inches apart that are horizontal. Draw two parallel lines about two inches apart that are vertical, that intersect the horizontal lines.

2. Decide which person draws X, and which person draws O. Also decide who goes first.
3. The winner is the first person to get one straight row either diagonally, horizontally, or vertically.
4. Take turns putting down one X or O in each square. First person to get three X's or O's in a row wins. At the same time, try to block the other players, while trying to get three in a row.

How to Make a Hand Puppet
Irving Wasserman's Fifth Grade Class

Shaping the Clay

Shape a piece of modeling clay or plasticene about the size of your fist. Make it into the general shape of a head.

Make a ridge to fit the puppet clothing which you will make later. To hold the puppet in place put it on a bottle.

Shaping the Features

You can shape the features two ways. The first way is to impress the puppet's face with your fingers or a popsicle stick.

Another way to do it is to make the features out of clay and add them on. Add eyes, nose, ears, and anything else you want to have on your puppet.

Making the Paste

To make up the paste, mix dry wallpaper paste (wheat paste) with water. Add a little water at a time to prevent lumps from forming. Then mix it to the heaviness of a thick milkshake. Mix about ½ cup at a time. Add a few drops of wintergreen oil to prevent molding. It can be bought in a drug store.

The Hands

Shape the hands like a mitt. Make a ridge to hold the clothing on the wrist.

The Papier-Maché

Tear three different kinds of paper into strips about ½ inch wide and 3 inches long. Use newspaper, green or pink sheet, and paper towel.

Applying the Papier-Maché

Before applying the papier-maché, put a light coat of vaseline on the clay figures. Cover a strip of paper

with the paste and wipe it off with your fingers. Put the paper on using a crisscross pattern. Use a popsicle stick for pasting in small places.

Completely cover your puppet with **one kind of paper, then the next, and so on until you have nine layers on the puppet's head and hands.**

Cut in Half, Remove Clay, Re-paste Head and Hands

Before you cut the head and hands in half, make sure they are dry and hard. This usually takes about two days.

Cut the head in half behind the ears with a knife. You will then have the face in one half and the back of the head in the other half.

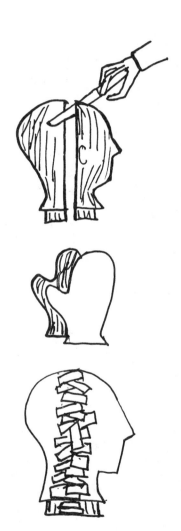

Cut the hands in half along the thumbs and around the tip of the mitt. Then take the clay out. Use a popsicle stick in small places.

To re-paste your puppet head and **hands put three layers of papier-maché crisscross** on where they were cut. Then completely cover them with a layer of paper towel. Let the re-paste completely dry. Now you are ready to paint.

Painting and Shellacking

Paint your puppet's head and hands with poster paints. After the paint is completely dry you can put a coat of shellac on both the head and hands.

Special Features

You can make hair, a mustache, or beard with yarn or string.

You can make pimples out of wool.

You can make warts out of nails.

You can make eyelashes out of straw or wire.

Putting Clothes on the Puppet

When you are ready to make your puppet costume, get a piece of newspaper that will measure double from your elbow to a little above your fingertips and about two feet wide. Use newspaper because you will probably waste a few sheets getting the right size.

Fold the paper in half. Draw your pattern. Staple it in a few places around the edge. Be sure your thumb and two fingers fit through the arms of the pattern. Then cut out the pattern.

Get a piece of material that you like that is twice the size of your pattern. Fold it in half. Pin the paper pattern to it and cut it out. Then sew up both sides of the costume. Do not sew up the arm **holes or neckline.**

In order to tie the costume to the puppet you need to make large enough cuffs and collar to thread through yarn or elastic. Tie yarn or elastic to a safety pin to thread it through the neck and arm seams. Then sew the hem or shape it into pants for a boy's costume. Now you can tie the head and hands to the costume.

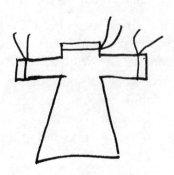

Ten Steps to a Patchwork Quilt
Irving Wasserman's Fifth Grade Class

Making a patchwork quilt is a way to use left over cloth as well as to have fun. Patchwork quilting has been an enjoyable hobby for hundreds of years. Women still have quilting parties. You only need a few things to get started.

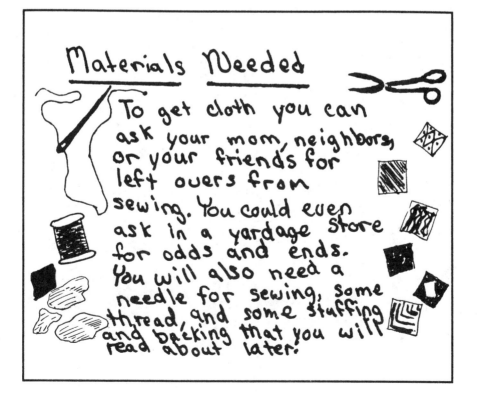

Materials Needed

To get cloth you can ask your mom, neighbors, or your friends for left overs from sewing. You could even ask in a yardage store for odds and ends. You will also need a needle for sewing, some thread, and some stuffing and backing that you will read about later!

The Way To Make The Top

Cut different kinds of material in pieces the size of this pattern (see fig. 1). Oversew the pieces of cloth together (see fig. 2).

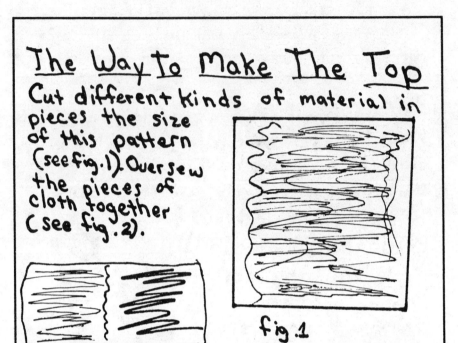

fig. 1

fig. 2

Continue oversewing pieces together until you have a strip as long as you want the quilt to be (see fig. 3). Continue sewing pieces together as you did in steps 1, 2 and 3. Do this until you have a piece the size that you need. This piece is called the quilt top (see fig. 4).

fig 3.

fig. 4.

The Way To Make The Stuffing

To make the stuffing you can use raw cotton, strips of sheet, layers of material, or a blanket. If you want your quilt to be fluffy, use old nylon stockings, raw cotton, or strips of cloth. If you want your quilt to be warm without being fluffy, you can sew the quilt top to an old blanket or layers of material.

The Way To Make The Back

There are a number of ways you can make a back for your quilt. One way is to get a large piece of material and cut it to the size of your quilt. Then sew it on. Another way would be to get pieces of material and sew them together until it's large enough to cover the back of the quilt and sew it on.

A third way would be to not put a back on if you use an old blanket for the middle section.

<u>Putting the Three Parts Together</u>
Put your top, middle section, and bottom together and sew them either in sections or all at once.

<u>Some Uses For Patchwork Quilts</u>

Patchwork quilts can be used for bedspreads, blankets, tablecloths, skirts, doll clothes and blankets, patchwork dresses, etc. There are all sorts of things that you could invent.

Mini-Encyclopedia

Organize an encyclopedia team with others. Look at an encyclopedia to see how it is put together. Then each person write about a subject that he or she already knows a lot about because it is a hobby or strong interest. Don't choose a subject that everybody knows a lot about. People read encyclopedias, after all, to learn things they don't already know. Illustrate your piece if you want. Together, go over all the pieces to suggest improvements and edit. Then put in alphabetical order, make a cover, and bind.

You can make a mini-encyclopedia alone by taking a subject you know really well, like horses or model airplanes or break-dancing, and doing your whole encyclopedia on it. Break your subject down into important parts, like key types of horses, models, or break-dance movements, or into key activities and objects in training horses, making models, or learning to break-dance. In other words, make a specialized *encyclopedia that will inform about your subject to anyone interested but not familiar with it. This could of course be done with partners if they are also experts in the subject.*

(The following examples were all part of a single encyclopedia.)

Armor

Shane Mecklenburger

Armor in the medieval times was mainly of six different kinds. Here are their names and definitions:

Banded mail. Banded mail is layered armor with some light chain mail (see chain mail), padding, and overlapping bands of armor in vulnerable places.

Chain mail. Chain mail is padded armor with overlapping, linked chains. It is fairly heavy, with the weight coming mainly on the shoulders. (There is also eleven chain mail, which is considerably lighter.)

Leather armor. Leather armor is just leather that is boiled in hot water to make it tough. Leather armor is usually worn in layers. Leather armor is also usually worn with chain mail.

Plate mail. Plate mail is armor (usually with chain mail under it) that is metal petal plates on the elbow, knee, chest, arm, back, shin, and thigh. Sometimes on the stomach there are overlapping bands so the man can bend. Otherwise, these are mainly on the knees and elbows. Plate mail is used in heavy combat and jousting.

Ring mail. Ring mail is leather and padded armor and sewn inside are small metal rings that make the armor bulky and heavy.

Scale mail. Scale mail is like ring mail but metal scales are sewn into the padded leather. And, like chain mail, most of the weight is on the shoulder.

Splint mail. Splint mail is light chain mail with leather that has grooves in it for plates of metal to hang in mainly the same places as plate mail.

Note that these are not all of the kinds of armor, but the main kinds. There are probably other similar varieties.

Break-Dancing

Chad Kingsley

Break-dancing originated about 3-5 years ago in New York. Breaking is a mixture of acrobatics, karate and dancing. Breaking is spinning on your head, doing flips, kicking your feet, flipping your legs, etc. The physical part most used in breaking is your arms. It's easy to learn. Just watch people that know how and then try it at home or elsewhere. Breaking is more popular in Evanston because it's just getting in from New York. Breaking has its bad points too. For example, one time when I was spinning on my head my body went down but my head didn't. I heard three cracks in my neck. It hurt for the rest of the week. That's only one of the examples that can happen while break-dancing.

Double Dutch

Tonnica Anderson

Double Dutch is a jumprope game people play at school or at home. Double Dutch was started by Dutch people who were playing with two ropes. Double Dutch is hard for some people because they don't know when to jump in. Also when turning rope for Double Dutch you have to turn right or the other person will get mad at you. Also when one rope goes up that is when you jump on the rope.

Fish
Robyn Barnes

There are thousands of species of fish. In the Great Lakes some of the most common fish are bass, perch and trout. In home tanks some of the most common fish are guppies, angel fish, and goldfish. The biggest fish in the world is the plankton-feeding whale shark.

There are two different kinds of water that fish live in. One is saltwater. Fish who live in saltwater are usually very different from the freshwater fish (that is the second water type). Some saltwater fish are anemones, clown fish and some kinds of crab. Some freshwater fish are angelfish, goldfish, and catfish. The smallest fish in the world is the goby.

Gymnastics
Debbie Rubin

The first step in gymnastics is to learn the basics: forward and backward rolls on the floor, walking forward and backward flat-foot and high-toe on beam, swinging on the high bar on bars, and straight, tuck straddle and pike jump off the springboard for vault. If you want to be a good gymnast when you grow up you should probably start at a young age. I started gymnastics when I was 4 years old. I'm tumbling some of the most dangerous things and pretty advanced back flips: 1) a Double Pike Back, 2) a Double Twist, and 3) a Triple Back.

Hair
Marilyn Belcher

Hair styles have been around for a long time. Just a couple of years ago no one except most women ever paid attention to their hair. But now mostly for punk rockers your hair can change your whole appearance. Not a long time ago the only really popular hair styles were the beehive and the afro. But now there are so many styles they can't be numbered because anyone can sit down and make up a style. Some favorite styles are punk cuts, chinese braids, curls, fish tails, and basket weaving. A perm is something we think will take hours and hours at a time. It only takes an experienced hairdresser an hour and a half.

Pigs
Amy Lehman

Pigs happened to be around when we humans evolved.

Pigs also happen to be extremely smart. I know because I took care of one for six weeks. She knew who I was and greeted me with an oink when I brought her dinner.

People have an almost instinctive dislike for pigs. Many people call others "pig" if they eat sloppily, but accurately pigs have a special order of eating. If I bring her the slop bucket and it's full of cream cheese, lettuce, potatoes, carrots and so on, she carefully picks out the cream cheese and eats it, then moves on to another thing. Gertrude just loves cream cheese.

Pigs love to lounge in the mud. They wait for it to rain and then run around wet and jolly. The reason pigs love the mud is because they have no sweat glands and the mud keeps them cool. People usually think of a pig as a menacing creature, but people who think that don't know anything about a pig. Pigs have short stubby legs, a fat body, largish head with floppy ears, and a snout. Of course, they also have brilliant eyes and an adorable corkscrew tail. Hardly the thing you could kill.

Pigs are built close to the ground because long ago they searched the dirt for food and water.

Rocks and Minerals
Emily Halderman

What are minerals and rocks? Well, minerals are the building blocks that form rocks, such as iron, sulfur, salt, water, and much more. Rocks make great collections. Different people collect different rocks. If you want to collect rocks, good places to look for them are by lakes, stores, garage sales, oceans, parks, etc.

Pyrite (Color: Gold)

Pyrite, or fool's gold, isn't really gold at all. But it is often mistaken for gold because of its gold color. It is found in almost any shape. It is often found with sodalite, a bluish-purple stone.

Quartz (Color: Clear)

Quartz is often found in clusters. Other times it is a mineral in other rocks. It is one of the most abundant rocks.

Moon Stone (Polished)
(Color: Milky White with Bluish Sheen)

Moon stones are a very beautiful kind of stone. Once polished they are considered gem quality (semiprecious). When you look at them just right you see a little glimmer. Otherwise, they are usually milk white.

Fluorite (Color: Anything in the Spectrum)

Fluorite is found in almost any shape. Its most common color is purple. It is found all around Illinois. Fluorite got its name by fluorescing in a black light.

Black Opal (Cut and Polished)
(Color: Everything in the Spectrum
with Black Background)

The black opal is just black. However, it also has sparkles in it called the opal's fire. The fire is all colors. It is considered semiprecious.

The process of making rocks takes thousands of years. Rocks are formed in different ways. Take the geode. Its exterior is dull and gray. This is because the outer layer of the geode is soil (petrified) and clay. hollowed interior has many crystals from minerals seeping gh the exterior. When broken open, a geode makes a good ornament or collecting stone. Another rock, limestone, is made up of different creatures. Different rocks have different scales of hardness. The diamond is the hardest. Talc (the rock in baby powder) is the softest. Graphite (the rock in your pencil) is one step higher than talc. You can find out what rocks are harder than others by using a steel file on them.

Many people wonder which is more valuable, ruby or emerald. The answer is emerald because it is rarer and may be the most valuable gem.

Soccer
Josh Spitz

Soccer is a sport that was made up in England in the 1800's. In a soccer game, there are two teams with eleven players who try to kick or hit the ball into the other team's goal. The team that scores the most goals in an hour and a half wins. All the players except the goalkeeper may use any part of their body to hit the ball, except for their hands and arms. Only the goalkeeper can use his hands and arms.

The players of a soccer team use different lineups for offensive or defensive strategy. Other lineups center around special abilities of a star player. Some lineups are made to take advantage of the other team's weaknesses.

There are four different ways of trapping and hitting the ball. There's the foot, that you can use to kick the ball, or to trap the ball by putting your foot on the ball, to make the ball stop. There's the head that you use to pass the ball to someone or to trap the ball by hitting it to the ground so you can kick or dribble the ball with your feet. But remember never to let the ball hit your head; let your forehead hit the ball. There's the leg to trap the ball by letting the ball hit your leg, and the ball will fall to the ground so you can kick or dribble the ball with your feet. There's the chest to trap the ball by sticking out your chest and letting the ball hit your upper chest, and while it's hitting your chest sucking in your chest. Then the ball will fall to the ground so you can kick or dribble the ball with your feet.

Advice Letter

Get with some partners and make up a name for your column, like "Dear Abby," based on the name of an imaginary counselor. Write a letter to him or her asking for advice abut a problem that is either real or sounds real. Tell enough detail and background of the situation to give the counselor plenty to go on. Put your letter in a box set aside for the advice column and take out someone else's to answer. You may or may not use your real name.

Run these as a column, perhaps a regular one, in a newspaper, make an advice bulletin board, or make a book of the letters. Get others involved and keep the column or board going.

Dear Labby

Barbara Friedberg's Fifth and Sixth Grade Classes

Dear Labby,

I'm so ugly everybody calls me Mutt Face. Including my mother and father.

Signed,
Mutt Face

Dear Mutt Face,

Tell your parents "not to judge a book by its cover." Try and show everyone else your good qualities. And they will forget how you look.

Labby

Dear Labby,

Nobody likes me! I am a social outcast. I try to be nice but they all look at me like I am weird. What should I do? I need some *good* advice!

Signed,
No Friends

Dear No Friends,

Are you shy? If you are, they may not notice you because you shy away from groups.

Get into school activities! You could meet people that way!

If people ignore and look at you like you're weird, they are not people who you would want for friends!

Playing by yourself can be fun! Pretend you are a famous spy or scientist. People will want to find out what you are up to.

Labby

Dear Labby,

My mom just got divorced, but she is getting married in a week. The man my mom is marrying is Peter, but I hate his guts. How do I tell my mom so that it does not hurt her feelings.

Yours truly,
Separation

Dear Separation,

Tell your mom that you hate his guts. It may change her mind a little. If it doesn't change her mind, live with the consequences.

Labby

Dear Labby,

I am getting treated like a six-year-old. I never get to stay home alone. I have to go into my room and do something quiet from 8 P.M. to 9 P.M. I can not cross Church Street alone. My brother can stay up as late as I can. I am ten years old and have talked about it with my parents. I have nothing to show for it.

Sincerely,
Mistreated

Dear Mistreated,

I think that this can be divided in two parts. It could be that they do not trust you. Are you careful crossing the street? Do you lock doors? Do you read and do your homework, or do you watch TV all the time? Think about it!

On the other hand, maybe you are being mistreated. I feel that if a person can be trusted, 10 is old enough to do all of the things you wrote me about. Spend the time in your room wisely, and show your parents you can be trusted. Do helpful chores around the house. Maybe your parents will change their ideas of you.

Labby

Dear Labby,

I don't know how to draw. Everybody can draw better than me. I can't write good either. What should I do?

Depressed

Dear Depressed,

Don't worry. If you would like to draw better why don't you take lessons? Maybe you should try and practice your handwriting. Mine isn't so good either. Maybe drawing and writing just aren't your best things. I bet you're good at other things. Try and find out what you are good at and do that.

Labby

Dear Labby,

I am the most popular person in my grade. Everyone looks up to me and depends on me. People think I'm great, but really I'm not. I'm afraid of a lot of things. I don't want to disappoint them. What should I do?

From
?

Dear ?,

Try to stop being afraid of the things you are. The best way I can think of is to try to live up to your demands. If that still doesn't work, confess your fears.

Labby

Dear Labby,

I am 13 years old. I am happy except for one thing. You see, I have nightmares. Every night, I dream about monsters chasing me, drowning, being very sick, dying and many more terrifying experiences. I wake up in the night screaming at the top of my lungs. I am scared to go to sleep, so I wake up bleary-eyed and tired, and I have nightmares anyway. Please help me!

Terrified at Night

Dear At Night,

Try not to think about your nightmares so much. Try to think about something nice and push your nightmares out of your mind. Hope it works.

Labby

Dear Labby,

I am into smoking and I can't stop. I am already beginning to have breathing problems and sometimes my parents get very angry. What should I do?

Breathless

Dear Breathless,

I recommend that you should see a therapy group of kids that have the same problem as you, and get yourself together.

Labby

Dear Labby,

My brother is a teenager. He goes to the high school, and after school ends he goes to swim practice. He gets home at about 5:30 to 6:00 o'clock. The problem is he never spends time with me. He is always with his friends, but I want to play games with him. What should I do to have him play games with me.

Signed,
L.B.

Dear L.B.

Did you ever tell your brother how you felt? That's really the best thing to do. If you did already, what did he say?

Labby

Dear Labby,

There is a kid in my class who likes me and who is always trying to be near me. He also thinks I like him but I really don't. How do I tell him that I don't like him without hurting his feelings?

Signed
?

Dear ?

I can understand the way you feel, and the answer to your questions isn't an easy one. First of all why don't you like this boy? What is wrong with him? Sit down and write the good things and the bad things about him sitting near you and trying to be near you. If you still think it's that bad that he sits near you, talk to him. Ask him to please not sit near you and to try to leave you alone. If that doesn't work, write back.

Sincerely,
Labby

Dear Labby,

My parents are getting a divorce. Their yelling makes me nuts. And they're such a good couple. I hate to see them apart. What should I do?

Crazy

Dear Crazy,

It is tough getting a divorce for your parents also. It may be just as tough for them as it is for you. The best thing to do is to try to ignore their fighting, which is also hard to do. Go outside or something. It helps if you can't hear them fighting. If you're too uptight to do much of anything then maybe call a friend and talk to them. It helps to talk about it with a friend.

Labby

Dear Labby,

I am an unemployed mother to two kids. They are babies. My old job was teaching 4th and 5th grade kids. I can not find any work. As you know, it is hard to find teaching jobs. I need to support my family. My husband was killed in a plane crash one year ago. I have been unemployed for 5 months. Please help me.

Signed,
Unemployed

Dear Unemployed,

I have great pity for you and I think I can help. For one thing I think you should get a husband when you get over your first's death. Then I think there's a job that I've seen for Dydee-smidee-idee cleaning service. Use that job until you get a teaching job. You can get any others on your own like babysitting or whatever your like.

Labby

Dear Labby,

I've had some problems. Boy, have they been bad. I've been married for 10 years this coming spring and lately my husband (I'll call him Ab) has been out late nights, every night. He comes home at 2:00

A.M. and sleeps till noon. He was fired from his job two weeks ago for coming in drunk.

Ab has been in six accidents since he started to stay out. I'm positive he's an alcoholic. I've tried taking, but no way. Nothing happens. I've got to get a job or we won't be able to pay taxes. He beats me, but I can't send him to prison. How can I make Ab better?

Signed Tax Free

Dear Tax Free,

I think you should call Alcoholics Anonymous and ask your husband to go just once. If he goes once he might go a lot more, and everything will be o.k. But if he doesn't go, try to talk it over and maybe it will turn out all right.

Labby

Dear Chuck

Chuck Bair

Dear Chuck,

I'm having a problem getting homework done. The assignments I'm given are never done in class. I go home and play until five or five-thirty. When I come home it's dinner-time and then I watch TV. When I go to do my homework I have all this pressure on me because I have to get it done and now. I like to play after school to get a break from writing and stuff like that. Reports are a real big problem. We get about two or three weeks to do it so I think I can just relax. I keep on putting it off. Then when it's due I'm not prepared for it. All the pressure is on and it's hard work. I need some advice soon or I'll be going downhill.

From,
Troubled

Dear Troubled,

I understand where you're at. When you come home from school with a lot of homework, have a snack. When you're done you can sit down and start your harder or maybe longer-taking homework. When you're done with that you can go and take a break for about an hour or two. Then come back and do your easier homework. If you have tons and tons of homework, get it done. If it's a report, do some of it every day. This will probably help you to get all your work done and you won't be under pressure.

Take My Advice

Ruth Feightner's Fourth Grade Class

I always have to walk the dog in the morning. My sister never has to. What should I do?

If you always have to walk your dog pretend you are sick, and you won't have to walk your dog. Or you can ask your sister to please walk the dog Mon., Wed., Sun., and you walk the dog Tues., Thurs, Fri., and Sat.

* * *

I get a cowlick and I can't keep it down. I try water. It doesn't work. What should I do?

If you get a cowlick you could put tape on it. If that doesn't work and water doesn't work, then try hair spray, but don't use too much. Or just get a crew cut.

* * *

I get in a habit of watching TV after school. What should I do? My mother is mad at me and does not like me watching TV.

If you watch TV too much you should get into a sport or call a friend. You could make a time for reading a book. And make time for doing your homework instead of watching TV. Or you could pick your favorite show and keep busy until it's on. If none of those work pull the plug.

* * *

My sister and I can never get along. We always get into a fight. Not that I care. It's just that I don't like getting hit. How can I not get hit?

When you and your sister get into an argument you should say, "Why are we fighting?" And if she says, "I don't know," walk away. But if she says, "Because you stole something," you should talk it out.

* * *

My brother always gets to stay up later than me. On school nights he gets to stay up until ten o'clock. I'm older than him and I only get to stay up till 9:00. IT'S NOT FAIR!!!

If I were you, I'd talk to your mom and dad. There are several things you could do—like, tire your brother out so he goes to bed and then you would be able to stay up later. Say, "Shawn's littler than me. Why should I go to bed earlier?" You could give reasons why. Well, good luck with my advice.

*   *   *

I have this problem. My brother and I always play football. He's always making up new rules and he cheats. What should I do?

Just tell your brother if he cheats you don't play. If that doesn't work you can cheat too.

Dear Patty!
Betty Mitchell's Fifth Grade Class

Dear Patty,
I have a problem. All the kids at school tease me because I don't wear all the fashions. I would wear Polos and Izods if I had them but my mother thinks it's silly to spend that kind of money on clothes. How can I make them stop teasing me? Please help!!!!

The Odd Ball

Dear Odd Ball,
You don't have to wear Polos and Izods just because other people do, but if it really bothers you I suggest you try T.J. Maxx or some second-hand stores. You may also try getting on some mailing lists, and when you do they send you information on upcoming sales.

Patty

Dear Patty,
I have a problem. See, I like this boy and I don't know how to tell him. Also, I like two other boys and all three of them don't know about it.

Problems

Dear Problems,
It isn't possible to really like one boy and also two others. You'll have to pick one.

Patty

Dear Patty,

I have a problem. A boy in back of me is always bothering me. I have tried to stop him but he still persists. When I go to the teacher he calls me a tattle-tale and teases me worse! What can I do?! Please help me.

In a no-way-out
situation

Dear No Way,

The only thing I can think of is to just IGNORE him! If it still keeps up just go to the teacher and ask them to talk to him but to not mention your name. If it *still* keeps up I suggest you move O-U-T!

Patty

Dear Patty,

Sometimes people get mean to me and gang up on me, and I get scared and cry. That's why people call me a baby.
What should I do!

Cry Baby

Dear Cry Baby,

Crying only shows people that they can upset you. People will always gang up on you if you show them that they can intimidate you.
Get tough!!

Patty

Review

After you have seen a film or TV program, read a book, eaten in a restaurant, seen an art or science exhibit, evaluate your experience for the benefit of others. Write a review. It's a good idea to take notes on your impressions during the experience. The general point of a review is to make a recommendation to your reader. So while describing the thing, make clear what you consider its strong and weak points, and back these up with evidence.

Read some reviews to get ideas about how description and evaluation may be woven together. Often it's useful to compare the thing you are reviewing to others of its kind. Some background information too may be welcome to readers if they are not familiar with some things about your subject, such as facts about an artist's life or about different kinds of computers (for a product review).

Put your review in a newspaper or post it up on a special board for reviews and book suggestions.

Which Burger Really Tastes Better?

Altran Reusse and Michael McGruder

When we got ready to turn out this edition of the *Lake St. Journal,* I started thinking about what I could do for my next article. I was still thinking about it when I got home that evening. Then suddenly, sometime between *Square Pegs* and *Private Benjamin,* I saw one of those Burger King commercials. It was the one where the little girl sits on a bench outside, telling us how much meat goes into a McDonald's hamburger. "Unbelievable!" That gave me an idea. I'll show McDonald's and Burger King how I feel. I'll review them both!

McDONALD'S—I went to the McDonald's on the corner of Dodge and Dempster at about 3:00 on Sunday afternoon. There were not that many people there at all, but the girl who served me was crabby and impatient. I ordered a Big Mac, small fries and a medium Coke. As I waited, I noticed that the place was spotless. When my order came, I found the Coke tasted good, but the cup was ¾ths full of ice. The fries this time were not greasy. The Big Mac . . . how can you describe the taste of a Big Mac? It's starchy and kind of greasy, but, oh, that first bite!

My rating: Coke—8; Big Mac—6; fries—9.

BURGER KING—I went to the downtown Evanston Burger King on Saturday about 1:00 p.m. The waiting line was very long, as it always is because of all the high school and college kids. The service was good. I ordered a Whopper, small fries and a medium Coke. The Coke was good but, like McDonald's, had far too much ice. The fries were good, too. The Whopper was really good! The thing that makes the Whopper great is the real vegetables and the fresh taste.

My rating: Coke—8; Whopper—9; fries—9.

In general, the thing I didn't like about Burger King was the incredible crowd. But comparing food to line, the wait was worth it! The thing I didn't like about McDonald's was the starchiness of the food.

Price comparison:

McD—Big Mac—$1.25   fries—50¢   Coke—55¢
BK—Whopper—$1.37   fries—55¢   Coke—61¢

The difference in price isn't that big for the value. So, putting aside all my sentimental attachment to Ronald and his pals, and forgetting that McDonald's is as American as apple pie, and that we all grew up with Big Macs, I have to say that Burger King is better than McDonald's. But don't worry, McDonald's, as long as there's a hungry kid, you'll have someone who'll buy your Big Macs.

Romance Strikes Again in the Record World

Leslie Brown and Altran Reusse

One of the biggest problems we have with buying records is that, out of eight or nine songs on an album, you usually end up liking about three of them. Paying $8.00 for an album and liking only three cuts is no joke. Especially considering the cheap quality of some albums. But recently, we found an album that has none of the above problems. In our opinion it is perfect in every aspect.

After spending 15 years with the Commodores, Lionel Richie did a smash hit with Diana Ross, "Endless Love." That song is a typical example of Richie's incredibly romantic style. His current album, *Lionel Richie,* is one we call perfect.

Side One

"'Serves You Right" has a nice beat, good lyrics, is original and gives a full sound.

Rating: Leslie-9; Altran-8

"Wandering Stranger." Both of us consider this song a favorite. Very pretty!!! It is an excellent slow-dance song and is SURE to make any candlelit dinner complete. With original lyrics, it is GREAT!!

Rating: Leslie-10; Altran-10

"Tell Me." Jimmy Conners sings backup on this song. We gave it 7 because it isn't quite what we expected from him. But it has full sound and a nice beat.

Rating: Leslie-7; Altran-7

"My Love." This one is *really* romantic. Kenny Rogers sings back-up. It is one of his newer styles. For some reason, it has more appeal to one of us than to the other.

Rating: Leslie-8½; Altran-10

Side Two

"Round and Round." This has a nice beat. Even though Lionel Richie is more of a slow-song writer, when he tries this fast number, it turns out right.
Rating: Leslie-9; Altran-9

"Truly." Since all of you have probably heard this song, you know what we mean when we say that it is very romantic. "Truly" certainly is that! It is very pretty and very dreamy but, surprisingly, it is not the best cut on the album. We think that it shouldn't be played on the radio so often. Maybe then it could be a little more special. A Classic!!
Rating: Leslie-9; Altran-9

"You Are." This number is fast but still good. Richie's wife helped make this one of the best songs on the album.
Rating: Leslie-10; Altran-9

"You Mean More to Me" and "Just Put Some Love in Your Heart." Both are short but sweet and to the point. They are very pretty.
Rating: Leslie-10; Altran-10

We are not completely sure about the meaning of the long note of thanks on the inside record jacket. One of us thinks that it refers to his last album. The other one feels that it simply shows the personality of the artist.

One of the things that adds to the quality of this album is the range of instruments Richie uses on all the cuts. Lionel Richie is so talented that he can mix the sounds of harps, violins, drums and electric guitars. He uses many, many different instruments and they have a devastating effect. Lionel Richie is a classic artist and this is an equally classic album.

OOO La La, La Salade

Elyse Glickman

Can you picture a restaurant where a salad can be made with ALL the vegetables and garnishes of your choice *plus* special hot table delicacies (except weekday lunches) and wonderful, fresh bread AND all you can eat? This fantasy place for both dieter and hearty eaters is a reality.

You'll love La Salade for the food. All the vegetables are garden fresh and trimmed, and there are wonderful pâtés, dressings and trimmings to perfect your salad (during brunch and dinner).

To complement your meal, take a cheese bagel. For a special treat, spread it with fresh butter. The beverage list includes mineral water and all the Coke you can drink with as much or as little ice as you want.

The things I most love about La Salade are its cleanliness, the low calorie content of its selections, and the prices.

La Salade
3938 Dempster
Skokie
679-6190

$4.77—Lunch with beverage
$5.59—Dinner or brunch with beverage

Cat Calls

Nina Billone

Suddenly the whole stage turned red, and colored lights flashed on and off. Two cats cautiously crawled out of a pipe. The trunk to a broken-down car opened with a creak, while more cats filled the stage.

My mother and I had seats in the mezzanine, which is just above the first floor of the Schubert Theater in Chicago. I was extremely excited because I was watching *Cats*.

The stage was decorated like a junkyard. There were four Rice Krispies cereal boxes about two feet high, a tennis racket, and a garbage can, but best of all there was a tire that was about four feet around.

After minutes of dancing, the cats all went back to their hiding places except one. He started singing, "I have a Gumby Cat in mind.

Her name is Jenny Anny Dots. Her coat is of the tabby kind with tiger stripes and leopard spots. . . .'' As he sang, the trunk to the car opened. Inside was a cat with tiger stripes and leopard spots acting out every move that the cat sang about Jenny Anny Dots.

Many songs went by such as ''Growl Tiger, Gus'' (the theater cat), ''Mongojerrie'' and ''Rumpleteazer,'' etc.

Then a very interesting song came on, ''The Rum Tum Tugger,'' which started out, ''The Rum Tum Tugger is a curious cat. . . .'' The Rum Tum Tugger was a teenage cat whose coat was black and stuck to his body. I decided he was my favorite cat. He acted a lot like our cat Benjy. The play ended.

On the way home I sat in the back seat of the car with my mind full of scenes from the wonderful play I had just seen.

I like cats a lot, and seeing *Cats* made me realize that other people understand cats the way I do and know that they are like people.

Wish

Write something you wish would come true for yourself or for someone else. Describe in detail exactly what you would like. Express your wish as a poem if you like. Maybe add a drawing.

Make a wish book or wish board with others.

Wish

Todd Delahanty

I wish I could fly like an eagle.
I would glide in the cool brisk wind,
Plunging down the deep valleys and
Soaring over the white-tipped mountain peaks,
Seeing all of the beautiful sights.
But best of all I would be free.
I wish I could fly like an eagle.

Wishing, Wishing, Wishing, Wishing, Wishing

Lisa Hoff

I wish I had a pony.
I wish I had a dog.
I wish I had a special dance,
Made just for me.
I wish I could talk to animals.
I wish they could talk to me.
I wish I had a special language,
Made just for me.
I wish I had a rabbit.
I wish I had a parrot.
I wish I had a special poem,
Made just for me.
I wish I had a wood flute.
I wish I had a gold harp.
I wish I had a special song,
Made just for me.
I wish I was an astronaut.
I wish I could reach the stars.
I wish I had a special spaceship,
Made just for me.

I Wish

Jody Harms

I wish I were magical, because then I would clean up the world and make it a better place to be.

I would make the moon a place where there would be six sections, all of them different kinds of land.

I would put a tropical forest in one section. There would be huge brown and white sloths and big hairy monkeys. There would be beautiful colored tropical birds flying everywhere. The rocky shelves upon immense cliffs towering above the swampy area below would hold monkeys of all sizes.

The second section would be spring all the time. The flowers beautifully blooming would cover the forest beds and grassy meadows. The redwood trees would peek out above all others, their leafy branches reaching out into the sunlight. Creatures in every shade of color would prance through the green leafy forests and sweet smelling meadows.

Yet the third would be just autumn. Bright earth tones would lace the branchy trees and float gently down to the leaf-covered ground. Squirrels, deer, bears, and other wonderful creatures would frisk through meadows and the forests, always preparing for hibernation that would never come (while in the meadows). The grassy landscape would turn red, gold, and orange. Frisky mice would run around playfully gathering nuts.

The fourth section would be winter, with stately empire penguins and snowshoe hares. The wolves would howl. You would be able to hear the crackling noise of a fire in the Eskimo huts. You would ski down crisp, snowy slopes.

But the fifth would be unlike any other. It would be an underwater world. Its creatures would be uncanny. There would be pink and purple serpents and green and blue serpents also. The fish would have magnificent tropical colors.

The sixth section would be a dream where whatever you wanted to happen would happen. But you couldn't hurt anything no matter how hard you try.

These lands would be just for people who really care about animals and their environment.

Editorial

Editorials express opinions about matters currently being discussed in a community. The matters usually concern whether some action should be taken or whether something already going on is right, like a well-known building being torn down or a school rule being changed. Read some editorials in different newspapers and magazines. If you want to get in on some discussion in your school or community, or want to propose some change, make a case by using all the reasons and evidence you can think of. Write these down in a way that you think will persuade your readers.

What's the best way to get your editorial to the attention of those you want to persuade?

Government Power, to Live and Let Die
Sarah Lieberman

Under the law I speak of, regardless of any handicaps, every baby must live as long as the surgeons can keep them alive. Babies that might have been better off dead have been aggressively handled and kept on respirators. Do parents have a say? Under the law, NO!

You, of course, see my point of view, but would you put your child through painful operations, operations that won't improve its life? I don't think so! Now these parents don't want to kill their child, only to save it from operations, handicaps, and perhaps special schools. Some of them die eventually anyway.

These parents are accused of not loving their children. These parents need to be understood; they only want the best for their children.

Shuttle Disaster Going to Stop Space Program?
Eli Rubin

At 10:39 A.M., just 72 seconds after it lifted off, a liftoff that began with joy, the space shuttle consumed itself in a gigantic fireball ignited by liquid hydrogen and liquid oxygen 28 miles in the sky. Aboard—the first 7 astronauts to die in *flight*. The first space shuttle to be destroyed in use. The first teacher in space—also the first to die. The pain that the families and good friends feel must be endless.

But the question is, should we take the risk of these unbearable pains being felt again? Should we continue sending civilians in space? Or humans?

Think of it this way. If those of you who think that space flight is dangerous wanted to bring this controversy up, why bring it up now? Why not in the early days of the shuttle? Like in the days of the Columbia? The risk has always been there. Right from the start. This could have happened on the first launch. This was bound to happen. I know this tragedy struck pain all over the world, but we can't let it stop us. Even the 7 astronauts who perished in a split second knew that the risk was there. And it's always there. Lurking, waiting. But, we can't hold the flight of the space shuttle "indefinitely." We must be bold and continue to explore the one thing that we could explore for billions of years and never totally understand—the universe.

Essay

Write your thoughts and feelings about some subject important to you. You may want to say how or when these thoughts started, what triggered them, like certain experiences you've had or witnessed, a conversation, an image. Maybe some things have led you to some conclusion. You might want to give real or imagined examples of your ideas.

Or just jot down for 10 or 15 minutes everything that comes into your head. Don't worry about correctness; just get down lots of fast notes. Then look these over and see if something in there might be pulled out and developed into an essay—a single thought or perhaps a chain or pattern of thoughts. Find out this way what's on your mind, and make use of it.

Post it up, pass it around, print it up.

If I Were One Inch Tall. . .
Sarah E. Marx

If I were one inch tall my whole life would be different. I never really thought about it until now.

If I were one inch tall, all animals except fish and other tiny things would be enemies.

I would have to build a ladder to reach doorknobs. Rings would be necklaces.

A great playground could be made up of a pencil for a pole to slide down on, a balloon for an earthball, a piece of thread to swing on, and bark to climb on.

For an exercise machine I could use rubberbands.

I would consider a dollhouse a mansion.

A toothbrush could be a great hairbrush.

For shampoo I could use a milliliter of hand soap.

And that is my feeling of difference between 4 foot 3 inches and 1 inch.

My Chinese Heritage
Grace Lin

My Chinese heritage is something very important to me. But I hadn't thought of it this way all the time. When I was little, I was taught to read and write Chinese by my mother. After we moved, I went to a school on Sundays where It was taught to read, write, memorize, and recite. It was exciting a first, but as most thing go, I soon lost interest. I began to ask a very common question, "Why?" Why should I come here? Why should I learn this? The answer to those questions came to me later while listening to a friend compete in a yearly speech contest. My parents gave me their point of view on the subject. It was this: "It is good for you to learn now to be proud of your heritage."

Chinese people have always been very polite and kind. Young children such as myself have always been taught proper etiquette and respect. My parents have always taught me to respect my elders and ancestors, as well as my teachers. I admit though, I have not been quite so responsible about the teacher part as the rest of it.

Honesty and patience are two virtues that are very important to us, because honesty and patience always bring success. To the Chinese, a good family relationship is very important. And in order to have that you must have patience, patience between parents and children, brothers and sisters. A family must have honesty, so the family will have harmony. All this can bring a family closer together, creating a strong bond between parents and children, brothers and sisters.

I have often been teased by my schoolmates about being what I am. I know I may look different, but I'm not any different from them in my ways of being human. I have feelings just as they do, though they may not have considered it. It used to bother me very much when they did this. But I gradually learned to ignore them or to defend myself at certain times, because I am proud of my heritage, and I'm proud to be Chinese!

Contemplation
Breeze Murphy

As I think of all I have been through in eleven years of my life, I wonder whether or not it was worth coming into this world—yes, this world, this beautiful world.

Walking along the shore has often helped me contemplate, watching the waves in tidal motion, filling the magnificence of the sea. The ocean, the cauldron of the world, is a driving force from which all life evolved. Its mist, minute particles of fine liquid evaporating into the atmosphere, is like an ocean in itself, floating in the sharp air.

My mind flows, too, but more like a meandering river, trying to grasp illusions of beauty, but my effort may be given in vain. For how can my spirit flow freely when images of pain confine it? Pain is something which all life must endure. But can pain be more than what one makes of it? Beauty, on the other hand, an illusory quality, held in the mind, is given to individuals who accept it. In its uniqueness, though, beauty is always accepted on different levels, according to the differing perceptions of individuals.

Beauty and pain. Freedom and confinement. Time and time-lessness. I contemplate. I am uncertain about the hearsay concerning the development of the universe in a massive explosion or of its creation by a supreme being. In a way, the universe and time began when I did.

Music
Felicia Sze

Music. Does that word have any meaning to you? It should. Music is the heart of our lives.

Many times when I fall asleep, I hear music I had never heard before. If I am awakened I can remember it and hum it by heart days afterward. Once I fell asleep in a concert hall and found that I had been able to hear the music through my dream! I have found out that my sisters also hear this. Some people hear voices as I do dreams.

The type of music you like can show up in your attitude towards others and your personality. I have met many people who just love classical music and they tend to be nice and generous. On the other hand, many people who like hard rock music don't turn out that well.

There is good music and bad music. Yet there are different styles, widely ranging. Some people cannot tell the difference between Baroque, Romantic, Classical, and Renaissance music, and others cannot tell the difference between hard rock, new wave, and jazz.

Life as it is would be totally different if we didn't have music. In books such as *The Phantom Tollbooth* by Norton Justin there are places where sound is banished. The book showed the importance of sounds—birds chirping, wind blowing, and other music-like sounds. It was then when sounds were abused that the Soundkeeper banished them. It shows how different life could be without sounds. I for one would be changed because much of my life is reflected off music, since I have been playing since I was three years old. Music takes up most of my life. I think I'd be bored to death without it.

Long days without light makes life dreary; it is the same with music. Music lights up many lives. Music gives many lives a job! Without music, we would be perhaps a very primitive type of people. Life and music go together.

Almost all my friends are musically joined somehow. People that are our best friends would be totally changed. We ourselves would be totally changed. I can list many ways one could be changed. For instance, one who was peaceful could turn into a mortal Ares. The angel of the class might turn into a bully. I could go on forever.

Ref. The Vermont atlas / David Delorme an

0 00 02 0244028 5
MIDDLEBURY COLLEGE